PRAISE FOR
Saint Germain on Advanced Alchemy

"In every age there are people whose sensitivity is sufficiently refined to perceive and commune with higher realms. In this extraordinary book, David Christopher Lewis brings us reports of a universe far more alive and sentient than most of us ever imagined."

—RICK ARCHER, author of the *Buddha at the Gas Pump* blog

"A man of our time and a man of tomorrow, David Christopher Lewis takes us to the altitude of heavenly spheres, bringing to humanity the joys and virtues of spiritual practice. In this book, you will experience the primordial spring of his clear and transparent teachings."

—MAMADE KADREEBUX, poet and author of *Destiny, Life in the Shadows, Book of Journeys,* and *Journey to Ancient Arabia*

"Grand spiritual teachings embodied in clear, elegant prose! This book provides a new benchmark on the laws and applications of spiritual alchemy, with thirty-three magnificent discourses by Saint Germain, meaningful commentary by David Christopher Lewis, and much more. Its teachings are apropos for today's mega-challenges and structured for practical use in one's everyday life—for anyone on any path. Bravo, Saint Germain and David!"

—KEVIN D. RAPHAEL FITCH, author of *Celestial Configurations of Africa and the Caribbean*

"In your hands you hold keys to transforming the consciousness of humanity from its base, leaden state into pure gold through the alchemy of love. With this book you can learn the art of becoming a center of divine light."

—WAYNE H. PURDIN, author of *Pharaoh of the Sun: Akhenaten and The Culture of Love*

Saint Germain

ON

Advanced Alchemy

HeartStreaming
in the
Aquarian Age

Volume 1

With Love,
Saint Germain

David Christopher Lewis

MERU PRESS®

For information, contact:
Meru Press®
PO Box 277
Livingston, Montana 59047 USA
Email: info@MeruPress.org

Library of Congress Control Number: 2015933029

ISBN: 978-0-9818863-5-0

10 9 8 7 6 5 4 3 2 1

Cover art by The Hearts Center Creative Arts Team
Cover and book design by Nancy Badten

Picture Credits: We offer our grateful acknowledgment for permission to reproduce
the following material: Illustrations by Mario Duguay: *A New Day, Conquering
Creativity, Divine Strength, Drawing in Happiness, Initiation, Learning from Life,
Light for the World, Listening to the Messenger, Marvel, Master of My Life, My Path,
Regeneration, Strength of Faith, Water of Life, Wisdom.*

Printed in the United States of America
For additional copies, visit: HeartsCenter.org

Notes and Disclaimers: (1) The information and practices presented in this book are
for informational purposes only. No guarantee is made by Meru Press or the author
that they will yield successful results for anyone at any time. Their application and
effectiveness are dependent on the individual. (2) Gender-neutral language can at
times be cumbersome. For readability, we have freely used *he, him, mankind,* and
man to refer to both male and female as well as to the Divine. The term *Man* (with
a capital *M*) refers to Mankind in general. *Brotherhood* refers to the Universal Great
White Brotherhood, whose membership in the heaven-world and in embodiment is
both male and female; here the word *white* refers to the white light of their auras. To
distinguish the soul from the spirit aspect of being, we often use *she* and *her* when
referring to the soul and *he* and *him* when referring to the spirit.

Contents

PART ONE

Instruction in Advanced Alchemy

by Saint Germain
with Commentary by David Christopher Lewis

Affirmations, Prayers, Fiats, and Chants

PART TWO

Answers to 33 Questions from Disciples

by Saint Germain
with Commentary by David Christopher Lewis

PART THREE

Alchemical Elixirs
33 Spirals of Divine Alchemy for Solar Beingness
by Saint Germain and Portia
with Commentary by David Christopher Lewis

Living in the Light:
Alchemical Art for Self-Transformation
by Mario Duguay

Foreword

by David Christopher Lewis

I first heard of the master Saint Germain and saw an image of him in the early 1970s when a friend showed me the book *The Magic Presence*, by Godfre Ray King. Although I did not read the book at that time, the image made a deep impression on my soul. In the spring of 1974, I found the teachings of the master as presented through The Summit Lighthouse activity. After attending my first conference in Spokane in early July of that year and hearing my first live dictation of the master through Elizabeth Clare Prophet, I immediately pursued earning the money to attend Summit University to immerse myself in the teachings of the ascended masters.

I attended Summit University from January through March of 1975 and then helped found the first official regional teaching center of the Summit in the Twin Cities of Minnesota. The following year, on April 8, 1976, I joined the headquarters staff in Colorado Springs. I moved with the organization as it moved, serving as a staff member for over twenty-two years. During many of those years, I served initially as the membership secretary and later as the director of the Keepers of the Flame Fraternity, a non-denominational and non-religious organization co-chaired by the Maha Chohan in the office of Keeper of the Flame and Saint Germain as the Knight

Note: Monograms with symbols are used to identify the three authors: *SG* for Saint Germain, *P* for Portia, and *D* or *DCL* for David Christopher Lewis.

Commander. I was responsible to maintain accurate membership records, send out dues reminders, and handle much of the correspondence related to the fraternity.

Little did I know during those years that my life would take a dramatic turn nearly thirty years later, by which I would commune with and serve the master in a much more direct manner. Looking back, I realize that while my years of humble service to the ascended masters through an outer organization were very important, the inner work on myself and the spiritual strides I was making during those years to expand the light within my heart and auric field were even more crucial for the fulfillment of my greater life mission and service to humanity.

On June 6, 2004, during a Sunday service in Livingston, Montana, at St. Mark's Church, a local branch of Church Universal and Triumphant, I had a mystical experience and what I now describe as a great awakening. I was taken up in spirit to a new and much higher level of awareness and there was a quickening within that resulted in the bestowal of a sacred gift that some term *locution* and others *clairaudience*. Although I did not fully understand at the time what had happened, in subsequent days it became clear that I now had the ability to commune more directly with the ascended masters through this gift as long as I would use it selflessly for the greater good of all.

The next day at my home in Paradise Valley, just after sunrise and following my morning prayers and devotions to God, I sat down to write a "journal of life" to document my numerous spiritual experiences so that I would never forget them. We had been encouraged by the masters to keep a journal in order that we would have the remembrance of these sacred times of transcendent communion with God if and when challenges would come in our lives.

As I put pen to paper and reflected on what I would write, a powerful presence and energy filled the room and the Master Jesus began telepathically dictating directly to my heart and mind my first *HeartStream*, a term the masters later gave these messages. This heavenly missive was personal to me, very beautiful, and was definitely not something that came from my own mind. Jesus asked me to continue to receive a message daily after a time of early morning meditation in silence, and said that more direction would come to me through other ascended masters.

Three days later, just after dawn on June 10, 2004, over seven months before the outer formation of The Hearts Center movement, beloved Saint Germain came to me for the first time. It was an electrifying experience during which my entire body was supercharged with light and I felt all aglow with his and my love for God. He gave me the following teaching:

> The radiance of the heart is the alchemical key in all experiments of the spirit. When you fully realize the intensity of this flame, nothing shall be impossible unto you. Your life will take on a miraculous aura of peace and divine ecstasy which is almost indescribable. Your inner knowing and growth will be most tangible to you and also to those around you. Ever has it been our cause to raise men out of mediocrity into the fullness of their divine potential. Yet most would have it not, having borne the hurts of past failures rather than looking forward to the glory of new and cosmic achievements.
>
> You have earned the privilege to receive tangible love from our hearts through your daily constancy, striving, and deep reverence for life. Now you must journey beyond the limitations of your finite self through new experiments in cosmic consciousness far beyond this world. When you meditate upon the stars, the nova, and the Hub of the known universe, you draw unto you those cosmic currents

that will literally change the essence of your cellular structure through a new and glorious brilliance of Christic patterns and a matrix through which we can pour more love to humanity. Pray for true humility, for in the light of Alpha and his great humaneness of simple devotion to the One Purpose is found the key to the All.

I was in awe after I placed my pen down, and I sat for quite some time contemplating his words and their charge of light to my soul. I kept these messages secret from all except my wife and one other trusted friend, for I considered them too sacred to share with others who would not understand what was now transpiring in my life and my inner walk with the Spirit Most Holy. My days working in my Paradise Artworks gallery in downtown Livingston were now suffused with a new radiance and purpose. It was as if I now breathed in the air of a different and more transcendent universe.

Saint Germain came again to my living room shortly after sunrise nine days later, on June 19, 2004. After reverently acknowledging his presence and sensing that he was ready to answer a question, I asked him what was the most important work that I could accomplish in this life. He replied:

> Beloved David, you are working my works daily—primarily in your inner spiritual work through decrees, prayers, and rosaries, and in constantly thinking about and meditating on God, the spiritual path, love, light, and community. Building a community of hearts united in my work of advancing my Aquarian ideals is the greatest work you can accomplish for me. Diligently strive to bring people together to glean divine wisdom, gnosis, and the raising of the Mother Light from the base to the crown through Buddhic devotion. A community of hearts is being woven together through the Holy Spirit's work.

Then, on the morning of June 26, 2004, Saint Germain came with this message:

> When you abide in love, I abide in you, for I am the embodiment of God-love as your Aquarian master. Portia and I anchor within the Earth the golden-age conscious-ness of the Father-Mother God, which they would have you also be. For when the many choose to become this love, Earth shall truly be Freedom's Star!
>
> We come to deliver to you vials of love to counteract the vials of the seven last plagues.[1] Contained within these vials are components of each of the seven rays as elixirs, dis-tilled down to the very essence and intensity of those rays. We are cosmic homeopaths, alchemists of the spirit, who bring to you the ascended-master antidotes to the perils within the Earth. These vials of love as concentrated quin-tessences of the rays will literally charge and change your beings in the twinkling of an eye when you imbibe them and allow a spiritual chemicalization to occur within you while maintaining your harmony, stability, and equipoise.

I didn't hear from Saint Germain again for some time, until suddenly I was awakened by him at nearly midnight on November 8, 2004. After I arose and had paper and pen in hand, he gazed intense-ly yet lovingly at me with those deep violet-colored eyes and said:

> David, the time has come for you to determine if you will be our amanuensis, for certain cycles of Aquarius are here and we are determined to make a mark within this Earth and initiate new spirals of victory! We fully under-stand your current situation, and yet we need you now to pen our words almost without ceasing, for the lightbearers need our current word to them for the ongoing and timely work at hand. The resources have been provided.... You

must go forth to carry our words and our message to the world. There is no time to dally or delay.... You are being called to come up higher and be fully trained by us. This will require your all, your very life blood and all the fruit that you have garnered over many lives. You must put behind you all concerns for business, abundance, and other personal and family matters, and take the next step. This will require a greater discipline, both internally and externally.

Of course this message shook my world to the core, and I realized that something dramatic and life-altering was occurring. I felt the urgency of Saint Germain's message and decided that, come what may, I would be obedient to the master and serve with everything within me. His words proved to be prophetic, because I had to surrender much of my life—who I was in others' minds—and be refashioned in a spiritual way to accommodate what the master intended to do with me in order that I could be the best servitor and amanuensis I could.

It was months later, in the autumn of 2005, that I realized that in 1994 I had written a letter to the Karmic Board* and offered to serve to fulfill the role of a certain individual who had decided to abandon his holy office within the Summit organization. We had been told that that individual had Buddhic attainment and was destined to do great things for the Earth. In my letter I had pledged to sacrifice, to work on myself, and to step up to the plate to become a vessel for the greater work. I also wrote at that time that my goal in life was to become a Buddha. I studied all I could about Buddhism during the limited hours I had available and I began to have amazing experiences in which I felt an inner shift into a more enlightened state of being.

From January 2005 until January 2008, Saint Germain came to

*Please see the glossary on page 321 for terms you may be unfamiliar with.

me, on average, once or twice a month to provide instruction on all manner of spiritual topics. He was always tangibly present, with an intense aura of violet-joy radiance coupled with a beautiful aroma that I would describe as violet-rose-honeysuckle, as he conveyed to me profound and poetic concepts about divine love, heart-centeredness, higher alchemy, and the joys of conscious living.

During February and March of 2008, Saint Germain and his beloved twin flame Portia* alternately dictated a series of beautiful teachings that they titled *A Spiral of Divine Alchemy for Solar Beingness*. These are included in Part Three of this book. In the summer of that same year, the master allowed a small circle of disciples to ask thirty-three darshan questions, which he generously answered; and these are included in Part Two of the book.

In the spring of 2009, Saint Germain asked me to conduct a seminar in Mount Shasta, a small city formed at the base of a sacred inactive volcano in northern California and the home of numerous new-age activities. Among these is the Saint Germain Foundation, which has published many transcendent teachings by the master as dictated in the 1930s and beyond through the messengers Guy and Edna Ballard, also known as Godfre Ray King and Lotus Ray King. And so on August 22, 2009, in a packed auditorium in Mount Shasta's Masonic Lodge, Saint Germain shared his teachings on advanced alchemy. Later, from May 1 to June 5, 2011, the master conducted a six-week Meru University[2] course in which he elucidated further on advanced alchemy. These transcendent messages are included in Part One of this work.

It has been my divine pleasure and privilege to receive both the teachings and the loving radiation from the master Saint Germain's mind and heart. These I now present to you for your spiritual edification and blessing.

---

*Please see the entry for Portia in the glossary.

The master intends that we publish volume two of this series within the next eighteen months. It will contain many of his additional teachings given over a ten-year period in over one hundred and sixty HeartStreams and will also include his new alchemical formulas for spiritual success, presented during a special event broadcast from Livingston, Montana, and simulcast to Mount Shasta, California, on May 1–4, 2014. All of these teachings are truly rich in the flavor of Aquarian love, prompting us all to heartstream to the world our own spiritual gifts, talents, and boons.

May the master's message raise you ever in the Light of God That Always Prevails!

David Christopher Lewis

January 7, 2015

Preface

My Sacred Formula for World Transmutation: Love, the Alchemical Key, Conquers All
by Saint Germain

Dearest Hearts,

My sacred formula for world transmutation begins with love, it ends with love, and within its very center is the flame of eternal love. Therefore you must begin every experiment that you desire to be successful on your knees before God, in love with your Presence, whereby you submit all to that eternal science of the spirit through which there is the ennoblement of the soul through integrity, through that which you offer in service.

It is only when there is the supreme understanding of your Source that each and every avenue will be open for you and the success of your alchemy may manifest. Truly, the grace of God is in the eye of the beholder who sees clearly that which may manifest through a heart apprised of this formula and beating in unison with the Creator.

Would you be co-creators with me? I ask. If you so choose, it will mean that from this day forward your every thought, your every emotion, your every movement will be seen as one that is in unison with the holy purposes of God; and that which you emanate—if you would be gods[3]—will be clear and true and sure of its effects upon life, of its cause, and of all that flows through the model that you represent as the one through whom the science of being occurs.

Many have studied the ancient mysteries and they can recite formulae here and there as to what could occur if they were to engage as co-creators. Yet how many have actually set their hands, their minds, their hearts to the task of employing God within the sacred space of light upon the altar, where there is the alteration of substance with the science of higher alchemy? This is where light, as the alchemical key, is always garnered and suffused into that which transpires so that the very glory of God may be seen and felt and known within the holy ritual at hand.

Did you know that you perform alchemy each time you sit in meditation upon your Presence and utter the sacred formulas of your prayers and songs? This is a higher form of alchemy; when understood, you intuit it as causative of the transformation that you seek—to be gods upon Earth. Often your minds are wandering and there is not the concentrated focus of the stream of your attention whereby the higher adepts can add to the equation and balance the forces of light and darkness within your own being and whereby the effects that you seek can be fully manifest.

When you engage, when your heart is full of the fire of the Supreme One and you are in awe of that which God has offered to you as opportunity to live a life of meaning, of service, and of support to the divine purposes, then that which is exhibited upon your altar is highlighted by cosmic energies, solar frequencies; and no matter what anyone else says, you may be that master alchemist through whom miracles ensue. Through your belief, your faith, and the laser light of seventh-ray joy, your victory is assured.

What is love? Many have spoken of it; few have penetrated its core or sustained within their hearts its momentum to transmute and transform in order to become God. The transformative power of the violet light and ray is love. The very frequency that wraps itself around that which occurs when you invoke my sacred formula is the light of change by the power of love.

When you know your Self, you will know love. When you feel the Presence of God blazing within your aura, then you can sustain love. When the surety of your wisdom, growing by experiencing the Divine within the laboratory of your soul, is manifest, then love becomes active, animated, kinetic in its force and power to recreate a world as you would like it to be.

The true recreation, or re-creation, of this coming age may be known through the joy of the use of the rays of God, especially the seventh, in all sciences, in all religious experiences, in daily life as a whole rather than separated into "my time for work," "my time for play," "my time at home," or "recreation." All life may be experienced within the universal understanding of the seventh age of holy reason, whereby the only reason for all that you do is to express love, kindness, holy friendship, and grace.

Every word that flows from your lips has a motive to support, uphold, and nurture. Every feeling that flows through your heart encompasses the very nature of God's essence through the movement of energy and light and sound. And everything that is studied from the book of the Law, both in the physical plane and in higher dimensions, may be grasped by the power of the Holy Spirit, who illumines that word and makes it vital, energetic, and real in your life experience personally.

Jesus said that all the law hangs on these two: to love God with all your heart, your mind, and your soul; and to love your neighbor as your Self.[4] This is true, and thus you can see how love, as the alchemical key, conquers all. There is simply no space for fear, no place for anxiety, no place for rebellion or ignominy in your life. The darkness flees from you because you emit the solar radiance of your Source; and there is no shadow and no night where you stand, because the supernal Christic light flows and glows from your being, one with mine.

I hear the questions of your mind before the frequencies of its emanations reach the higher octaves, and I answer each query with my ray of love, through which you may discern for yourselves the answer. The Socratic method, whereby the master elicits from you your own true inner wisdom, is the way of Aquarius. We will draw out of you your inner genius, for it must be forthcoming in this age. We will magnetize and, where necessary, sterilize that which flows through your aura for the highest purpose of your soul: to know and experience God.

I have been waiting for you to become who you are for a long time. Isn't it time that you listen and obey the inner voice once and for all, and know your Self and awaken fully to your Buddha nature?

I am increasing the heat of transmutation within your heart now to a new pulsation of cosmic love if you will have it burning there for the duration of your time upon this Earth. Yes, I say, let it burn! Let it be enflamed! Let it be exemplified in the lives of the fiery ones who are called Keepers of the Lightning because they dare to touch the very sky and know the light of God. Let Prometheus be your middle name, for we would have fire-bearers in our midst.

Zarathustra, come and touch the fiery coals of love upon the lips, the hearts, the minds of these your sons and daughters. And let every alchemy be fulfilled within the landscape of love, the light-house of love, the lea, the glade, the holy glen of love through which we will walk together, hand in hand, in silence, knowing that the breath of God is present in the air and that the angels witness the sacred space of love that we create and recreate each moment.

I am your Knight Commander. I command you to love with a cosmic fiery heart, through which you may know your Self as gods and goddesses.

Saint Germain

PART ONE

Instruction in Advanced Alchemy

by Saint Germain

with Commentary
by David Christopher Lewis

Establish the Platform for Your Advanced Alchemical Works

Students of Higher Alchemy,

The transcendence that appears in your domain when you are tethered to the reality of life that is God will win for you a new consciousness. I come to give you the next step in the process of Solar development which, when applied, will bring to you untold graces, cosmic abundance, and all that you require to be a full-fledged son or daughter of God, one with the creative spirit of all life.

Alchemy, as the all-chemistry of God,[5] is meant to allow every creative spirit the means and the opportunity to enter into the creative process of life. Therefore, those who practice true alchemy, which always sets the evolutionary process of all life ahead of the gain of the ego-center, will understand the necessity to sublimate personal glory, outer development, and inner development to the spiritual upliftment of the world and its peoples.

One is blessed when one blesses others. The natural law of flow states that when that flow is fully operative within the domain of a soul, then the pure radiance of God's light may continue unabated so long as the aperture of self is wholly pure. Therefore the true alchemist is completely unselfish, and the current that is established within his being becomes a conduit for greater and greater energies of the Godhead.

Testing occurs by the masters of wisdom to determine what quantity of light can be channeled through a lifestream and also the quality of that light as it descends from the God Presence and contacts the auric flowfield of the practitioner of truth.[6] A certain stability, a certain polarity of positivity must be maintained for the flow to continue unabated. This requires balance of body, mind, and spirit; of love, wisdom, and power; of the constancy of right motive, right thought, and right action.

Ongoing education and training are prerequisites for every alchemist of the higher order. This process begins in earnest when the student has surrendered a certain portion of his or her human consciousness to accept and become a greater portion of his or her Divine Self. Once the student has sufficiently mastered the emotions (energy in motion within the chalice of being), stilled the mind, and purified the body, then the science of alchemy will become more easily understood and actualized.

Those who think that they can precipitate anything and everything out of thin air when they have major unresolved issues within or with others are fooling no one. Those who seek to take heaven by storm,[7] demanding of the universe the mastery of *siddhis*,[8] or spiritual powers, before they are activated gradually through the spiritualization of consciousness, will only lose at every turn.

Thus, it is paramount that one hitch oneself to the star of an ascended-master sponsor, who can moderate for that one every level of advancement and monitor the use of energies, the acceleration of light, and the resulting internal realignment that occurs as one progresses toward immortal perfection.

The expansion of the heart through devotional practices of prayer and meditation and the emphasizing of purity and grace are the first steps which will ultimately lead toward developing true spiritual prowess and a victorious sense of God-wellbeing. Therefore, establish first and foremost the platform, the altar, upon which all your alchemical work will proceed. When the Bible and other ancient Scriptures speak of various prophets establishing an altar upon which sacrifice occurred, it was often simply the preparation and invocation of a holy flowfield around those beings.

Once the space is hallowed and the lower self is sacrificed, or surrendered, then the scientific practice of alchemy may ensue. If you have not fully looked after certain details in setting about you the necessary circle of fire, then there may be intrusions, delays, or outright interference with your work that will require calling forth extraordinary cosmic energies to neutralize and overcome.

How often have you experienced the fact that some friends or acquaintances with the best of intentions couldn't perceive the intensity of your spiritual path and therefore, through doubt and human questioning, they set you up to fail so that they could prove to you that your path doesn't work? How often have inquisitive minds penetrated your aura and temporarily rendered your alchemical work null and void until you could establish such a positive and blazing aura of protection and develop so great an inner sanctuary of fiery love around your heart as to ward off these intrusions?

Therefore, learn and use the science of invoking the crystal-diamond tube of light as well as a solar sphere of fire and a triple ruby dome of light around you.[9] (See "Crystal-Diamond Tube of Light," page 85; "Opening Invocation for Prayer Services," page 86; and "Solar-Sphere Invocation," page 87.) Seal your aura and being in the cloak of invisibility so that no one may interfere with your sacred work and time in communion with your ascended gurus. Develop a plan whereby you set aside quiet time when you will not be disturbed and you will be free to work for at least one-half hour or longer in deepest concentration on your goals.

With practice, the establishment of your spiritual flowfield will become second nature to you and you will know, believe, and act with a spirit of indomitable victory at all levels, dear hearts. This, in and of itself, will be key to your work in higher alchemy.

Therefore, no matter what your religious or spiritual background may be, use the tools we have given to first create a chrysalis of spiritual fire around yourself and then practice seeing and sustaining this light at all times. When you have developed a sufficient energy pattern around yourself, then prepare for the next teaching that I will give you on developing God-power for the increase in your abilities and work with the angels to save sentient life upon Earth.

Ever yours as we move forward with chin held high and with spirits soaring, I am

Saint Germain

Knight Commander

DCL: It is only within the past several years that in the New Age movement we have started looking at ourselves as co-creators. Now this essential concept is permeating the world: We are co-creators with God.

The Aperture of Self

Saint Germain says said that when the alchemist is unselfish, God's light can flow unabated through the aperture of self, the open portal through our attention. The aperture is the heart chakra wed to the mind, or crown chakra; and our attention is what allows us to focus. No matter what we are doing, being focused and present is the whole key. For example, if the person who checks groceries at the store is exuberant and full of love, that energy uplifts and blesses people.

If you have been praying and decreeing for some years, you may feel that you understand the science of flow through your prayers and decrees. You may be able to establish a connection almost instantaneously wherein you feel the light flowing through you. It takes a while to develop that connection. As you cleanse your aura and the light flows through you, your aura expands. And then, through this larger aperture, you can draw down greater fire and emanate it to the world and the planet. It doesn't happen all at once.

I'll share my own experience to help clarify this process. Within a week of my joining the staff of The Summit Lighthouse in Colorado Springs, I was asked to lead the staff in giving a decree we used to reverse the tide of anything negative or harmful that is occurring. I had only given that decree once before that day, and I discovered that the long-time staff had a much greater momentum of giving it than I did. I could not sustain in my being what they were invoking through theirs due to their mastery in decreeing and in giving that prayer. I felt discombobulated and that I wasn't doing anything. They were doing everything; they were doing the work of that prayer.

It was a really humbling experience and it was great that I had it. After that I didn't lead prayers again for a while, because I didn't have the momentum the others had. That experience gave me insight into the fact that I hadn't yet developed the power that I felt flowing through the others.

Those of you who attend our events who are not used to praying or decreeing with a group may have a similar experience. Perhaps at times you can't keep up with the speed of the words. That's okay. It takes time and development to build that momentum. As you master things, you will feel the expansion of that aperture of your auric flow-field whereby you are able to deliver to the world greater and greater God-power of the frequencies of God's love and light and wisdom to bless life.

Be forgiving with yourself. Don't expect it to happen overnight. Even those of us who have been praying for twenty or thirty or more years are always learning new things about the science of the spoken word and how we can be clearer vessels through which God's light can flow.

In his book *The Tipping Point,*[10] author Malcolm Gladwell says that it takes ten thousand hours to become a master at something, to understand it from all different facets and relationships and angles. The book gives examples of tremendously successful people, including Bill Gates and the Beatles, whom people thought were simply in the right place at the right time. They were, in some respects, and yet they also put in the time, they did the work.

Some of us have decreed ten thousand hours; if we haven't already become masters of it, we are becoming masters. Maybe things won't take as long for those who are in tune and aligned with Source and are clear channels for the light to flow through them. For most of us, though, we still have to put in the time. We may have done it in past lives as monks, as nuns, as lamas, yet when we come back we have to learn it again in a new mode.

Testing Determines the Quantity and Quality of Light the Alchemist Can Receive

Saint Germain says we are tested to determine both the quantity and the quality of light that can be channeled through us. We are all tested; to think we are not observed by our sponsoring masters is folly. They observe us continuously in order to help us, and this testing is a loving unfoldment of their mindfulness to gently urge us forward. That is how our sponsoring masters work. If we give the master permission, things can be intense, and that master may goad us to help us pluck out our human momentums. Generally, though, most of us appreciate the gentler way.

We stamp the light that flows through us with our consciousness and the purity of our being. I've had experiences of leading decrees where I felt this power flowing through me and I've also had times when I didn't have the mastery to qualify it with the highest emanations and qualities and virtues of God. Over the years I feel that I have gained a lot more mastery in that.

When you are in a prayer or decree session and there is tremendous energy and power flowing in the entire room, it's possible at times to feel carried away by it, even lightheaded. This is why exercising the physical body is so important. If you are just in your head or if you're not balanced in your four lower bodies, you can't retain that light, you don't have the mastery in the four quadrants of your being for that light to be anchored in its full intensity in the Earth.

Physical exercise is essential to anchor yourself in the physical plane and create a strong and supple chalice to contain the light of Spirit. As you master your physical body, you will know your spiritual self better. Engage in some sort of physical activity every day, if you can, or at least a few times a week, to garner energy in your physical body. I do the dishes and laundry, chop and haul firewood, mow, garden, and do all sorts of things around the house and property, because when my mind is cognizing spiritual concepts I have to anchor them in the physical plane; otherwise I could be living in some other plane and would not be as effective or practical here.

Balance the Various Aspects of Your Threefold Flame

For the flow of light to continue unabated to the alchemist, he or she must maintain a certain stability and positivity, a certain level of balance. Saint Germain mentioned three different aspects of the threefold flame that require balancing: body, mind, and spirit; love, wisdom, and power; and right motive, right thought, and right action. Here's another key: In mastering the emotions, stilling the mind, and purifying the body, we have another aspect of balancing the threefold flame. Emotions relate to the pink plume; mind relates to the yellow plume; and the physical body relates to the blue plume (structure is physical, blue).[11]

Saint Germain cautions us to have right motive in all that we do. If we do something for personal glory, we won't receive those gifts. If we try to raise our kundalini, or sacred fire, to get these gifts, we won't be able to sustain them without purity of heart. The ascended masters help us to self-moderate and they monitor us. You may already know which master you resonate most with. Whoever it is, you can trust that master to be there for you and to help you consistently and constantly.

Providing knowledge and practical tools to help students achieve balance and to advance on their path and in their alchemical journey is what Meru University is all about—lifelong learning of wisdom from ascended-master realms.

Clear Your Flowfield, Establish Your Magic Circle

The prophets desired some symbology for establishing the flowfield for their work and they used an altar and other symbols. Clearing the flowfield is an important part of establishing the altar for the alchemy to take place. One way to set a flowfield is through establishing a "magic circle."[12] This concept was popularized, with some Hollywood compromise, in the 2010 movie *The Sorcerer's Apprentice*.

Before any event I establish the flowfield. Sometimes I do this in my mind, through intention. At other times, especially before a class, I do it physically as a ritual. When I enter the room where the event will take place, I clear the area, in part by using a bell *(ghanta)* and thunderbolt *(dorje* or *vajra)* and by burning incense. We have to protect ourselves and do the work to establish our altar, the place where alteration, change and transmutation occurs.

By giving the prayers "Crystal-Diamond Tube of Light" and "Opening Invocation for Prayer Services," you can invoke protective energies so that you are ready for the challenges of the day. With constancy, you can reach the point where within a few seconds you are still, the crystal-diamond tube of light is around you, and you are firm in your flowfield and sealed in light. If you aren't yet able to achieve this, you can get to this point. It just takes constancy, doing it day by day, every day.

2

Wield Engrams of Fire and Fohatic Light
in Your Creative Process

Those Who Are Progressing in Higher Alchemy,

Having attained a certain equilibrium in invoking the sacred fire to sustain a flowfield of cosmic love around you, it is time to bring to you the next step in your determined work as initiates. This work involves the wielding of certain engrammatic formulas for the dissolution of greater darkness in the world and in your own past.

As ancient patterns of karma are transmuted within your electronic belt—that area of your subconscious where the records of all misdeeds reside until converted into positive energy—you become more light. And as the light of your eye, your mind, and your aura begins to glow with a new radiance and you are able to sustain the necessary quotient of fire from ascended realms, you enter into a newfound freedom to be a co-creator with God. This freedom is not license to do as you choose; it is an opportunity to enter into the planning and outpicturing of greater God-directed works to free other lifestreams still caught in the maya of illusory living.

Dear hearts, the preparation required and the sacrifice necessary to become a God being is fraught with attempts by the sinister force to bend your consciousness and entice you to enter into an interdimensional rift of darkness in a netherworld existence. Many who were almost knocking at the gate of immortal freedom have been seduced into accepting a lesser state of existence whereby they have replaced their divine birthright with the dregs of that glorified ego state that seeks praise, power, and self-identification rather than the gnosis of pure light.

Thus, be careful as you are daring in your desire to soar to new levels of experiencing the spiritual realms. As your vision is opened and your heart is expanded, you will be required to view all with a certain nonattachment and objectivity. The Buddhic way, the Middle Way of maintaining that cosmic equipoise of nonreaction, allows you to keep tethered to the reality you seek. Therefore, maintain your devotional aura and be both guarded and humble in your acceptance of greater graces delivered to you as you begin an accelerated communion with ascended masters, angels, and devas of great stature and light.

See yourself at the nexus of an hourglass where above you is the heaven world and below you the material world. Utter the Hermetic axiom, "As Above, so below." Visualize the divine ideation of your Higher Self being mirrored into manifestation in the world of form. This cosmic magic occurs through the nexus of your heart one with God's, and it cannot fully outpicture unless you are centered in the stillness of purity—pure reality.

As an alchemist, the more you know of all the sciences, the more easily you will be able to speed up the process of precipitation into the Now of immediate change, wherein the normal cycles of life in your realm are compressed, and etheric, mental, emotional, and physical cycles are annihilated into a point of final acceptance.

I again recommend the study of the atomic architecture of crystals, the absorption and transfer of light-energy in photosynthesis, and the vibratory rates at which the molecules of the substances you require in your work quiver. 3-D representations or to-scale models of what you desire always allow the convergence of more energy into the final point of precipitation. Advances in the use of imaging that bring the play of light, shadow, proportion, and structure into an accurate representation of your goal should be utilized by artists of the spirit who would rather create a new world of purity than a chimera of darkness.

Alchemical change is not some notion of a mindless wizard who desires to abrogate the laws of cause and effect. It is a higher science of glorifying God through the valuing of every erg of energy and through seeking ways to hallow space by the focused use of that vibrant light that went forth in the Beginning to stir the cosmic void into motion. Study the Hermetic sciences and the Emerald Tablet[13] to understand engrams of fire that are keys to your use of fohatic light. Through the perfect voice of love, send forth the divine issue of compassionate transmutation where darkness, when illuminated, simply vanishes.

Know the divine afflatus of the breath of the Holy Spirit—pure fire that impels atoms, cells, and electrons into perfect harmony, health, and happiness. Close off the sensual world of despair and human questioning. Invite the rarefied thought processes of the Elohim, the cosmic creators of planetary spheres, to take up residence within your life and being.

Fohat is star-fire light corralled and channeled to effect an immediate and powerful transformation. It requires the energetic use of the voice (throat chakra), the diaphragm (solar plexus), the heart, the third eye, and the Higher Mind. Create in your mind's eye visual representations in the form of symbols of your desired results. See as a thoughtform the progressive stages of outpicturing these results, with the stages strung together like knots on a string. Make the call to your Higher Self to utter the specific words that will then set this string on fire through your powerful and impassioned prayer, using the power of the energy within your sun center (solar plexus) to ignite the first symbol on the string.

Through the fiat you give, a ray of perfect ruby love-energy will explode from your heart and then travel through your throat chakra using the keys locked in your third eye in the thoughtform you've created in higher realms. The fire then ignites each stage of the progression on the string like fireworks, and each successively burns until the full string is glowing. This is the key to getting more spiritual bang for your buck through the harmonious and powerful use of all your chakras and resources.

In due time I will reveal certain geometric patterns that will be helpful to use as you visualize perfection come to Earth through your heart and mind. You will receive, at the behest of your Real Self, certain symbols, keys, and formulas that will allow you to more easily precipitate God-good in your world.

Instead of long hours of penitent prayer asking repeatedly for mercies and graces to come to you, through the powerful uttering of short, fohatic verbs highly charged with cosmic intent you can rend the veil between the material and spiritual worlds and bring into manifestation your alchemical dreams.

Blessings to those who will press on in the science of joyful living in the Now of God-love. Truly and always yours for alchemical transcendence, I am

Saint Germain
Aquarian Master of Fire

DCL: The *electronic belt* is where our karma resides. It's an area shaped like a kettledrum that is roughly from the navel down. All of our good energies go up in spirit to our causal body and the karma gets stuck in the area of the electronic belt. Clairvoyants can see this kettledrum effect around people, and it is more pronounced around those who are less conscious or who have a heavier karma. We all have at least a bit of karma left; otherwise we wouldn't be on the Earth.

At some point on the path we are all tested to make sure we maintain our humility. This testing is ongoing. We have to be on guard because it is easy to slip—these are subtle things. We have to be in integrity, remain humble, and give God the glory for everything. We have to try to sublimate our human propensities and train our focus on God. We have to be careful what our motives are. Is our motive self-serving or is it to be of service to others? The gifts that we receive are sacred and are intended to bless life. If we misuse them, we may lose them.

Saint Germain's caution applies to all and it bears repeating: We must be careful what our motives are as we dare to soar to new levels of experiencing the spiritual realms.

Create a Precise Model in Your Mind's Eye

The key to alchemy and precipitation is to annihilate all of those other processes into one point of acceptance, "I accept now, O Lord, your light"; and there is the gold, so to speak, right in your hand. Knowledge of the natural sciences can be helpful. The Bulgarian spiritual teacher Omraam Mikhaël Aïvanhov[14] went back to school and studied the sciences, and then he could teach on any subject. He penetrated to the very core of understanding the depths of those sciences infused with his higher understanding from the framework and vantage point of spirituality.

When you know the sciences, you can see so many awesome relationships. For instance, in chemistry class, when I finally understood the relationship between atoms and molecules, it was cosmic. It's all about us and our relationship with God and with each other. If you were to go back now and study biology, chemistry, physics, or another science, you would be so much more able, through spiritual gnosis, to see things in a new light.

You can create a precise model in your mind's eye, a superstructure of what you desire to precipitate. Doing so will help you to fill in that model with substance so that it can manifest. This is part of alchemy. If you have a blueprint of anything in your life, the more defined and clear and specific it is with all the details, the better you are able to manifest it. Architects create scale models and blueprints of structures they design. To be an architect is to be an alchemist; it involves creating the whole structure in design form before it gets clothed in reality with substance. To build a structure, builders require blueprints showing every detail precisely, including electrical details, plumbing details, everything.

Alchemy is not like Harry Potter taking a wand and doing something that is not according to the laws of the cosmos. Saint Germain is always specific in how he utilizes energy for the highest purposes of light. The difference between magic from the human level and divine magic, the alchemical light-work of the masters, is night and day.

Meditating upon the Elohim, the Lords of Creation, and attempting to conceive and perceive as they do begins to bring some of their thought processes into play through our mind. When we pray or sing to the Elohim, the stream of their awareness can come to us and we start to see things the way they do—from a higher and more objective perspective, from all angles and planes. The more objective we become, the more compassionate we become. We no longer judge people from one little facet of their whole being. We naturally become more tolerant and no longer sweat the small stuff.

Fohat Is Star-fire Light Corralled and Channeled

Saint Germain defined *fohat* and gave us keys for harnessing it in our alchemy. You create a thoughtform of a progression from here to what your desired result will be on a cosmic scale. You have little "firecrackers," like knots on a string, which are indicative of the stages of the progression, of what will lead to the next thing and then the next so that the end you conceive of will occur. You release fiery energy—*Ha!*—through your fiat powered by your solar plexus and tempered by love. You charge that first knot with energy and, like a firecracker, it goes off. Each one successively goes off. And then, on a cosmic level through this fohat, the end result is accomplished.

A *fiat* is a short powerful call such as this: "God, come and help the Earth now!" The fiat "Archangel Michael, save me!" is a call you can use in a crisis. If you are in danger or close to being in an accident, utter that fiat with fohat. Power your fiat with a charge from your solar plexus. This is not a reactionary release of unbridled emotional energy. It is controlled, and it animates your word with a thrust of God-power that allows what you call for to come forth.

We all have projects, alchemical things we are working on. This process of harnessing and releasing fohat is how the master explains to do it with a charge. Meditate on this. Work with it, try it. If you desire something enough and you storm heaven in the right way, with right motive and fohat, it can happen. This is higher alchemy. This is for adepts. If you can conceive of the end from the beginning, this is how you do it. If you are involved in a project and you know from experience what it will take to accomplish it, you can compress all that into one powerful laser-like frequency, *fohat,* and allow it to be manifest instantaneously.

3

Activate the *Siddhis* through Resonance

Students Progressing in the Alchemy of Higher Love,

Grateful I am that you have perceived the divine fruit of cosmic love as manifest within you. Grateful I am that you have taken to heart the pure teachings on divine alchemy and begun to spin within you a chrysalis of fire so that in your meditation you are contacting that inner purity that will win for you immortal perfection. Grateful I am that some among mankind are rising into that divine estate where God does grant the full blessing of perfect love, which casts out all fear[15] and unknowing and replaces it with a stream of radiance from his own heart.

Beloved ones, we now move upward into a new level of cosmic alchemy. Having practiced the keys that I have given on the accelerated use of the science of the word in releasing fohatic fire, you are now ready to embark on developing the guarded activation of the *siddhis* in other chakras. The employment of these gifts and graces may only come when, through balance of heart, mind, and soul, you have placed beneath your feet any desire for personal gratification or the elevation of self in glory and honor.

Thus, the next step is for you to develop a practice of meditation on perfecting the original release of light of the upper chakras, wherein, in perfect balance, they create a humming action in perfect resonance.

You have uttered the sacred AUM, yet few have fully realized the totality of this key to universal harmony. I now release this key to you. The sacred AUM is the sound of creation. It is the universal note of God's being. It is the fulfillment of all even as it is released in both tonal harmony and in geometric symmetry. The AUM is the emergence of God as light in manifestation. It is the concentric flow of radiance as a cosmic stream issued forth through the voice one with the inner silence of the soundless sound.

See the AUM as a perfect *yantra** resonating within each chakra. Each chakra is a cosmic resonator and in and of itself is a creator. Thus, you have seven Elohim creating within you as your own chakras, one with the greater Elohim who created the worlds in the beginning. When you know yourself as God, fully God, then you are the Creator, the Preserver, and the Destroyer[16] all one within; you are God in manifestation within your own body, one with the Cosmic Egg.

See the AUM amplifying the activation of the light within each chakra, accelerating the spinning of the petals of each chakra. There is created a harmonic resonance as each chakra spins at its highest rate of vibration, one with each Elohim. As this resonance occurs, the AUM is both amplified and sustained within you and issues forth from you. Captivated by this tonal radiance, you merge with the bliss of the Infinite that is already within the seed of the sound of creation within you. From this point of perfect bliss, you enter the seed of creation. And from this seed, all is possible unto you, for you are God where you are.

Thus, in perfection, you are the Alchemist, for there is none other than thee. And in this seed, perfect alchemy is your only desire, your only way. You are the Creator and the creation as one. Your seed ideation, then, is instantaneous, for you are the manifestation of the All of your own identity as God. This is the knowing and the perfect attunement that every ascended being, one with God, has. This is the

yantra: a geometrical diagram used in meditation

mystery of creation that is reserved for those who have sublimated the desire for anything, for it is subsumed into the nothingness of the All of God. There is nothing besides God. You are God.

Dear hearts, Jesus and other masters who walked the Earth with this knowing of their own nothingness, even as they were one with God the Father, could perform any feat because of this inner harmony of perfect resonance with the Light. At the command of the pure Son of God, all the elements obeyed, because the Son was within and of those elements, which are also God. Therefore, God obeys Self and is Self-fulfilled in the Word become flesh[17] in one who is obedient to the Inner Light.

Only in meditation upon the One will you discern the perfect AUM manifest in your chakras. Only in the seamless gnosis of Self as the All within will you resonate in the harmony that you seek as a divine alchemist of the spirit. Therefore seek the music of the spheres first within if you are to manifest the outpicturing of the AUM without in perfect works of creativity. Seek and know the resonance of immortal life that is already yours through the science of acceptance, which comes through alignment and grace.

We will continue our alchemical studies on the science of perfect acceptance as we move forward in the art of living, moving, and having our being in a living, liquid crystal-diamond of light. As you prepare for the next lesson, visualize the crystal rays flowing through and within and around the liquid crystal in which you live. It is ever changing. It is ever evolving. It is ever glowing with the radiance of the God Presence that you are entering day by day, hour by hour, as your heart is one with mine.

Ever your champion to fulfill your reason for being a true alchemist of the spirit, I am

Sanctus Germanus
Progenitor of Worlds of Cosmic
Love-Wisdom to All

DCL: In the previous chapter, Saint Germain defined *fohat* and explained how to engage and release fohatic fire by first creating a string of images and thoughtforms and then using the fire of fohat, the fiat within fohat, to charge them and see them manifesting. Once you have practiced that and taken the master's teaching to heart, you are ready to move on to the next step.

Saint Germain has purposefully reiterated in these first few HeartStreams, just as he did in the first two alchemy books, that people must have the right motive in their use of the higher alchemical sciences of light. Because of the power in the science, people without right motive could turn these practices around and use them for great darkness.

The Hum of Perfect Resonance

Some of you have experienced what Saint Germain referred to as the humming action of the upper chakras in perfect resonance. When you reach this state, either through meditation or through your giving of mantras and decrees, you can feel the resonance. There is an engagement of the upper chakras together as one to exhibit a great power and energy field. This is an important concept. Imagine a pulley action similar to what you see with a car's fan belts; this will give you a sense of how the chakras work in resonance.

In The Hearts Center, in our preambles and closings to prayers and decrees, we often chant the prayer *Om Mani Padme Hum AUM.* When we chant the AUM, we accentuate three sounds: the *A* (signifying Alpha), the *M* (signifying Omega), and the *U* (signifying you) in between. When your voice is at rest, there is a natural closing of the mouth. So, to chant the AUM: First, with the *A* sound, you open the mouth to accept the light-energy from the Cosmic Egg, from the Source. The *U* sound in the middle of the word, with a vowel preceding it and a consonant following, ties the two together. With the *M,* you seal the sound flowing through you by that intonation where the sound is fully embedded within you. You close your mouth and then the vibration resonates within you. The *mmm* sound is associated with happy feelings; for example, when you eat something tasty you might say, "Mmm, that tastes good!" With the *mmm* sound manifest through the AUM, there is a natural levity of light, of acceptance within your being.

In addition to chanting, you can visualize the AUM as a perfect *yantra.* A yantra is a kind of geometric design or mandala, an energetic matrix that manifests in the ethers as you give a mantra. Combining a yantra with the release of fohat increases the power of your word.

Saint Germain's teaching empowers us to realize ourselves as creators and, within us, to realize our chakras themselves as creators. Our chakras are both cosmic resonators and creators. As we move through our day and we are in our purpose, manifesting our purpose through our sacred work, our chakras are spinning and creating light-waves. They are creating divine tonal qualities that are emitted to the cosmos. Everyone who comes within our purview and within our auric field receives the blessing of these tonal qualities and yantras that are resonating from within us. This is higher alchemy. "Praying without ceasing"[18] is an aspect of this alchemy in that our chakras themselves, as resonating centers, are in effect praying within us as we offer ourselves to the cosmos as cosmic resonators of light.

Pay attention to what you are feeling as you are hearing this teaching, as you are singing the song of your own soul and spirit within your chakras, as you are being buoyed up by the master Saint Germain, as you are feeling the integrity of these words and the empowerment of yourself as a co-creator and as a cosmic resonator.

Know Yourself as God

Each one of us is the Creator, the Preserver, and the Destroyer.

More and more I hear from individuals who are rising in their awareness of cosmic consciousness and understanding that they are God and that they can worship God within. This is not meant in an egotistical way; it is with the full humble acknowledgement that God is present within them and within each one.

To be one with the Elohim requires a step-up of our conscious awareness to accept the fact that God at the Elohimic level of co-creation can exist within us. When we begin to accept this and to actually work with the Elohim within ourselves, we are entering into that oneness with the Elohim that allows us to be true co-creators. Saint Germain's teaching that you are the Creator and the creation as one expresses clearly what so many people are beginning to experience more and more. I'll share a simple example.

Early one morning, as my wife and I were giving *Kuan Yin's Rosary of Mercy*,[19] I had my eyes open occasionally and I saw cowbirds and red-winged blackbirds eating from the feeders outside. We especially enjoy watching the colorful finches, and at one point my wife said, "Oh, I wish the finches would come back!" Well, about a minute later, the house finches were back at one of the feeders. I saw that as an instantaneous manifestation of desire coming to fruition.

Know yourself as the All within. Whatever gets you back to the state of your oneness with Alpha and Omega, your God Parents, continue it. Meditation can be especially helpful. Once, while I was listening to a recording of whale sounds, I had a cosmic experience of being in the womb of Omega back before I incarnated in matter.[20] Experiences of oneness may come from time spent in the etheric retreats during sleep or from ancient memory. The reason you typically recall these memories when you awaken in the morning is so you can work with them. Keep a journal next to your bed so you can jot down these memories while they are fresh in your mind.

The Science of Acceptance

Heart Friends Learning to Accept More of the Infinite Within,

It is with great joy that I bring to you an understanding of the science of acceptance as a most salient and powerful means of divining the alchemical purposes of the Father within you. For when you fully employ and master this tool for your cosmic realization of holy purpose, your life will never be the same.

The parable of the prodigal son[21] is one that speaks to each one who has gone out of the way of full acceptance of the divine birthright. The Father fully desires each child of his heart to become a joint heir[22] of all the riches and gifts of the Spirit. The Father desires to extend the full manifestation of the kingdom of heaven to every son and daughter, for this is what a true God Parent does.

Many among mankind have accepted the lie that life is a struggle, that it takes a supreme level of sacrifice to win anything of a divine nature, and that God is a miserly sort of fellow who requires us to beg for all that we receive. Nothing could be further from the truth. God in all his greatness desires simply to extend the fullness of all riches of the Spirit to each one. And it is through engaging in the science of acceptance that you will finally realize this accelerated opportunity to partake of the divine offering.

Acceptance is a science, for it requires knowledge of certain cosmic laws, including the laws of correspondence, congruence, and harmony. Acceptance is a science because it is through a determined response to these laws that the fullest application may be manifest in the world of form.

When you accept the admonition to be a son or daughter of God,[23] you first must realize that you are capable of playing that role. You must sense with your whole being that you are worthy, that you have what it takes; and that through the cape of ability, which you may don, you may step upward fully into the functionality of a pure son or daughter of the Divine One, radiating spiritual fire and fulfilling your reason for being.

Unfortunately, many among mankind have been stung by the lie that all are sinners and must grovel before a wrathful potentate to ask forgiveness and mercy. I say that God long ago granted you the fullness of himself when he gave you his own Presence of perfect love, which still vibrates above you in the same immortal stream of radiant light-energy as when you were first ideated in God's cosmic mind. It is only through the lie of separation that mankind has accepted his mortality and thereby has also realized in his own unreal world the bane of that limited life in that world of illusion.

Acceptance requires the courage to stick one's head through the clouds and know that God-reality that has always been there, hovering just above you. It requires knowing that the glory that awaits is for each one and not for only one Son of God or the few who, through some freak of nature, have been granted a special grace. Yes, acceptance is the fate of each one who seeks to make it his own through a conscious act of will, knowledge, and love of the God-good that is ready to be received for the asking.

The science of acceptance requires a certain understanding of vibration, where you come to realize that if you desire what heaven has to offer, you must begin to come into harmony with those vibrations of perfection. Therefore, your life must be ordered and congruent with certain levels of cosmic joy wherein you no longer sink into states of morose thinking, densifying your mind and emotions into a depressive state and again thinking of yourself as less than a divine spirit.

The science of acceptance necessitates your congruence with holy purpose as you see the playing field of life as opportunity to win greater levels of grace, which may then be shared with all. Competition drops away as internal harmony is accentuated and all around you feel that you have come to the inner resolution of who you are. And through your refined aura of wholeness, you are now capable of being a more proactive contributor to the spiritual evolution of divine awareness on Earth.

· Acceptance is merging with the spirit of who you are within the greater aura of God. Acceptance is knowing that because one elder son or daughter of God has shown you the way, you can and simply must walk that way home to God's heart. Acceptance is believing in the worthiness of God to be thyself in action, for you cannot become immortal by thinking that it is humanly possible—it is only possible in the reality of God being you. You must be humble enough to realize it without claiming that you did it or that you were somehow more special than others of his children.

Beloved ones, it is time to accept who you are. There is no other choice that is acceptable now. This is not blasphemy, because in your holy acceptance of God where you are, you are by congruence also accepting all others as God where they are. When all see the joy of this process, the true party of divine glory may begin, and the Divine King will welcome all who have taken his invitation to heart and come to the table to receive what is rightfully and righteously theirs.

Yes, all have been the prodigal ones, and all must return to the Source. I am here to receive you, to bathe you in the violet flame, and to dress you in new garments of grace that you may wear in the presence of the Divine One because you have answered the call and come home. Having been received fully as heirs of all spiritual blessings, may your alchemical words and works expand as you now employ your newfound freedom to be a co-creator with God.

Ever yours in the great symphony of life as musicians for the Infinite, I am

Saint Germain
Director of Advanced Classes
in Alchemical Love

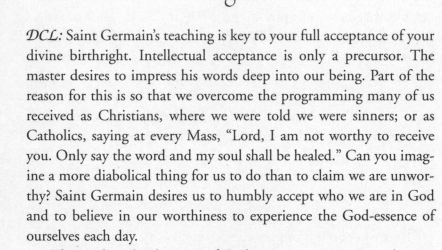

DCL: Saint Germain's teaching is key to your full acceptance of your divine birthright. Intellectual acceptance is only a precursor. The master desires to impress his words deep into our being. Part of the reason for this is so that we overcome the programming many of us received as Christians, where we were told we were sinners; or as Catholics, saying at every Mass, "Lord, I am not worthy to receive you. Only say the word and my soul shall be healed." Can you imagine a more diabolical thing for us to do than to claim we are unworthy? Saint Germain desires us to humbly accept who we are in God and to believe in our worthiness to experience the God-essence of ourselves each day.

Those who take the reins of God-power as co-creators, who create things rather than waiting for someone to tell them to do it, are progenitors. When you move into integrity by acceptance of who you are in God, you create a sphere of energy that also allows everyone in your sphere of influence to accept all that they are in God.

The Laws of Correspondence, Congruence, and Harmony

Saint Germain noted three aspects of acceptance—the laws of correspondence, congruence, and harmony. The law of correspondence states that our outer world is a reflection of our inner world—as within, so without. It is a slight variation of the Hermetic axiom, As Above, so below.

The law of congruence states that things equal to the same thing are equal to each other.[24] This is an axiom of mathematics, specifically geometry, and it is also true in spiritual science. You put A over B, and if they are coequal and congruent, then they are one. From a mystical standpoint, if we are synthesizing God within ourselves, then by that process of synthesis we become God in manifestation. This is congruence.

Harmony is the law of the universe and is also one of the divine virtues. Harmony denotes the balance of the masculine and feminine aspects of Alpha and Omega. Within the law of harmony is a host of subtle aspects of beingness that facilitate the emanation of God's quintessences throughout the universe, especially through the music of the spheres. Through meditation, you can translate to your spiritual life all that you have learned about harmonic scales, chromatic scales, and chord structures. Because of the cosmic law of harmony, which perfectly balances justice with mercy, we can be assured that there is no injustice in the universe. Karmic reciprocity, or the law of cause and effect, is the playing out, or outpicturing, of the higher law of harmony.[25]

5

Accelerate Your Vision
into Full Realization

Ascending Ones Who Would Behold the Truth of Life,

I would give you now the next course in your diet of divine inspiration. This heavenly meal consists of a teaching and a quintessence on the principles of accelerating your visualization into the domain of full realization.

As you know, vision is required in order to see the end results of your alchemical work. Many of you are just beginning to gain footholds in the realm of pure vision whereby, through the path of the Middle Way, you see the goal before you and do not allow elements of duality to sway you to the left or to the right of your course. This is necessary for attaining the state of oneness whereby pure seeing becomes first the acceptance of and then the final precipitation of your goal.

I have previously given you the ritual of the Cloud,[26] whereby the energy of creation is coalesced around the seed idea of your creative purpose and accelerated in focused attention until all is light around you. The end result of this work is the bringing into your domain the light of Spirit in a tangible manifestation of God-good.

Now your work is to learn the art of commanding energies of cosmic proportions into manifestation through the blending of your aura directly with your divine Buddha nature so that you, as God, create in the Now, without any interference from without or any acceptance of lesser energies to distract you from the process.

After you have accepted the totality of your Real Self as the active principle in your life, then through the entropy of limitation in time and space there is the tendency to sink back into the domain of unknowing, where you lose this realization in moments of detachment from that pure state of being. The key now is to no longer struggle in this process. Instead, through meditation day and night, stay within the aura of the Divine as the creative one that you are.

Beloved ones, this is the final test of all true initiates in the process of becoming immortal—to maintain the humility of Godhood in the process of the final purification whereby all human consciousness is subsumed into the divine estate. Many have fallen during this cycle, thinking that through a superhuman effort they could sustain their perfected consciousness, whereas it is only through the art of cosmic identification through sweet surrender that one may be trued and aligned into the crystal of Self.

This is why we have given you the visualization of the liquid crystal-diamond of light, which, when fired by your heart flame, will eventually become the full diadem of cosmic perfection. If you could see higher beings who have dwelt in immortal perfection for eons, you would see them as starry crystals of light, for they have accelerated the science of being to such an extent that their alignment with the original design of perfection is complete in all ways.

The master Omraam has taught that in the Golden Age the science of Surya Yoga will include all other yogas as methods of union with God.[27] This is true, for when all is realized by the advanced student, the science of alchemy ultimately boils down to the art of becoming a Sun center of divine light. This is the great joy of cosmic realization.

Therefore I suggest that the serious student study the words of this master of wisdom, who was truly sent by Brahma as the Pure Son to convey to a world the initiatic science of becoming Suns of God. In his words you will discover the inner science of advanced alchemy that is written in nature and is only fully cognized by those who see, through meditation, the seed reality of the perfected design. Meditate on creation through the Solar fires of the Sun of being. Meditate on fire as the creative principle in all alchemy. Meditate on how, through identification, you may become a Sun and live and move and have your being in immortality forever.

Ever yours for the transcending of cycles into perfect love, I am alchemically changing the cosmos as we speak.

Saint Germain

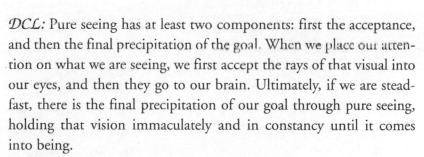

DCL: Pure seeing has at least two components: first the acceptance, and then the final precipitation of the goal. When we place our attention on what we are seeing, we first accept the rays of that visual into our eyes, and then they go to our brain. Ultimately, if we are steadfast, there is the final precipitation of our goal through pure seeing, holding that vision immaculately and in constancy until it comes into being.

Mother Mary was tested before she was given the assignment of bearing Jesus as the Christ Child. She was first required to hold the immaculate concept[28] in her being in order to determine whether she would waver or remain constant. Diversions were sent her way to try to catch her off guard, and these were purposeful. She proved true to her course, and thereby she earned the right to bear the Christ, the Manchild, within Jesus the boy.

Mary demonstrated her mastery of the science of pure seeing, immaculate vision, first by accepting the goal and then by remaining steadfast until that goal precipitated into the physical. This is our work. It is intense, concentrated, focused work to learn the art of commanding energies of cosmic proportions into manifestation. Those of you who have prayed and decreed for many years know the dynamics of this science, because you feel the currents and the frequencies of God-power flowing through your chakras.

When you are able to sustain thoughtforms and the action of light by uninterrupted focus upon a particular visual, goal or engram, then it manifests. You feel a release through your chakras, a great flow as the light coalesces into those essences that are captured by your attention. You put a sphere, a circle of light, around what you are co-creating with God. And because you are a co-creator with God, God infuses it with energy and it precipitates. It is a very powerful co-creative action to engage in meditation at the level where you are affecting worlds of cosmic proportion.

The Mystery of Surrender

If you have trouble reconciling yourself in the highest way, if you feel any blockage, if you feel at all that your human ego is somehow getting in the way of your oneness with your Higher Self, you may recite the prayer *Sacred Surrender: Ritual of the Divine Interchange*[29] and feel God's light and energy flowing through you. Allow the words of this beautiful ritual to pour through you in praise of the One. See how surrendering to God brings you back to your reality as a God being.

Another practice that can facilitate surrender to the Divine is the act of prostration. Prostration before the Divine is employed in various world religions in varying degrees—for example, in Islam during the five obligatory prayers performed daily, and in Catholicism during the rites of ordination to holy orders. The act of prostration, practiced once in a while, can get you into the mode of complete surrender to the Divine. If you can, practice it somewhere private, perhaps in a safe place in nature or on the grass in your own backyard.

If you do try it, see what connection you make with the Earth and with the cosmos by allowing all of your chakras to be connected with the earth, engaged with the earth and with the Earth Mother. You may be surprised at what occurs. You may feel a connection you have not felt before. As a child you may have lain on your back or on your stomach or rolled on the grass or done things in nature. In that carefree act, you were really in a state of simple surrender to the All within nature.

Fire: The Creative Principle in All Alchemy

Alchemists have long used fire as an important component within their experiments. Saint Germain provides us the wherefore and the how of harnessing the power of fire in our own alchemy: "Meditate on how, through identification, you may become a Sun and live and move and have your being in immortality forever." Identification is a very important component of this process, for as we identify with God, we become a Sun.

We must first feel worthy and validated enough to be called a Sun (Son) of God and move out of the domain of the not-self and the feeling or thinking that we are sinners. We must be bold enough to become engaged in higher alchemy. We could not have received these higher alchemical teachings until we had moved past the Piscean Age and the old order of the dominance of the priestcraft and those who put themselves in positions of being the intercessor between God and us. For these intercessors, even when they meant well, were displacing our relationship with our own Christ Self and our Godhood.

We must take that power back by claiming our divinity from the perfected essence of our Godhood, not from the human ego. When we do take that power back, we can work the alchemical works. We can do those greater works that Jesus said we would do because he went to the Father.[30] Jesus ascended into his own Solar Presence and into the Presence of God the Father.

Saint Germain boldly stated that he was alchemically changing the cosmos as he spoke. He instructed us to "meditate on creation through the Solar fires of the Sun of being." Ponder this: You are a co-creator with the Divine. The Solar fires of the Sun of your own being are constantly burning and emanating light just as the physical sun does. Will you be bold enough to change the cosmos, with Saint Germain, as you speak?

6

Become the Instrument
of the Divine Alchemist

Aspirants of God-consciousness Pursuing the High Road,

Training is the key to mastery. Training as the sharpening of the mind that leads to the perfect acuity and acumen of Godly virtues is what is required of my students. Training whereby you hone the spiritual senses so that all that you experience is the reality of creative joy, a life lived to the fullest, is my goal for you.

Advanced alchemists enjoy a good read, a good regimen, and most of all, a good session in disciplining the self to become the instrument of the Divine Alchemist. Although this may take many forms in various cultures and climes, the result is the same—to bring light to a world in need of illumination. Those who have left their mark upon the ages determined that a lasting legacy was necessary, and that this required the all of their giving each day. To overcome the inertia of the gravitational pull of human living requires that the divine life be invoked and sustained.

As you pursue the alchemy of a life lived for a holy purpose, realize that those who made it before you have carved a pathway that will make your journey easier, even though the conditions are unique during each trek home. Just as many great lights have set markers and signs along the way for you, you may do the same by clearing the path of boulders and brambles that have blocked your path.

Some remain anonymous in their attainment of cosmic consciousness, preferring not to draw the attention that often magnetizes forces that can oppose their victory. Most have learned that leaving a clear roadmap for others is worth the extra strain, taking their cue from the Buddha, who returned from nirvana to help others navigate the sea of samsara. These are the forerunners that can teach you of the surest pathway and train you in the use of the equipment and in developing the skills that you require.

Beloved ones, it is to your advantage to develop a relationship with one or two masters of wisdom who can take you on as apprentices until you gain the full mastery of the next level of your Godhood. A true master will work diligently with you and prepare you for that next series of initiations, caring more for your development than for your attachment to him. When you have progressed to the point of requiring greater teaching, it is always his pleasure to introduce you to one who can train you in the next series of lessons and teaching.

In many cases, great masters with supreme attainment have taken it upon themselves to hold back in their own development of greater levels of cosmic consciousness for the very purpose of aiding many more to attain their immortal perfection. These have developed a clear lesson plan and know the surest footings for you at every turn, and it behooves you to listen, obey, and benefit thereby.

In the process of adhering to the master's lesson plan as you are discerning greater levels of self-mastery in the natural unfolding of your own evolution, your keen feedback always helps that master to refine his training or to apportion it in perfect increments for your best and highest experience as well as for those following you. We therefore applaud those who document their alchemical training, clarifying what has been most beneficial for them in their studies and work. Regardless of what ray you serve on, the recording of your experience will be helpful for many coming after you and it will also serve as a legacy for your own children and spiritual students. In clearly defining your unique means to overcoming, you thereby add to the great wisdom teaching that may be shared in future generations by teachers whom we are even now contacting and raising up in consciousness.

Think what this world would be like if all that the Lord Buddha or Lord Jesus did and said was clearly recorded and documented with numerous eye-witness accounts! Much of the miasma that has clouded their lives and works would be cleared away so that a clear methodology of the path of adeptship could be read and studied by all. Alas, much of what was recorded was either lost or tampered with and misused. You see in your world the effects and results of this travesty.

Strive with me to study what has been recorded in holy verse that still remains, and determine how through your own efforts we may together leave a greater legacy of light for the millions. Those of you with skills in writing, compiling, and editing are required to prepare this teaching for a new class of students who are coming. Those of you with skills in public relations and the media are required to develop programs and means of transmitting to the world the new word of wisdom that we bear.

Work while ye have the light.[31] Confide in us and we will lead you. Seek to collaborate with those whose skills augment or complete your own. Get moving in the business of bringing to bear in your world the next best plan to reach those among mankind who are ready to hear and study our words. Your efforts will be rewarded as you one day gaze into the eyes of those ready for the fruit of your service to life and recognize your own self in former days of waiting upon every word of your master with that joyful expectancy that creates the excitement of new discovery.

Become alchemists of the Word made flesh[32] this day, clothed by you in new garments of beauty for all to see.

Ever your divine paramour and the lover of your soul, I am goading you with Morya to make it happen now!

Saint Germain

DCL: The term *paramour,* though it often carries a derogatory meaning, was originally used in the thirteenth century by women to mean Christ and by men to refer to the Blessed Mother. Saint Germain, as our divine paramour and the lover of our souls, is ever-present and unwaveringly supportive of our soul's advancement.

Discipline the Self unto Adeptship

What is meant by disciplining the self? Showing up and doing your spiritual or body-mind practice consistently, even when you may be tired, is a disciplining of self. Way beyond that, though, beyond just putting in time, is being engaged and focused. This is the highest discipline—being on spot, focused on God, your heart trued to his, your mind shutting out the distractions of the world and abiding within the mind of God.

Saint Germain's teaching is for those who are becoming empowered and self-realized as God-men and God-women to the extent that they will in turn inspire others to take heart and grow into their own adeptship. We are about the creation of adepts. The Hearts Center was founded so that people can be re-emboldened to be who they are, to become adepts, and then to go forth and victoriously share the masters' teachings of light to move us into the Golden Age.

Be Forewarned and Forearmed

Transformative Ones,

In the annals of the Universal Great White Brotherhood, there exist records of various cosmic beings' interactions with Earth, including its very creation and its seeding with life substance. At a certain point in mankind's evolution, it became necessary for the establishment of protective bands or belts around the Earth to seal her from the intrusion of certain alien and intergalactic forces who sought to use her resources and life for ignoble purposes.[33] The history of all, if fully known by mankind, would give you pause to consider how much of science fiction is actually the outpicturing of a level of truth from the unconscious memory of the various root races and their mingling and ongoing evolution toward Godhood and a golden-age civilization.

The reason I bring this to your attention during my course in advanced alchemy is that many of you, when beginning to open the portals to your own cosmic consciousness during your alchemical experiments, will contact these records and memories, and you must be equipped with the spiritual tools to deal with them. Those who are not fully realized and who thereby do not have instant access to the akashic records[34]—which are simply the fullness of the Mind of God in its subtle vibratory resolution—must rely on those ascended or unascended masters who have the ability to read them to lead them past certain blocks and warn them of impending dangers in their spiritual journey.

Blessed ones, to be forewarned and forearmed is the requirement of the hour. For in the working out of karmic cycles at the end of one age and the beginning of another, certain cosmic forces come into play. The Lords of Karma do attempt to help mankind make the leap to evolve fully from one level to the next in their spiritual attainment. It therefore behooves all to have teachers from among our realms who can clearly show them the way, leading them through cosmic portals of understanding, dividing the Word, and lending their energies of perfect love.

Calling upon the Lord through rhythmic prayer, mantra, and intoning the sacred sound of the AUM, augmented by the use of visualization and the sacred fire breath[35] (see page 91), is required of those who would attune their consciousness to the Lord of the World and his plan for planetary change. Striving to uplift all through an example of purity through the use of the sacred science of alchemy is required of all advanced students. Therefore, the convergence of various spiritual schools' understanding and use of the science of invocation through the spoken word is coming to the fore even as the ancient memories of how cosmic beings create and sustain worlds are also revealed.

Dear ones, all true mystics intone the name of God in their own tongue, for in the sending forth in sound of the sacred seed syllables of that name, the creative fires are keyed into action and the universe is obedient to the word of the son or daughter of God. Once you have this key, it is imperative that you never misuse it in any statement of imperfection. Always raise your voice on high first to praise and honor the Lord and only then to effect his assistance in your alchemical work. Realization occurs when one is one with the Word. Enlightenment comes when the light shines throughout one's entire being. Perfection comes when the heart sings fully in unison with the Divine.

There is no reason to fear forces or flowfields of darkness that at times ring themselves around you simply because they are witness to the growing auric light that you bear in your quest for divine union. An awareness of their presence and of your own ability to attune fully to a higher energy pattern that allows you to rise above and beyond their limited mental state is necessary for your ultimate victory. Some may attempt to catch you off guard and then implant certain viral probes within subconscious layers of awareness to slow down your progress and attainment. It is then that you must wield the sword of the Word in the fullness of a knight of the Spirit, to slay those interlopers of death who would denude you of all your creative work for the Lord.

Therefore I say, use the word if you would become the Word. Send forth the sound of cosmic joy as you utter fiats of truth to clear a pathway for God-love. Use the sacred science of invocation as you intone perfection in your world, for the Word must be made flesh daily, again and again, before the Lord's full appearing within all.

There are certain secret alchemical formulae that are known only to those who can be trusted. These consist of both symbols and syllables in an ancient tongue which, when combined and uttered in humble knowing, instantaneously produce the desired results in the world of form. This is not magical mumbo jumbo; it is the distillation of the keys to the alchemical fires of heaven brought to bear in a more direct manifestation for the elect because they have elected to serve mankind. It is like using a kind of cosmic stenography wherein a shortcut to the full-blown manifestation is developed because one has first mastered all the steps and stages required for that attainment.

A certain knowledge of Sanskrit, Hebrew, and Latin will assist you in preparing for the release of these secret formulae. Those with mastery of all three languages who also have a knowledge of occult (hidden) science would be of great help to the serious student of alchemy. In time I will release certain keys to your advancement based on your own personal use of the gnosis already transferred in all previous lessons.

Yours for the victory of intuitive learning where your mind is merging with mine more each day, I am Holy Brother for all who would know me,

Saint Germain

DCL: Over many eons of time, Earth has been home to a diverse array of civilizations, races, and evolutions. Esoteric tradition identifies seven primary *root races*—seven distinct groups of souls, or live-waves, sent forth from the Father-Mother God in different epochs. Members of each root race share an archetypal pattern and a specific aspect of God-consciousness. The first three root races lived in golden-age civilizations, fulfilled their divine purpose on Earth, and ascended. Many members of the fourth, fifth, and sixth root races are embodied on Earth today, learning lessons, balancing karma, and fulfilling their divine purpose. Recently, members of the seventh root race have begun embodying on Earth.

Those of us from the fourth and fifth root races have been on this planet for a long time. Saint Germain implied that many of us were embodied in Atlantis or Lemuria when a group of intergalactic beings came to Earth and attempted to seed Earth with the DNA of their evolution, including strains of darkness that were not benign. Saint Germain brings this knowledge to our conscious attention so that, forewarned, we can ally ourselves with the masters and receive their guidance, protection, and assistance.

The record of everything that has ever occurred in our physical universe—every word, deed, thought, and feeling—is stored in an etheric dimension known as *akasha.* Clairvoyants and those who have higher vision can see both the good and the bad. Still, they can choose to create a screen around the darker energies of the astral plane so that they don't have to look at them all the time. They can be peripherally aware of those energies through a kind of peripheral higher vision, and they can focus on their Presence and on the higher light-energies of the etheric plane in ascended-master realms.

Adepts and those with developed soul, or psychic, faculties can read the akashic records as easily as they might read a book or watch a film. You may have read or heard about various masters who could instantaneously read akasha in order to perceive what was about to happen in the lives of their disciples, and who would warn and instruct them in what they required to know in order to pass their initiations. The masters assist us in this manner today, typically through messages or inspiration that we receive on the inner. By maintaining a state of listening grace, we stay open to their guidance and instruction.

Thirty-three Levels of Teaching

Saint Germain spoke of *dividing* the Word—that is, working with the teaching, parsing it, seeking to understand the nuances of what the master is saying, even the wisdom between the words, between the lines. When we look at something from different views, we often achieve new levels of understanding.

The teachings of the masters are presented on thirty-three levels. Each time we read them, we receive fresh insights. If we re-read a book some years after we first read it, our experience can be almost as if we had never read it. As we bring to each reading the wisdom and knowledge we gained earlier and applied practically in our life, we continue to receive new insights and new levels of understanding.

A Key to Communing with the Lord of the World

Saint Germain gave us a key to communing with the Lord of the World. Gautama Buddha holds that office, and in that capacity he sustains the divine spark within Earth's evolutions and nurtures our potential for higher consciousness. Calling upon the Lord through rhythmic prayers or mantra, intoning the sacred AUM, and using visualization and the sacred fire breath are all components of attuning to the heart of Gautama.

We in the West now have many opportunities for giving Eastern mantras, singing *bhajans,* and intoning the AUM and the names of the deities. Having been primarily Judeo-Christian in the past, the West is now eclectic, international, global, cosmopolitan. In larger cities, we see people from all over the world and from diverse cultural and religious backgrounds. I believe we are moving into a time when over half of the people of many nations will accept the law of reincarnation and understand what is occurring with "the Shift," the spontaneous evolution[36] that is manifesting.

Intone the Sacred Name of God

Saint Germain has said that when you, a son or daughter of God, consciously and lovingly intone the name of God, the creative fires of heaven are keyed into action and the universe is obedient to your word. You summon great power when you speak the name of God in English as I AM THAT I AM. The Lord God gave us this name when he spoke out of the burning bush to Moses, saying, "This is my name forever, and this is my memorial unto all generations."[37] Saint Germain's entire "I AM" teachings through the Saint Germain Foundation, also known as the "I AM" Activity, in the 1920s, 1930s, and beyond, really began to clarify this science and led to the use of the I AM name in very powerful fiats and declarative affirmations.

When we learn of the power inherent in God's name and we begin to use "I AM" statements, we realize that in our higher understanding we can no longer righteously say the words "I am" and follow them with something negative. Saint Germain says it is imperative that we use the name of God first to honor and praise him, only then to enlist his assistance in our alchemy, and never in any statement of imperfection. Negative "I am" statements will coalesce what we affirm into our world in some way. An important key for us is to catch ourselves before we say something negative, and to replace it with a positive affirmation. Yet, even as we are mindful to do this, we can also be mindful that perfection is more about our hearts and our motives than it is about mistaken words or actions.

The Word Made Flesh through Invocation

We make the word flesh through invocation, through anchoring that word through our voice one with the Word, the Logos. The ascended masters are beyond time and space, and they have access to the Word, the Logos. They use tones and symbols and syllables in a number of different languages to create specific desired results. And those syllables, through their vibration, can have a powerful effect for change, for transformation.

In their HeartStreams, the masters sometimes intone a chant in an unknown tongue. We may at first be taken aback by the syllables and sounds they are chanting, yet sometimes they have explained afterward that through those chants they were creating something, or that they were blessing us, or placing electrodes of light within our higher mental body or our etheric body, or that they were cleaning out something from our astral body.

It would be an interesting study for someone to compare all of the HeartStreams where the masters, through divine glossolalia, are speaking in tongues, to study the key tones and syllables they use, and to attune to what they represent and to what is actually occurring. If you know Sanskrit, Hebrew, and Latin, you may be able to figure out some of this. It will take study. It will take being a sleuth, looking at cryptograms to figure out the underlying message. I believe that someone sometime will do this, perhaps someone who is a master of languages and has something to share with future generations about what the masters were actually doing when they were intoning these chants.

8

Accelerate into Cosmic Consciousness with the Crystal Rays

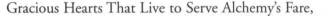

Gracious Hearts That Live to Serve Alchemy's Fare,

I am instructing you in the art of advanced alchemy, which is for those progressing on the path of divine love manifesting within you as increased compassion for all life. As your spiritual training ensues, the refinement of your sensitivity to the light-emanations of love-wisdom from your Divine Presence through the nexus of your heart should be increasing day by day. It is only through the acceptance and allowance of these higher energies to flow through your chakras that you may understand the higher laws of divine alchemy.

The action of the crystal rays is little understood by mankind. These rays are the conveyance of the senses of the Godhead to those who qualify themselves through deep reverence for the things of the Spirit. Hidden from the baseness and crassness of mortal consciousness, the qualities and action of the crystal rays allows the adherent to qualify light in an extraordinary manner for the raising of all life in the four quadrants of being. These quintessential energies, which are only discerned by the pure in heart, allow the acceleration of love-wisdom to occur through the five chakras of the hands, feet, and secret chamber of the heart so that one is literally catapulted into new dimensions of cosmic consciousness.

Often the spiritual alchemist may lose outer sense consciousness and swoon in a divine bliss born of the pressing through his being of the energies of the crystal rays, which are not native to the lower vehicles of selfhood. This can be somewhat disconcerting at first, until one has reached a level of adjustment whereby the divine energies activate higher nerve centers throughout the spiritual body, which then allows that one to live more as a light-being than an earthly being.

True mystics will understand whereof I speak, for they often dwell within two worlds, the human and the divine, seeing the pulsing of the energies of the aura of mankind and aware of the transmission of thought patterns and the interplay of both spiritual and astral (lower magnetic) energies within the worlds of all. Thus, as the crystal rays are activated, it is as if the dial of one's sensitivity to all vibrations is turned up exponentially and one no longer lives in a fleshy body—one lives in a new body of light. This can be somewhat disconcerting to the devotee at first, for it requires a departure from normal human sense consciousness, and it becomes more painful in many ways to continue living in a limited body. The mystic desires to stretch the consciousness into other realms of light, leaving the outer form to travel on wings of light to other worlds and higher spiritual highways with beings attuned to those octaves.

Those in whom the crystal rays are activated live in an almost dreamlike state, detached from the cares of this Earth, communicating with elemental life and nature spirits and angelic witnesses with ease, and they may seem to be somewhat aloof to life in the flesh. If you study the lives of many saints and mystics, you will discover this very real conundrum for them, for when one sees God one may no longer live as human. This time is one where the mystic must remain both vigilant and tethered to the reality of godly service in the Earth, for to loose oneself prematurely from the daily responsibilities of completing the rounds of karma yoga may necessitate returning to an unpleasant round of life whereby one must be "grounded" in order to fulfill one's obligations to all.

I urge all in whom the crystal rays flow to have concrete plans and an ordered schedule in your life to meet the demands of your calling and profession, whereby the true mastery of each phase of your spirituality is anchored in works of love manifest as tangible benefits to your fellowman. The Lord of All requires practical adepts who seek to leave footprints in the sands of time[38]—a documented path and a shining example to family, friends, and community of a life of love in action through compassionate works and deeds.

The crystal rays allow the soul to rise. They activate healing at a deeper level, at the root of problems, rather than dealing with the outer symptoms. They allow one to discern how karma, having been balanced to a degree where one is beginning to be loosed from the magnetic pull of the Earth, can be completely overcome to the point where the laws that one operated under previously no longer hold sway, for they have been superseded by higher laws of love-wisdom. This does not mean that the law of cause and effect no longer exists; it means that one is no longer bound by the activation of that law within, because there is nothing within to tether one to the Earth.

Some are fooled by sinister forces to believe that they have arrived at the gate of immortality when in fact they are host to all manner of discarnate entities that give glowing utterances of one's supposed high attainment. These are not true devotees who have sublimated their human propensities toward flattery and psychic thralldom; they are hollowed-out ones who have become havens for a host of problems. Cast aside all thoughtforms of astral reasoning issuing from these harbingers of darkness lest you listen and become hoodwinked into believing their ill-conceived lies.

Listen instead to the voice of divine reason effused by your Real Self, whose pulsing heart is always available to ray forth cosmic heartstreams of living fire through your being, cleansing you of past patterns of limited thinking and of any temporary lapses you may have on your spiritual journey. Claim divine alchemy working through you at all times. Use the laws I have conveyed through living a disciplined and ordered life of service to your fellowman. Apply and self-correct and meditate with great expectations for divine love to act more fully each day and hour through your words and works wholly sanctified by the angels.

I am your advocate and coach in the mastery of the crystal rays. Call to me and to Mighty Cosmos[39] and we will deliver the goods of spiritual gnosis as you are able to receive them. Yours ever in the practice of advanced alchemy, I am

Saint Germain

DCL: We can qualify light in an extraordinary manner in our four lower bodies right now. An effusion of the light of the five crystal rays can be ours right now through Saint Germain's mind-connection and heart-connection directly with us as we study this course in advanced alchemy. Each of us can commune directly with the master to receive the continuous heartstreaming of his consciousness, his love, his heart fires.

Inner Refinement Leads to Outer Refinement

As we change our diet—both our food and what we read and take in through other means—many of us have noticed that we can no longer live the way we lived in the past. We cannot take in certain substances or be engaged in certain activities without a detrimental effect, sometimes a huge one. We are becoming more refined beings, and because of that inner refinement, some of the denser things that we used to do or partake of no longer serve us.

This reminds me of the story about Ramakrishna going into Samadhi as he meditated upon the Divine Mother in numerous forms and seeming somewhat aloof as his body sat or stood still for hours on end when he was in this state. His disciples had to tend to him to keep him alive and fed so he wouldn't wither away. This may not be practical for most of us in the West, yet it demonstrates that we are much more than our physical bodies.

Divine Service Is Practical and Down to Earth

As spiritual aspirants, we of course desire union with God. At the same time, we know that service and practical, compassionate and loving work is the key to our victory, our union with the Divine.

When I travel to certain places, such as Mount Shasta or Sedona, I notice how many psychic shops, mediums, and UFO-type activities and groups there are and how many people who do channeling attempt to reach the ascended-master levels. Unfortunately, the vast majority of them are hoodwinked by discarnate spirits who do not have the high attainment that the masters have. Because the channels talk around issues, they open themselves up to astral entities and they don't have the grounding for their own higher attainment to unfold through a practical, balanced, disciplined path.

Lest anyone think that these psychic channels are speaking the words of the masters, here's a key: If there is a lot of flattery involved, you can be assured that it is not a true teaching. The masters goad us and love us and call us *beloved,* yet they don't flatter us to involve our egos. Individuals who are engaged in divine service for the ascended masters are always practical, grounded, and down to earth, not living in the skies. The proof is by their works.[40]

9

Call Forth Energies
of Cosmic Light Substance
into Your World

Gracious Ones Who Are Increasing in Cosmic Consciousness,

Attending to the spiritual requirements of mankind is the work of the Universal Great White Brotherhood, which includes three kingdoms—angelic and archangelic beings; all ascended sons and daughters of God; and the Elohim, highly evolved, powerful light-beings who wield vast stellar energies to sustain the spirit-matter cosmos. These three kingdoms of created beings work in perfect harmony in the blending of love, wisdom, and power on behalf of all sentient beings evolving through time and space to merge back with their Source.

Those of you who know the names of higher beings may key into their identities and vibration and call them forth into service in the domain and affairs of mankind. By free will, all have the opportunity to make wise choices in the judicious use of the energy that flows through the nexus of self, the heart, in either moving upward into the light or continuing the rounds of rebirth until the ultimate choice is made to merge with the cosmic stream of light that is the outpicturing of the Creator's being everywhere. Spiritual beings who serve the One God, the Universal Spirit of Love, may assist mankind when they are invoked, for only through your conscious willingness and desire through prayer and meditation will they enter your world to aid your path to wholeness.

The mystery schools of the Brotherhood have always held in high esteem those who have brought the light of truth from higher spheres into the world for the enlightenment and freedom of mankind. There exists ample proof—in certain tomes of ancient wisdom, within mythology, and even in the subconscious memory of the race—of the knowledge of highly evolved spiritual beings who may be implored to help raise the consciousness of all Earth's evolutions into a golden age of wisdom.

If the true history of the evolution of life on Earth were known, men would be amazed to see how, through the direct intercession of spiritual beings, your world has been sustained. Evolution does not occur through a chaotic or synchronistic synthesis of elements and energies that somehow merge to become what you see today as the miracle of life within mankind and within all of nature. An ordered plan and cosmic scheme has always been in play in your world, for if divine laws of balance and harmony were to be withdrawn from the manifestation of life, all would collapse into a cosmic void and be no more.

Value life as an opportunity for soul growth, for many who have passed through your world in the rounds of rebirth regret the poor choices they made. They yearn to return to the arena of action where free will holds sway in order to mend their ways and to serve life until they, too, evolve into higher worlds of light. You may assist these embodied souls by becoming an example of purity and love and through conscious service in teaching them the spiritual truths that you now accept as second nature on your journey.

Your work in higher alchemy may be accelerated through the correct application of the laws of conscious cooperation with ascended beings. This includes maintaining a certain disposition of humility, expectancy, and joy in receiving from our octaves the light and teaching that we would convey to you. It also requires that you employ the advanced instruction we give only for the greater good of all sentient life.

Thus, I admonish all serious students of alchemy to study and learn the science of invocation and prayer, whereby you may accelerate the balancing of your karma through the invocation of the violet fire of freedom, mercy, and forgiveness as well as the other colored light-rays, which will be useful in all your spiritual experiments. Learn from those who have mastered this science. Learn the nuances of calling forth the higher energies of cosmic light-substance into your world through the naming of divine benefactors and the rhythmic intoning of the sacred sound of life through prayers, mantras, and songs of adoration, gnosis, and God-empowerment.

Through the activity of The Hearts Center or other ascended-master-sponsored activities, you may become acquainted with this sacred science that will allow you to take years of struggle off your path and to increase the light in your aura whereby you garner more and more of the energies you will require to earn your own ascension at the close of this or the next embodiment, by the grace of God.

Beloved ones, soon many more among mankind will be chanting the songs of celestial praise to the Father-Mother God, invoking the servant-sons and daughters who long ago made the choice to return to his heart. Jesus and Mary, Gautama and Krishna, Confucius and Kuan Yin are only a few who continue to aid mankind in a most tangible way to return to the All-in-all. You, too, can be of great benefit to many when you master this alchemical art, which will then no longer be so mysterious. It will become a natural and pleasant part of your daily routine when you understand the beauty and harmony it engenders in the auras and lives of all.

I am your cosmic benefactor as you pursue the upward climb to the summit of being, ever seeking to grace the lives of all with love-wisdom flowing through your heart and mind each day. Yours for the manifestation of pure alchemy always, I am

Saint Germain

DCL: In our alchemy of light, we pray and call to God and the ascended masters and angelic host to increase goodness and light on Earth. Unfortunately, point/counterpoint, there exists a dark alchemy of nefarious ones, black magicians, witches, warlocks, and those possessed by demonic forces. Through sinister incantations and chanting and by placing their attention upon the astral plane, these adherents of darkness invoke fallen angels, Beelzebub, Satan. They work the works of darkness through their misuse, perversion, and inversion of the methods we employ with devotion and goodwill to work the works of light.

The science of the word, which we use for good, can be turned around by adepts on the dark side and used to invoke their dark masters, their quasi-gods. A modern example is the evil emperor in *Star Wars,* whom Darth Vader and others call *master.* Such things exist. And like the evil emperor, these dark ones, in order to shroud their true identities and control their subjects or others whom they use as tools, often set up systems whereby beings who are less advanced in the mastery of darkness do not really know who they are.

Our ascended-master brothers and sisters and elder light-beings do reveal to us who they are, although they may not give us their inner names. For example, the name Divine Director is not that master's inner name; it is the title of his office. Metatron is not the inner name of the master we know by that name. The inner name of some ascended masters contains the key to so much power and light that they do not reveal that name to us. They do this to protect their light and power from misuse as well as to protect us from the karma that would ensue should we misuse that light.

True Alchemy Proves the Law through Practical Works

We have free will on Earth, and therefore heaven may not enter directly into our domain without our permission or request. This is cosmic law; we must pray and ask for heaven's assistance, even if our prayer is an inner plea from our heart, reaching to the Source of all God-good. Free will is highly significant in our physical domain, in our life. We might think it would be better to live in the heaven world, the etheric plane, yet in that plane there are not the same opportunities to balance karma that we have while in incarnation in the physical plane. Here on Earth we are in an *involutionary* cycle— we have the opportunity to get involved, to get to work and master our initiations.

It is great to meditate and to live in Solar light. At the same time, it is important that we work the works of God in form. Practical people, those who have shown their mastery by their works, by minds that are acute and very developed in more Christic thought, are able to synthesize the higher truths through practical works and to glorify God in form. Some of us have had embodiments in the East where we meditated in caves, or in the West where we withdrew into prayer in cloistered monasteries and convents. This kind of extended meditation is beneficial at a certain level and at certain times, and yet in this life most of us have been called to the West to prove the law of beingness in conscious, practical works. This is true alchemy for today's initiates.

Higher Alchemy Is for the Greater Good of All

By correctly applying the laws of conscious cooperation with ascended beings, we accelerate our higher alchemy. Saint Germain repeats this admonishment over and over because it is essential that we know it and live by it: We must always glorify God and always use our alchemy for the greater good of all life.

Another key is to learn the nuances of calling forth the higher energies into our world. This may seem second nature to those who have been praying in this manner for many years, yet there are always other and higher levels of mastery in the science of the word. It takes more than length of service and outer knowledge to master these keys; gnosis and the amount of love you put into your service also count. As you consciously employ and master the aspects of this science that have already been given, you will be given new keys and shortcuts to invoking even greater light. For example, Saint Germain gave us a shortcut when he explained the use of fohat as a key for greater God-mastery.

Shortcuts and keys from the master are the shortening of days for the elect[41]—the shortening of our days of balancing karma by the use of the violet light through the science of invocation. As we transmute our karma, we increase our ability to wield sacred light-energies for God-good. Again, for many this teaching may be second nature, and yet it is important for these concepts to be reiterated and anchored for devotees who will read Saint Germain's instruction in the future.

Transform Obstacles into Stepping Stones

Omraam Mikhaël Aïvanhov offered a perspective on alchemy in his book *Life and Work in an Initiatic School: Training for the Divine*:

> This question of purity is very far-reaching, for, in reality, it is not enough to work at one's own purity; we also have to be capable of transforming the impurities that come from our surroundings: from the food we eat, the air we breathe, even from the thoughts and feelings of other human beings. We have to learn to transform all the criticism and hatred that the other people throw at us. You cannot imagine the stones and rocks that have been thrown at me from every direction—mountains of them! But I have found a way to transform all those rocks into precious stones. The gems that I give you every day are the stones that were once thrown at me. This is true alchemy. Since the earth is capable of transforming ordinary stones into gems, why should we not learn to do likewise? It is simply a question of remembering to do it; you have all the power and forces you need within you. Even the philosopher's stone, the stone that transforms

everything into gold, is within you. Convince yourselves of the truth of what I am saying, for until you adopt this philosophy, you always will be unhappy and vulnerable and every little criticism will discourage you.

You have not understood the significance of an obstacle. Why do ships float and move through water? Because the water provides resistance. And the same is true of aeroplanes: the air provides resistance. It is not possible to advance without some material resistance. You have to understand that obstacles and difficulties are natural phenomena, and that those who know how to make use of them advance and perfect themselves much more quickly.[42]

Even in our relationships with our beloved ones, God in his great wisdom allows for things to occur by our freewill choices that create temporary conflicts or situations that allow one or more of us to respond, to react. And then, through dialogue, through discussion, through communion with each other, we resolve the issue or situation. We learn from that situation or experience and we move higher. Hopefully we pledge to do better, to be more conscious, to be more aware, to be more loving, kind, giving, and forgiving.

It is the nature of life that there is movement, change, the dynamic of things occurring that require our attention and our interaction. Life is not perfect insofar as having no challenges or having smooth sailing. We require challenges in order to move into higher consciousness. As Omraam stated, it is important that we look at obstacles and resistance as stepping stones to our attainment and our greater personal development and self-gnosis.

10

On Purity of Heart and the Inner Sciences

SG

Heartfriends Whose Love for God Is Expanding Daily,

Treasure the love of the Infinite One for you. Treasure the radiance that continues to flow day by day and hour by hour from the Source of all life into the chalice of your heart. Treasure the ongoingness of life and the cosmic resonance of God's heart into which you may tap to receive all the blessings that you require to fulfill your mission to life.

Higher alchemy is all about tuning into the purity of God's cosmic stream of love and, through attunement with that energy, learning how to manifest more of that flow through your chakras, your spiritual centers. The radiance of God's heart may only be expressed in purity, for it is inviolate and is only available to those who have learned to resonate with the great pulsations of that heartbeat in rhythmic and cadenced order, riding the waves of the cosmic stream unto the shores of perfect calm and peace.

I would give you this day another key in discerning the higher way of the all-chemistry of God, the Source of all life. It is this: that the higher dimensions of vibration may only be entered into by the pure in heart whose every breath speaks of light, whose every thought speaks of wholeness, and whose every desire is to do the will of God through heart, head, and hand.

When you can discern the dove of the Holy Spirit as the active presenter of that purity of heart and motive, then you may also be one who can present to the world the light of cosmic joy and wholeness through the divine musings of your Higher Mind attuned to the All-Mind.

Alchemy involves understanding the inner sciences that are replete with the spiritual relationships between all life and how, through entering into the heart of the crystal symmetry of the diamond and becoming that core of white light, you may then draw forth diamond substance into your world. Likewise, when you know the pure Sunlight of cosmic love-wisdom as the core of the substance you call gold, you may then become a conduit through which gold may be precipitated in time and space.

The great mystics and sages of all ages have had the ability, through meditation, to enter into the heart of every matter, every outpicturing of matter in all of its variegated manifestations. Once one has become one with the Sun, then one may be that Sun to all within the manifest world of one's life for others to then also experience that Sun Presence in their midst. Once one has become one with the Sun, one may become the essence of love at its core.

The reason we implore you to be in attunement with your God Presence at all times is that through your entering into a deep relationship with the heart of God through your own individualized God Reality, you then become one with that point of reality everywhere. Then you can attune to the vibration of the seas and merge with them to walk on water.[43] Then you may command water to become wine,[44] because you know the vibration and composition of that wine through having tasted and become its essence. Then you may command the winds and the elements,[45] because within them you live and move and have your being attuned to the God-energy at their core, one with their spirit.

Discerning the future is not so difficult for those who have entered into the heart of humanity through attuning the strings of their hearts to the great harp of mankind's evolutionary journey through time and space, which is simply a slice of the eternal Now. Hop from one string to the next on this great harp and you will see the full outpicturing of the cosmic chords that God plays through the consciousness of all living beings with the interplay of their karma and dharma, their desires and hopes, their dreams and visions. The future renderings of choices made by each soul are foreshadowed as cloudy patterns that may be discerned by the astute one who learns to read the signs, symbols, and writings of akasha even as the etheric blueprint of each soul's mission vibrates at very subtle levels around that one and may be seen by those whose inner sight is opened.

Cosmic wisdom must become the daily fare of mankind if a golden age is to manifest in your world. This requires raising your consciousness past the trifling distractions of earthly living and beholding the inclusiveness of all life forms, lifewaves, and life-energies within the cosmic scheme that are outplaying their roles and acts upon the stage of life. When you get the whole picture, then you can see beyond a two- or three-dimensional view and begin to enter into the center of every view at once, merging your mind with the minds of Elohim, who know all in the eternal Now.

Cosmic alchemy first requires the mastery of terra alchemy. When in balance you understand all the principles of the outworking of God's desiring within matter, then you may enter spirit to discern how the Father principle may be creative from the higher realms. Yet, even in our world, the divine seed must be impregnated within cosmic substance in order to sprout forth into manifest reality. Without the Alpha-Omega action of giving and receiving, there is no co-creation and therefore no alchemy.

Do my words seem too ethereal, my friends? If so, meditate upon the seed concepts behind them until you can discern their inner meaning. For then, in that aha or eureka moment, you will have the key to performing the advanced alchemical feats that will allow you to bring more of heaven to earth through the richness of your new understanding of holy grace and total surrender to the allness of God-being.

I am Saint Germain, wooing you to my heart to know the inner law of your being, which, when fully cognized, will win for you new rounds of cosmic happiness and joy such as you have not experienced since you descended from angelic realms long ago. I give you my joy this day, for in the violet heart of cosmic joy you will know the smile of the Divine One, who awaits with expectancy your smile, your laughter, and your love.

Saint Germain

11

Intuit the Divine and Know the Limits of Sharing Alchemical Gifts

SG

Alchemists of the Spirit,

Intuiting the Divine is the goal of each true alchemist. Engendering the expansion of the reach of the Eternal One into the affairs of mankind, and of mankind into the affairs of the Eternal One, is our work. As Above, so below—the maxim of spiritual alchemists—reminds us of those godly principles that must be employed for the betterment of sentient beings at all levels, meeting the requirements of real men, women, and children and assuaging the hearts of each seeker of divine grace.

I have been called a charlatan, a miracle worker, a quack, an avatar. No matter the outer label, I am a lover of God and a servant of each soul who seeks liberation from the shackles of existence at lower levels of consciousness that keep it tethered to unreality. The use of alchemy to benefit the Solar and *soul-er* evolution of life should be at the center of all your scientific applications of the principles that I convey.

Divine gnosis, wherein you attune to the original design of the Godhead for each one who comes your way for assistance, is the only meaningful way to discern how to use the bounty of spiritual energies that you find available to you at all times and in all places. For you will be tempted to give where it may not be lawful to do so, and to precipitate things and conditions that will not ultimately benefit the advancement of the souls of those who ask for your help.

Each one whom the Lord presents to you in the course of your alchemical work comes for a reason. This reason must be asked of the Higher Self of that one through simply asking the person what it is they require or what is their question. Then pause to silently ask permission of the God Self of that one for what is acceptable to bring forth by cosmic law, taking into consideration the karma of that one. Where grace and blessing are not merited through humility and a certain surrender of the human will, you will be shown that only a certain action may occur or that specific outer results may first require a greater level of that one's personal inner work and striving. In some cases, a question will be forthcoming for you to give to that one to ask if the necessary commitment is now willing to be made in order to receive the gift of heavenly intercession.

Dear students, God is good and would never deny the soul the graces that will lift that one from mortal thought and feeling into our realms. Likewise, as a just steward, you must be the eternal watchman to ascertain what alchemical relief may be acceptable to God for the ultimate reunion of each soul with her own Real Self. Thus, it is often better not to act if there is any question as to the true motives of the one who comes to you or if, through a clear sign from your God Self or of discomfort in your solar plexus, you discern that the time and place are not correct for you to use God's energies on behalf of this one.

Alchemy is an exacting science, for just as the specific amounts of various substances and conditions are required for chemical reactions to occur, so the law of cause and effect will determine at each juncture what is the best use of heaven's resources. This requires that you master the art of discerning divine intent through meditation and self-emptying so that there is no guile or malintent within you as God's servant first and Man's second.

Gracious ones, it is through this key that you will avoid a mountain of grief and of having to undo certain work that you at first may feel driven to perform, and which, upon reflection and holy attunement, you realize is simply not God's will. Therefore, sharpen your sensitivities by the ongoing development of cosmic consciousness through the use of what are known as the *crystal rays* in your spiritual work. These rays, or cosmic streams of energy, have been discerned and used by the saints and sages of all ages who have first balanced the energies of the seven prismatic rays within themselves. They are more rarefied and powerful and thus are hidden from the use of most of mankind, for they are also a great tool for sudden and transcendent change within the lower realms of earthly existence and may only be discerned and used by higher initiates.

These rays may come forth through your invocation to the being known as beloved Mighty Cosmos. This great, divine lord delivers to the Earth and to other planetary homes the energies from many solar systems, amplified through their travel through the great Cosmic Void of the Holy Spirit in interstellar space and through his own cosmic awareness of God as the All–in–all. These rays are unseen yet powerful change agents that precipitate a certain action of the raising of the Mother energies, or "night" (occult or hidden) energies of the spirit. These rays, if misused, could cause the very destruction of worlds, and therefore they are only revealed to those who have first sublimated all desire for personal or egoic gain and proven their ability to maintain harmony.

Purity is the key to alchemy. Love is the key to draw forth mercy from Above. Self-effacement and humility are the only means to the divine ends that you seek. Often those with the greatest gifts to offer mankind are misunderstood, shunned, and denounced as incompetent or as devils, when they may have brought forth the very solutions to the human problems that may only come when people are ready and willing to accept them.

I am Saint Germain. The God-freedom of all is my reason for

being and the joy at the heart of all that I do. You honor me and your own God Self by supplanting all tendencies to limit who you are and by becoming the true alchemists that you are meant to be. Go and use your God-given talents and abilities to grace this Earth and her evolutions. Rise and know the Eternal One today!

Saint Germain

The Sacred Exchange of Energies between the Heaven World and the World of Matter

Blessed Hearts Who Would Know the Deeper Mysteries of God,

I am Saint Germain and I come again in this hour to proclaim the eminent victory of your soul when you have chosen to be the flame of freedom. There are many students of higher alchemy in the heaven world who would work with you on a more personal basis to move forward the plans of the Divine Director for the alchemical change to a golden age on Earth.

The science of mankind in this day and in this hour is lacking in the true understanding of certain principles as a foundation which, when embraced and understood, would lead all scientists into new discovery, gleaning the secrets of the universe and then using the sacred sciences toward the betterment of all life.

God has shielded mankind from the deeper mysteries because the spiritual attainment of most has not kept abreast of the development and advancement of scientific learning. Yet some are required who hold within their consciousness a strong tie to the heaven world, whereby there are conveyed keys to your divinity that, when fully employed by greater numbers of mankind, can move forward the race. And then the mass consciousness itself will be dissolved into its spiritual counterpart, which is the community of the Holy Spirit.

When mankind understand the soul as the seat of the flame of freedom within, then all will be clear. For from this seat, wherein the violet light does emanate and the interlaced triangles of the six-pointed star are congruent with the six petals of this chakra in the "as Above, so below" matrix that you understand as students of higher alchemy, the divine world impregnates the human and the human reaches up into the divine. From the point within the center of the interlaced triangles of this matrix, the soul may be known by you.

There is a reflection of this seat in your world within ours. And therefore, as you understand the third eye as the seat of the divine consciousness that looks upon the soul in the reflecting pool of the energy of the Mother embracing all, there is seen, Alpha to Omega and Omega to Alpha, the interplay of cosmic energies through the figure-eight flow descending and the Mother flow rising to greet the Father and the continuous interchange in this sacred figure-eight of the stream of reality in both worlds. Therefore, you are eaten up of God and God receives the food of your own nature; and likewise, you consume the divine substance, anchoring it in the planes of Mater so that more of the suchness of divine beingness can manifest in your world.

Through this sacred exchange, all the qualities and resources of heaven may be available to you for your alchemical works, practices, and experiments. Likewise, within the heaven world, as you engage in the sacred science of alchemy, more of the sublime within your world is available to the Divine One as the substance of the Mother is drawn and magnetized into the Above for the Father's use. There is a push-pull action of the Tai Chi within this sacred exchange. Thus, one cannot perceive from which level there arise or descend the energies and substance of the All. For when this interchange occurs, a field of flux is established; and if you could see or slow down the vibration of an atom, you would not know at any point where exactly the shell exists except for a fleeting moment outside of time, outside of space itself.

Physicists have begun to understand the greater laws that God has set as a platform for the evolution and involution of all. And yet, truly, not all is known, for mankind is still bound in sense consciousness to the Earth and not free within the confines of his consciousness to rise or move as a stream of energy throughout the cosmos. Yet some, when fully understanding the laws of nature and then transcending sense consciousness, can move anywhere, everywhere or be at many points simultaneously. Thus, one who has the attainment of perfect alchemy can disappear, walk through walls, tread on water, perform seeming miracles. This is the daily fare of divine beings, for they have transcended lower sense consciousness, which you yet seek to do.

One of the first principles of understanding the acceleration of consciousness and perception within your being is resonance and attunement with the Divine. Where there is no resonance, then the Divine may not resonate with you. Where there is no attunement to the heaven world, then naturally the Divine may not attune or reside where you are. Therefore, do not misappropriate who you are, for then God cannot appropriate himself within you. Where there is convergence through the understanding of divine principles within, then the *you* with a small *y* dissolves into fulfilling the *why* of being within God.

I teach perfect alchemy as the all-chemistry of the All, whereby every particle of being is known within. Would you know the cells within you, sensing all from within a single cell of your big toe or your brain? Even in the conscious awareness that resides within each cell, there is the divine experience. If you could, through your meditation, enter into this divine experience within the microcosm of your own being, then through congruence with the Divine you would know the All of God within.

Therefore, look not so much outside of yourself or to the vast outer reaches of the galaxies of star systems to understand the nature of all, for the nature of all resides within every particle of self where you are. The admonition "Know thyself" is a mystery to some, yet for those who have truly discerned that God is within every particle of being of the self, the mystery of life may be understood. Worlds within worlds within worlds are you; worlds without worlds without worlds am I.

Now let us exchange seats. And as I inhabit the sphere of your being and you rise to understand cosmic awareness, there is the liberation within you of all unreality and there is the proliferation of God within me into the allness of yourself. When your chakras are aligned, seven and five, first as resonating suns spinning, balanced, trued, then you may call forth my chakras to be superimposed over yours for the acceleration and the full ennoblement of your God centers into divine centers.

There is a point of vibration that I may not descend below in working with you. Therefore some, when I come, do not experience the totality of the flame of freedom who I am. The key for you is to know yourself within each chakra as purity's fire, as freedom's light. And when trued and spinning freely, unencumbered by the molasses of impure thought and feeling or the substance of non-perception, then, warmed by the sunlight from within, each chakra may resonate with mine and you may be called Holy Brother, Holy Sister.[46]

Take the gift of freedom that God has given you and use it wisely. Why have you accepted non-freedom within when the Lord gave you free will, blessed hearts? Freedom to be—as one of the first principles of life—when fully understood and embraced, will allow you to fully become God. You are free now, you see, if you accept your freedom. There is no time and space outside of freedom, for freedom is and is not bound by mortal illusion. When you say "I am free," if there is not within you the acceptance fully of the flame of freedom that is true, then your words have no resonance or meaning. If, however, you understand the nature of freedom, then when you say "I am free," all limitations dissolve and *you are free!*

Be free to pursue the divine experience always by accepting the Divine experiencing you always. Are you in the heart of God or is God within your heart? Both are required.

I am the heart of freedom for the Earth. Resonate with me and be true alchemists.

Saint Germain

DCL: The concept of the sacred exchange is important to understand. Even as the resources of heaven are available to us in our experiments and experimental works, our research is available to God. As we master ourselves, God is accelerated, completed, and expanded, and our substance is drawn up into the divine world. Whenever anyone ascends into the very living presence of the Father aspect of God, it expands the universal awareness of the All. The Father and the Mother are aspects of God, who is universal, undifferentiated, masculine/feminine as one unified Being.

One purpose of alchemy is to glorify God. By glorifying God, we bring light into the equation of our alchemical experiments. God, being glorified, is expanded. God has an aha experience each time one of his sons or daughters experiences the bliss of oneness with him, and it is reciprocal.

This "as Above, so below" reciprocity is part of why God created the cosmos. If God were to experience the creation by himself without any part of creation experiencing itself, it wouldn't be as rewarding. Just as God lives within us, we live within God. God is blissing out, so to speak, through our experience within him, within her.

The Purpose of Divine Ritual

Beloved Friends of Higher Alchemy,

In the avenues of light that we walk in the heaven world, there exist special foci of light as remembrances of the eternal grace with which the Divine One has blessed us. Each of these is both an out-picturing of a specific creative rendering by a divine being and also a powerful spiritual talisman that allows a concentrated action of the sacred fire of God's glory to vibrate at etheric levels of beingness. It is the joy of every ascended master to be responsible for the precipitation of one or more of these cosmic creations, and so great expectancy and spiritual honor always accompany any of these new manifestations of heavenly beauty that come forth in our domain.

So it also is in your world, where often much pomp is shown when a new endeavor is begun and then completed, with a groundbreaking and/or a dedication ceremony attended by various dignitaries occurring at both junctures. This is as it should be, for the seventh-ray action of divine ritual is both endearing and meaningful when it is entered into with a sense of holiness and a cosmic pause that allows more of the divine nature to be experienced in the stillness of the Now.

Some among mankind have rejected outright all affectation for the various accomplishments of individuals or institutions along life's path, seeking instead to go within and focus all of their energies in internal, spiritual attainment. I understand this mindset, for often the regalia that is displayed only promotes the outer egos of those being honored. And yet, there is a just and proper place both in your world and ours where and when the divinity within each one who has attained to a new level of spirituality is magnified during these events, which are often sponsored and attended by great cosmic beings who increase the love-fires within the hearts of all present.

Hearts of fire, one aspect of the seventh ray that is often overlooked or misunderstood is this action of cosmic ritual whereby, through the worship that also may occur at these times, there is the interplay of higher spiritual energies and the creating of a permanent record in time and space of these sacred events for the glorification of the divine ego of Godhood within each created being. This is what is meant to occur during each sacrament that the various churches have celebrated for hundreds or thousands of years. Concurrent with the outer ritual that you see manifest, there is the attendance by many angels and spiritual beings at each of these sacramental ceremonies. Each communicant is thus sanctified by their presence of divine love and light.

If you could see into our realm to observe the sharing and caring that occurs for each of your souls by your sponsoring masters and often thousands of supporting angels, you would truly be amazed at how much God dotes on you as one of his created beings. You see, although God is Light and Spirit, God is also very personal in his manifestation of love for you outpictured through the individualized beings that inhabit the vast universe of his conscious awareness of life.

Take time to enter into a deeper spiritual communion with the souls of your family members and friends each time the opportunity presents itself for you to be with them during those times when you celebrate special days, such as birthdays, baptisms, graduations, marriages, and all the various holidays that you have. These are truly meant to be holy days where the divine essence of each one is magnified through the lens of your focus in attending to the joyful sense of community that surrounds each of these experiences. And if you take the time to call forth the presence of the angels and masters before and during these special occasions, we will be there to make each one a treasured time of intimate communion with our hearts as well.

It is always heaven's desire for the lighter and more beautiful aspects of God's grace to be lowered into your world for your uplift-ment and support. There is no reason for any among mankind to feel bereft of the divine compassion and understanding that is always available for the asking.

Therefore ask, that you may receive our guidance.[47] Knock, that the door may be opened for the eternal light to shine upon all your works. Seek anew our inspiration each day through attuning to realms of cosmic knowing through meditation upon God's divine joy and the ritual ("right-you-all") of the divine interchange that is always occurring right within your own heart.

I am always with you as you pursue the higher alchemy of communion with the One.

Saint Germain

A New Matrix for Quicker Precipitation

SG

Friends of Freedom across the Earth,

The flight of your soul is magnificent to behold when on wings of light you ascend, witnessing the rarefied heights of freedom's light truly as one ennobled within God's kingdom here below. I am Saint Germain, and I come to give you a lesson this day on the alchemical fires of the soul and how, when you employ the sacred science of alchemy within your own life, the Lord God does witness all and his Spirit merges with yours to accommodate your experimentation with that which can move you toward the perfect union you seek with the Beloved.

Alchemy, as the all-chemistry of the Lord, allows you access to every element within the cosmic periodic table—truly that which is offered upon the banquet table of light by angels and masters who understand the science of the creation of form and formlessness and of the precipitation within any realm of that which is ensconced around the seed of light of your imaging forth of perfection.

When you are composed in God, fully within his being, then all power, wisdom, and love are yours to command, and you can be confident that your creation will be that which the Lord God will work through you as a servitor of fire, a servant son or daughter of love. Therefore, experiment and try that which I have given you in the way of a new matrix for quicker precipitation of that which you seek.

I have always advocated that first you seek God in all things—his virtues, his qualities, the resonance of his fire within your heart. Once you have established the flowfield of cosmic love where you are, then command the elements of the universe into action, into the vibrancy of perfection within the creative realm in which you abide. For it is mete that you should have all you require to survive and also to thrive, to excel, and to rise to greet the opulent ones of heaven, whose radiance of fire is always surrounding them and which should always be within your domain.

You have access to every created element. When you understand the periodic table—the metals, the gases, and those radioactive elements for which you would have to accelerate in Spirit far beyond your consciousness to maintain harmony and balance within your aura, and all those substances which, in perfect balance, form a world upon which you abide and through which you breathe the breath of God's Spirit—you may attest to that which is true, that which is real within each element, within each atom of that element as the perfected sun center, the radiant beingness of God within that substance. The interplay of magnetic resonance between substances you must understand. Yet, first know that which is within you as pattern, as design, as the Most Holy One's seed ideation of who you are as a God-created being.

When you understand the Self, then you may understand the suchness of all substance and how it may be employed in combinations through your spiritual experimentation for the victory of the alchemy of your life. Mankind has been given much by the Lord, truly endowed with all that is necessary for both physical and spiritual opulence within this domain. And yet few understand the words of the master, "I come that all might have life, and that more abundantly."[48]

This day I call you to prove the abundant consciousness within your life that many of you have put off in some manner. Prove that it works through attesting to the light within yourself that you invoke and also emanate, that you know is real, that you know is God. It is time that many more servitors prove that which I was witness to as the Wonderman of Europe and sustain the radiance of the Presence of God where you are. This is the requirement for all true alchemy to manifest. When you hold a circle of fire, of presence, of love within your flowfield, then naturally you will be able to perform and to precipitate that which it is mete for you to do.

Some relegate the perfectionment of this craft, this science and art, to a future time of their immortality. Is this my way or your way? I say this day that there must be many more alchemists upon Earth for a golden age to appear, those whose consciousness is rarefied and purified both by the violet-flame action of prayer and mantra and by the crystallization within form of the alchemical fires from your Presence in manifest works, in active principles made plain and real for others to see, to behold, to witness as what you have mastered in the way of the spiritual path.

The proof of your life is in how you live, where you live, your surroundings, and the tangible reality of that which you have brought forth through study and through the application of the teachings of the holy masters of wisdom. For those of you who want for this or that, I ask, "Have you truly applied the law at all levels of your being?" If not, join me and the alchemists with the God of Gold, with Fortuna and many ascended masters whose great desire is to see you bring forth that abundance of the Spirit and of form in the here and now.

You are happier when abundance flows through your consciousness in all ways as the joy of the spiritual path that can be shared with many. When your resources are greater, then you can share more with many heartfriends across the Earth. Therefore, ramp up that which can be the substance of things hoped for,[49] of things seen and felt, of those smelled and tasted. For others will, through your proof of the teachings, come your way when you have made them real before their very eyes, I say. Cosmic alchemy awaits those who prove the law at each level of the science of precipitation.

If you would be cosmic alchemists with me, then begin at the beginning. Precipitate the amethyst, the Maltese Cross, the pyramid, and the sphere of fire. Once you have learned more of this art, then I will return to give you more, blessed hearts of fire.

By the power of Omri Tas' love, I seal you in cosmic amethyst dust and the fragrance of violets from my heart.

Saint Germain

Affirmations, Prayers, Fiats, and Chants

The following prayers can assist you to establish around yourself a radiant flowfield as a chrysalis of spiritual fire. Please give them as often as desired until you feel ensconced in a sphere of divine light.

Crystal-Diamond Tube of Light

Om Mani Padme Hum AUM
Beloved I AM love divine,
Blaze your light, around me shine.
Cosmic crystal rays of fire
Pulsing, flowing, you inspire.

Violet joy now smile through me,
Raise me up and set me free.
Singing, spinning, burning bright,
Grace me in your mercy light.
Om Mani Padme Hum AUM

Opening Invocation for Prayer Services

In the name I AM THAT I AM, beloved Alpha and Omega, Four and Twenty Elders, Elohim, twelve archangels and your archeiai, all saints robed in white, my own guardian angel, and precious devas and nature spirits of earth, water, air, and fire around the world:

I see now a mighty crystal-diamond tube of light around me, sealing me in the light of God that always prevails. I accept a solar sphere of fire, a cloak of invincibility, and a triple ruby dome of light around me now. I feel the blue-fire radiance of Archangel Michael and Faith protecting me 24/7.

I accept the clearing of my auric field and chakras by the violet laser-light frequencies of Aquarius, the balancing of my threefold flame, and the alignment of all my spiritual bodies. I feel Solar and cosmic consciousness manifesting through me now. I reclaim all fragmented or lost soul parts and I cast into the flame all human sense of lack, want, desire, and suffering, including past karmic entanglements. I see my divine plan joyously fulfilled with courageous love manifest in every thought I think, every decision I make, every word I speak, and every action I take. I accept the twelve gifts of the Holy Spirit in my life and the blessings of God flowing to my loved ones, extended family, heartfriends, co-workers and all sentient beings on all worlds throughout the cosmos.

Lord God Almighty, Brahma/Vishnu/Shiva, use me throughout this day as your humble instrument for blessings, healings, graces, and divine intercession to manifest around the world in miraculous ways to glorify and magnify your name I AM THAT I AM. Amen. AUM.

Solar-Sphere Invocation

In the name of my beloved mighty I AM Presence and Holy Christ/Buddha Self, I invoke and envision a corona of energy from Helios and Vesta around my aura as a garment of light that is a precursor of my eternal Solar body. I now spread my wings as I feel the cosmic impulse of the light of Helios and Vesta before, behind, and around me, hallowing the sacred space of my life. I now draw forth around my form a sphere of light through which this cosmic radiation may be the new food of the spirit. I see my being as spherical, for this is my true nature; and I feel the cosmic radiation as a new communion of the Spirit.

Visualize a sphere of white light around your form as you draw with your arms a circle around your waist and a second circle from head to toe. Feel cosmic radiation nourishing you as you say these words:

Through the holy breath, I ingest the prana from the Sun into my etheric body and accept the Solar breath of Helios and Vesta as a transfer of the breath of Alpha and Omega. I now imbibe and breathe in this Solar breath, increasing the golden, liquid light in my bloodstream.

Breathe deeply three times. Then say:

I intensify the action of this solar sphere and Solar breath by drawing this light into the center of my heart and into the secret chamber thereof, where the flame of God abides. I draw the plumes of my threefold flame higher and envision myself as a Sun of God, radiating love, light, and life to all.

Give the prayer "Crystal-Diamond Tube of Light" (see page 85) one time.

Visualize light radiating to all of life in your neighborhood, city, state, nation, and the entire planet, especially into specific situations that require a transfusion of golden, liquid light.

Wash the Earth in Violet Fire!

by Beloved Holy Amethyst

Om Mani Padme Hum AUM

In the name I AM THAT I AM, beloved Divine Director, Saint Germain and Portia, Afra, Archangel Zadkiel and Holy Amethyst, Kuan Yin and all angels and masters of the violet fire:

I pray for the washing, cleansing, spinning, raising and sealing of the Earth and its evolutions this day with the violet fire, for the transmutation of all karma, burden, suffering and substance that opposes the dawning of the great golden age of Aquarius, and for the enlightenment and victory of all lightbearers this day.

Wash the Earth in violet fire! (4x)
Cleanse the Earth in violet fire! (4x)
Spin the Earth in violet fire! (4x)
Raise the Earth in violet fire. (4x)
Seal the Earth in violet fire. (4x)

Om Mani Padme Hum AUM

Fiats to Ignite Your Alchemy

I AM Light!

I AM the fire of God manifesting here and now!

I AM instantaneous, God-victorious love blazing throughout the cosmos!

I AM lighting up this world in Solar joy!

I AM courageously changing my world into all Light, all Love!

I AM victorious in my work fulfilled now!

I AM a ray of hope blazing to all who have lost hope now!

I AM charging forth light into every nation, continent, lake, river, sea, and ocean now!

I AM the truth revealed to all mankind now!

I AM pure love blazing around the world now!

Chants to Experience Your Chakras as Cosmic Resonators

OM

Om Mani Padme Hum AUM*

Om Ah Hum Vajra Guru Padma Siddhi Hum

AIM HRIM KLIM CHAMUNDAYE VICHE

Sarasvati: OM AIM SARASVATYE NAMAHA

Lakshmi: OM SRIM LAKSMYE NAMAHA

Kali: OM KRIM KALIKAYE NAMAHA

Durga: OM DUM DURGAYE NAMAHA

Om Mani Peme Hum Om*

AUM

---

* The mantra means "Hail to the jewel in the heart of the lotus." Om Mani Padme Hum is the Sanskrit pronunciation; Om Mani Peme Hum is the Tibetan pronunciation.

Ritual of Surrender

Dear Lord, I AM love because your love lives within me. I AM wholeness, I AM rich with the eternal spirit of life, and it now fully becomes who I AM. O God, I desire only to know your Presence in me at all times as you work your holy work through me for your purposes. I thank thee, Lord, for hearing my prayer.

As Above, so below, I am experiencing the great interchange of the figure-eight flow. I imitate you, the Divine Giver, mirroring your own gift of Self to me by giving back the all of myself to you. I release all so that I may become the All and then begin a new spiral by releasing the All again and again unto all.

I open wide the door of my heart and consciousness as I say:

Centered in the One I AM, pure beingness in light,
Reality is all I know, now perfect in your sight.

Forever living one in thee, my godhood I decree.
Accepting in totality your essence clear through me.
In joy I give my all to you; now back your currents flow.
Drink me while I am drinking thee; pure love you now bestow.

All unlike God falls away. O Presence, only thee!
Our consciousness now one in bliss for all eternity!

Release of the Sacred Fire Breath

Visualize a six-pointed star centered over your threefold flame in the secret chamber of the heart. See the name of God, I AM THAT I AM, written across it in living flame. Maintain this visualization as you give the following breathing exercise once, three times, or in multiples of three for the purification and balancing of your four lower bodies by the sacred fire breath of God. Each breath consists of four steps: inbreath, hold, outbreath, hold.

1. The inbreath begins in the etheric body to the count of eight.

2. The first hold energizes through the mental body to the count of eight.

3. The outbreath releases through the emotional body to the count of eight.

4. The second hold anchors in the physical form the balanced action of the Father, Mother, Son, and Holy Spirit to the count of eight.

Give the sacred fire breath three or more times.

Divine Director, Lead the Way!
Om Mani Padme Hum AUM

In the name I AM THAT I AM, my beloved Holy Christ/
Buddha Self and Holy Christ/Buddha Selves of all lightbearers,
beloved Great Divine Director, Gautama Buddha, Saint Germain
and Portia, all ascended and cosmic beings, legions of angels and
archangels, Elohim, Buddhas and bodhisattvas of heaven, I pray:

1. Divine Director, come to us
   Within your sphere of light.
   Divine Director, show to us
   Your aura blazing bright.

Refrain: Divine Director, lead the way!
   Our victory is won today.
   We don your cape and jeweled belt.
   Your awesome power now is felt.
   Reveal the plan for all the Earth
   As we are raised in cosmic worth.

2. Divine Director, wield for us
   Blue-lightning bolts of fire.
   Divine Director, give to us
   Your wealth of God-desire.

3. Divine Director, blaze through us
   Your heart of diamond blue.
   Divine Director, raise in us
   God-power pure and true.

4. Divine Director, share with us
   Your vision free and clear.
   Divine Director, claim with us:
   Ascension fire is here!

In the fullness of your cosmic joy, we accept this prayer manifest here and now with full love, wisdom, and power; anchored in the earth, air, fire, water, and ether; and tangibly manifest in our lives and in the lives of all evolutions of light throughout cosmos!

Om Mani Padme Hum AUM

I AM My Victorious Abundance Here and Now!

1. I AM my victorious abundance here and now!

2. I AM my magnanimous heart of God abundantly giving and receiving from my eternal fountain of life.

3. I AM the reality and physicality of my abundant gifts and graces of the Spirit.

4. I AM my Self-realization of Godhood as my abundant life.

5. I AM shining my Solar awareness of beauty, grace, and effulgence to bless my life and the lives of all my heartfriends.

6. I AM gratitude in action, precipitating my victorious abundance here and now.

7. I AM an opulent servant-sun of God and my abundance flows as an eternal spring.

8. I AM blessing all through my heart, full of love; my mind, full of wisdom; and my hands, full of sacred works of godliness.

9. I AM demonstrating my full mastery of the laws of alchemy through victorious love.

10. I AM my spirit of givingness even as I receive every perfect gift of God that blesses me every moment.

11. I AM my tree of life bearing twelve manner of fruits of beingness as God's holy virtues.

12. I AM whole as I daily and hourly integrate Victory's abundant cosmic energies into my auric field.

13. I AM living, moving, and being within the harmonic center of Victory's six-pointed love star of abundance!

14. I AM a blessing to all life through my heart of gold and my abundant consciousness.

15. I AM a crystal being, assisting our Mother Earth in her perfect work of being Freedom's Star.

16. I AM living in a harmonic field of Solar light through which Victory shines forth Venusian streams of God's abundance.

17. I AM breathing in the golden Solar prana of Helios and Vesta and emanating my Christic essence 24/7.

18. I AM dynamic, charismatic, and prismatic because Victory's abundant spirit shines within and through me!

19. I AM an alchemist of spirit, an adept of soulfulness, and a master of solar energy flow!

20. I AM accelerating my victorious sense of abundance and manifesting all I require to fulfill my sacred labor.

21. I AM a star-fire being, emanating light waves of cosmic abundance and engrams of victorious love-wisdom beauty.

22. I AM raising all life through my victorious smile, my victorious aura, and my victorious example of divine opulence.

23. I AM partnering with beloved mighty Victory to use Gautama's 2011 Thoughtform to continuously bless life.

    To view Gautama Buddha's 2011 Thoughtform in full color, go to HeartsCenter.org/Broadcast/Visuals/YearlyThoughtforms/tabid/648/Default.aspx.

24. I AM perfecting the science of cosmic flow by giving and receiving Solar light through my victorious heart.

25. I AM a Solar scientist following Omraam's example of living in the presence of divine light, love, and joy!

26. I AM my new paradigm of beingness in Solar light, love, and joy; and I AM grateful to be my new me!

27. I AM the light of Victory as my own effulgent light manifests through God's abundance!

28. I AM God's graces of the Spirit, of the Eternal One!

29. I AM a living temple of Victory through the 360 degrees of my Solar awareness.

30. I AM distributing the light of God equally to all life through the impersonal impersonality of the Spirit and through the personal personality of the Mother Light where I AM.

31. I AM the effulgence of the One because I know my Source.

32. I AM, through my cosmic resourcefulness, lovingly distributing my graces of the Spirit in all domains through my heart fires offered on the altar of humanity.

33. I AM my effulgent life realized within every sacred work that I offer unto humanity through my consecrated life.

34. I AM blessed by the one God-power, God-wisdom, and God-love of the Almighty.

35. I AM God's three-in-one fire blazing through my heart in perfect balance and industrious, indomitable harmony.

36. I AM God-love, -wisdom and -power restored in my domain as God in me sees them fully realized within every heart, within every soul, and within every spirit through a childlike attitude of divine gratitude, grace, and beingness.

37. I AM offering myself in a continuous stream of love-wisdom-power fire.

38. I AM my Venusian qualities of holiness and cosmic presence anchored within the Earth as she resonates with a new frequency of holy communion through cosmic cycles.

39. I AM manifesting a new golden-crystal age consciousness day by day, and I realize it within me as an anchor point of light for the Lord as I live and move and have my being within liquid crystal-diamond light.

40. I AM fanning forth cosmic frequencies of God's abundance and opulence, and all now feel this flow of light.

41. I AM the firing of the antahkarana, the great grid of light across this world and universe, which is maintained moment by moment through my own abundant victory consciousness.

42. I AM setting forth upon the table of the Lord my highest gifts and works—that which God has vouchsafed to me as my talents—and I multiply, multiply, multiply them a million times over through my experience in all of my lifetimes.

43. I AM now manifesting through these gifts and works my highest potential for my Lord.

44. I AM manifesting and realizing my highest Selfhood as a Solar being, proffered to the universe in great God-joy!

45. I AM my full Solar mastery here and now.

46. I AM giving again and again as I surrender all unto my Lord.

47. I AM seeing that which God sees clearly as who I AM.

48. I AM beholding all life perfectly, joyously, and deliciously.

49. I AM manifesting my light of perfection through all of my spiritual senses.

50. I AM WHO I AM. I AM THAT I AM. AUM.

PART TWO

Answers to 33 Questions from Disciples

by Saint Germain

with Commentary
by David Christopher Lewis

1. What is the path of alchemy?

SG: The path of alchemy is the science of divine love practically applied. Divine love applied with power is co-creativity through work and service to a holy cause. Divine love applied with wisdom and understanding is compassion in action and may involve sharing lessons learned through discernment. Divine love applied with the comfort flame of the Holy Spirit sees a need and acts to alleviate suffering. Alchemy as the all-chemistry of God utilizes all the elements of God's consciousness that you can access through the flame of divine love to precipitate into matter something of spirit—something of grace, beauty, harmony, and happiness.

For the serious student, the path of alchemy is one where you are subsumed into the very heart and bosom of God, and through oneness with his heart you may employ all of the energies entrusted to you as a co-creator to expand the universe as God's experiencing of himself. Co-creation is the key on this path; and at every level the student learns how to increase his ability to refine himself and thereby draw forth greater and more refined works of the spirit. The path is a graduated one, as are all true paths of oneness; and as initiations are passed, greater bounty is offered to the student from which to draw cosmic resources for his experimentation with light. The path of alchemy is the path of co-creation, because it understands that of ourselves we can do nothing;[50] it is the divine light, the active creative power of God within, that we work with to ideate and co-create something magical, something magnificent, which always glorifies God and magnifies the Lord.

The path of alchemy is the path of the initiate, one who initiates spirals of light and love through the nexus of the heart attuned to the heart of God. Nature is the great initiator that the Divine One has set before you to teach you the way, the truth, and the life of this path, and so you may learn much of the laws of alchemy by observing nature. God has embedded within the creation the essence of the path. If you attune to nature's message by observation and intuition, you will have ample knowledge and instruction to fulfill your grand alchemical experiment, which is the absorption of your being into the all-chemistry of God's universal being through affinity, oneness, unity. Adhering to the Law of the One, you have the allness of God's promethean fire at your disposal to co-create lovingly, with a majestic sense and with mystical awareness. In this sense, as alchemists you become spiritual mystics, fully involved in employing the gifts of love to serve and raise humanity in light.

The path is guarded and guided by many celestial beings. At each level there are a number of guardian spirits who witness the lesson to be learned by the student and who act both as observers and as a protective, overshadowing presence to assist that student. This is the true nature of all teachers along the path: They provide you with the resources to experiment with light within the laboratory of yourself; they provide you what you require as you pursue this sacred science.

The teacher gives you a lesson plan that you are expected to follow within the context of free will and your own personal evolutionary path as a part of the one path toward the heart of God. Thus, there is at each level a lesson to be learned and a trial to be won. Each one experiences this lesson and trial intimately within the context of his or her own evolution, and in this way God experiences himself through each created being differently, uniquely. This broadens the scope of God's own Self-awareness through his created sons and daughters, and in this process the universe itself constantly expands.

These guardian spirits, as teachers, have certain parameters that they must work within in guiding souls, and every ascended master understands this within the context of his own evolution and his work with his own teachers. It is as if each teacher is also a student and apprentice upon his own path; and there is a cosmic distribution of energies and the cycling of cosmic resources, which are then graduated to the various levels beneath that one. This is hierarchy; this is the path. For true seekers of divine knowledge, the spiral staircase of their own evolutionary trajectory is made clear by those who offer their service to mankind. Each of you, both as student and as tutor of those progressing on this path at the level just behind you, may employ the energies and resources that your teachers give you in guarded measure so that all will evolve according to the disciplined cycles that are part of this unfolding matrix of evolution.

Thus, you may call upon your teacher. You may have one principal teacher and a number of tutors along the way. Consider that various ascended masters have hundreds and even thousands of students. They require tutors and assistants who bring their lesson plans into the domain of the student in such a way that the plan may be personalized for each one. These tutors and assistants report back to the guiding master. In the case of alchemy and the path of alchemy, I, Saint Germain, have been sanctioned by Alpha and Omega to be for the Earth in this age the master through whom the initiations of alchemy flow. Thus, all true students of alchemy as the cosmoscience of oneness in God come under my divine tutelage, blessed hearts.

DCL: The lesson plans the masters give us are usually given on the inner, although they could be given on the outer. We often won't realize right away what that lesson plan is; it is for us to discern and intuit, and as we do this we are expanding God's consciousness. The entire hierarchical structure of the universe outlines the path as we ascend in awareness. We reach different levels of the path through this ascending process; it is like school on Earth.

2. How do I determine which alchemy to work on?

SG: The simple answer is: Ask! You may ask: "How may I serve you this day, O Lord? What is the most optimal use of my time and energy and the resources you have provided me through my heart-centered awareness here and now, O my God?" Ask the question and then patiently await the answer and it will come through a muse's inspiration, gently offered to your mindful heart.

───── ⚜ ─────

DCL: It is so important that we ask for direction from our ascended-master sponsor before we engage in any major alchemical project. For, although we might choose to do any number of things, it is to our benefit to learn the most important alchemy to undertake at any given time, before we commit our time and resources to a major project. The reason for this is that we may think something will be to our benefit, and yet the master, from his or her higher level of understanding, may see that it would be to our detriment to carry that project through. The masters know what is best for us, for our divine plan, for our greater collective mission, and for the world. We can ask for direction from the Divine Director[51] or from whichever master we resonate most with. Or we can simply pray, "What would you have me do, O Lord?"

3. How can I make the most progress on my spiritual path?

SG: Your greatest progress is made when you are aligned with your True Self through following the lead of your heart and being obedient to the still, small voice[52] within—your conscience and inner guide. The kingdom, or consciousness, of God is within[53] and is your real source of all knowledge, wisdom, and truth. Obedience to this inner voice is paramount. Studying the mystical teachings of the ascended masters East and West provides a foundation for right choices. Following the Eightfold Path of the Buddha and the mystical teachings of Christ and devoting yourself to the purposes of the Universal Great White Brotherhood through loving service to life provide great impetus to accelerate into the pure state of being that is the sacred space of divine love. The Holy Spirit will guide you to all truth. Your guardian angel will urge you to improve and make progress. And your ascended master sponsors and tutors will teach you the essentials if you will meditate daily and intuit each next step on your path with great joy.

Blessed ones, progress is only made when you attune to the very heart of your Source and strive with great God-desire to fulfill your reason for being. This may be accomplished in many ways, for the pathways are many, and yet there is a true and noble God-pathway home to the heart of the One God. Seeing your God Presence as the source of all inspiration, joy, and vitality—not striving from the human level—will move you swiftly along the currents of this pathway home.

Pilgrims along the path often come to bends along the way where they must navigate that which will take them upon those currents to the very Source. Often rocks and brambles lie in the way, and it is best to avoid them in order to make swift progress. Thus the ascended masters, as your elder brothers and sisters, show you how to paddle, how to avoid those nefarious elements arising from your own unconscious that at times could take you far afield from the swift currents that you seek always to engage.

Studying the true teachings of the ascended masters is key for making swift progress. For when you have within your sphere of understanding the keys to overcoming, then you may make right choices. Thus, serious students daily study the Word and discuss that Word with their heartfriends, seeing how it may be employed within their lives, discussing the tests that have come unto others who have gone before them and how they overcame those tests using the sacred science of alchemy to clear the way for the soul to rise at every level.

Going upstream is more difficult than going downstream; it takes great effort—not of the human, as I have said—and a certain allowance of your Divine Presence flowing through you. The currents of our love, of God's love, are all that is required. Attuning to these currents and employing them day by day through the seasons and through the rays is what you must discern as necessary for you on your path.

In addition, your communion with angelic and archangelic ministrants of fire is key. When turmoil comes within your emotional body, attune to the heart of the angels and feel their presence of love for you personally. Often they may give you, through their inspiration and through their mastery of God's feeling body that they utilize, great resources of light to move you beyond human emoting and unto feeling the pressures of the spirit of Godly love within your soul that are necessary for you to be victorious.

Progress for each one is different, and none should judge another for where they are along the pathway of life. What seems for one a simple test to pass may be for another a test with which that one a has had difficulty for lifetimes—and yet that test could be the very key for that one in order to fulfill the final mandate of his or her own God Presence for complete and total illumination, God-awareness, and liberation. For you, other knotty issues arise that you know not of from your outer perspective. Thus, it is best to dwell in the sanctuary of your heart in holiness, seeking only that which God desires to fulfill through you day by day.

DCL: To make great progress, study with each of the chohans.[54] Get to know them personally. Ask for your soul to be taken during sleep to their schools of light, their retreats in the heaven world. Even if in the past you have asked the chohans to sponsor you and have asked to study with them, ask again. Saint Germain says there are higher levels of beingness about which they can teach you. Each chohan is key for you at whatever level of spirituality you now currently reside on your path. Depending on your desire and your ability to maintain harmony and your connection with your Source, each one will give you keys for passing your tests at each level along your way.

Failure of initiations is often a result of misqualified emotions in the feeling body. What a great resource we have when we attune to the archangels and the angels, who manifest the feeling nature of God to give us their resources to overcome our challenges. From our limited human perspective, we may look at an individual and think, "They're blowing it, they don't get it"; and yet they may have mastered every other initiation on the path and this one thing, when they get the victory over it, may mean their ascension. We can't judge anyone for anything.

Our prayers should not be a supplication asking for all manner of things from God. When our prayer is simply, "God, I desire to serve you. How can I serve you?" it sets the whole stage, inspiring us to know how we can serve at the highest level. Then our prayer is no longer a constant stream of desires from our human self. It becomes simply, "I accept God's will in my life. I am true to that will. Thank you, God, for allowing me to serve you. Inspire me with ways that I can serve you better." That becomes our holy prayer.

4. How can I make my life meaningful amid those who do not understand my spiritual path?

SG: Keep the inner mysteries you are experiencing secret from those who do not strive towards oneness with God. As you attune to the heart of your ascended gurus and teachers and receive their instruction, training, and evaluations along the way, their guidance, admonishments, and praise, your life will become meaningful because you will see it in the context of the lives of all devotees of light throughout this world and all worlds.

Your life gains meaning when its purpose is perceived within the purview of the Lord God, who sees you as a co-creator. Thus, understanding that alchemy is co-creation with God, you instantly see the meaning of your life: that you, as an initiate walking the way towards personal soul freedom, can experience life in all of its wonder and glory and joy toward the end that you seek, your union with God. Every day becomes meaningful and holy and filled with cosmic purpose when you see it as an opportunity for growth.

Within the context of movements such as The Hearts Center, whereby all who partake of what we release are striving together toward one end, your life has greater meaning because you are within the context of a greater body of alchemists. It is one thing to walk the path alone, or seemingly alone. When you walk it hand in hand with others with whom you may share your insights and your struggles, you receive the added benefit of the striving and consciousness of others to round out your own understanding along this path.

Community makes life more meaningful for many who struggled when seeking on their own for years before they found others with whom they could communicate on a par. Relationships on the path are key to giving your life meaning. Building these relationships is what community alchemy is about. For you see, within the greater classroom of all devotees, you may grow in greater understanding than when you limit yourself to performing experiments on your own in your own private laboratory.

When you see how others employ the energies of God in their own course, you receive a greater action of the glorification of the God-flame and the crystallization of that flame within the world as you know it, having first observed it in the lives of others. This is why we establish communities—for the ennoblement of holy purpose within all lifestreams and within specific graded classrooms along the path. Our classrooms are filled with conscious individuals.

5. Why and how does the violet flame work?

SG: The violet fire as the seventh-ray action of the Holy Spirit contains God's essence as love-power merged. The power of love to change is at the core of the violet fire, for violet is composed of pink (love) and blue (power); and this blending of love and power accelerates each of these flames to a level beyond its individual frequency. Based on the gradation of violet utilized and depending on how the student employs the violet fire, there can be either a greater action of love's mercy or of love's power.

The violet flame works because, as the alchemical flame of the Holy Spirit, it is the flame of divine love applied to help life, and so the Creator is invested within the living light of the flame itself. God has placed a living essence of him/herself within the violet flame that activates it. It is a pulsating fire that, as one of the five elements, embodies an aspect of universal consciousness.

Because the flame is alive, it has a vital force of energy backing it, which itself empowers those who utilize it to co-create. Applying the violet flame in any situation facilitates the work of the Holy Spirit to be accomplished and fulfilled through the nexus of our hearts. The Holy Spirit is the active energizer of God's applied love in our world. Through the invocation and use of the violet flame, all true alchemical works manifest and become permanent because of this universal, omnipresent awareness of the Holy Spirit.

The violet fire works through a blending of the flames of power and love. When these merge, the result is not what you know as friction; a certain transcendence occurs through the interplay of these two frequencies into one that allows the core of past karma, negative influences, and darkness to be consumed. The violet flame is a powerful divine solvent for transmutative change wherever and whenever it is lovingly called forth as a blessing to life. As a cosmic eraser, it consumes the misqualification of light within four dimensions of being. This action occurs because of the nature of the flowfield that is established through invocation of the violet fire and the way in which the misqualified substance is cast into this fire through the whirling of the electrons, which occurs through the acceleration of consciousness. There are higher frequencies beyond the fourth dimension that require an acceleration beyond what you know as the violet flame within your field of vision and understanding. To employ these energies requires cosmic consciousness beyond the time-space continuum. I received a dispensation to release the knowledge of the violet fire to mankind within this four-dimensional plane of being which you cohabit with other lifestreams.

The seventh-ray action of the Holy Spirit contains, at a certain level, all of the six frequencies that come before it. One reason the violet fire works so magnanimously is because, in a sense, the other six rays are contained within the seventh ray, even though you would consider, through the rainbow colorations infused, that this would be within the crystal, or white, ray. And yet, it is the seventh ray, as the fulfillment of the six rays that precede it, that actually contains them all. This is why it is so essential to employ the violet fire within your plane for the wrapping up of cycles, for the consuming of the cause, effect, record, and memory of karmic causes within the four planes of being. Simply visualizing the violet fire allows a certain action to occur. When you add invocation through the throat chakra, that action is precipitated in Mater, within the world of form that you know.

Thus, as you visualize violet fire affecting karmic causes, an action occurs in the mental and even the emotional and etheric planes. To bring that action into the physical requires the use of the throat. This is why I released the creative principles of its employment through the "I AM" Activity, whereby many have benefited from the absorption of their karma into this fire and then its adsorption, purified, back into their consciousness, returned unto them as new energy for their use. You see, when darkness is consumed in the violet fire, the core of what that darkness had surrounded is reinitiat-ed as light substance and energy that you may then use again for holy purposes. Some only consider *putting* things into the violet fire; they do not consider what occurs when this substance of darkness is *consumed* in that fire.

The key I give to you this day is to re-garner misqualified energy unto yourselves for greater alchemical works. As you reclaim that which has been tainted—stained, as it were, imprinted with human nonsense—then the higher sensibilities of God's awareness through the core of that light-energy may be reemployed in perfection as it was originally intended to be utilized by lifestreams in their alchem-ical experiments. Thus, each one who invokes the violet fire is really one who reclaims God's light over and over on behalf of himself and all evolutions.

DCL: Energy is neither created nor destroyed. We don't destroy ener-gy when we invoke the violet fire; what we do is transform the dark-ness that has surrounded something of light. That is the blessing of the violet flame—we feel the release as the darkness is transmuted and then we have more light-energy to work with.

6. Can DNA be changed through alchemy and the violet flame?

SG: The divine DNA is the blueprint of your Self-identification as a God being and co-creator with the One. There is also a shadow DNA of the lesser self, which has been carved out and created over lifetimes through your conscious cooperation with illusion. Thus, the process of your merging with the Divine is a continuous process of change and transmutation.

The DNA that you have embedded within yourself as a being liv-ing in this plane of existence is limited and is a result of all past choices of all lifetimes, even of a certain strain of genetic material that you have allowed through your acceptance of yourself as mortal. When you begin to understand, through the process of Self-identification with the God-flame, that you are truly an immortal being of spirit rather than a body, then the natural strains of your divine blueprint begin to be activated once more within your consciousness.

The more you self-identify with these cosmic traits—characteristics of nobleness, beauty, and joy—the more quickly your human DNA is transmuted into the divine strain of perfection. Thus, mankind en masse live with a certain consciousness (as you would call it, a *mass consciousness*) that is partly based on the lowest common denominator of the DNA, which is the genetic representation from which humans evolve in consciousness on the path.

As more and more of mankind awaken to their God Source, the divine strains are spread across the evolutionary scheme, first into the subconscious of mankind, raising the mass consciousness a certain cycle or level. Then, when enough of mankind have awakened, there can be a catalytic conversion of consciousness through a supersaturation of the mass consciousness seeded by divine beingness, whereby the entire solution is raised in spiritual fire. This is our work through you as some of the first fruits of those who have finally pulled your heads out of the sand, emerged from the cocoon of the lower nature into the Reality, the Sun Presence of God.

Yes, the DNA is transmuted through the action of divine alchemy and the violet flame through your prayers and invocations; and the transmutation is accelerated through your conscious awareness of this process rather than its simply happening unconsciously. Study and know the light-essences embedded within your own DNA and genetic material through meditation upon your Higher Self. Your Higher Self will expound on what current science teaches on this subject.

The violet fire is the surefire way to permanently create a bridge through which you may emerge from past limitations and connect with your higher reality. The violet fire activates a higher energy flux at every turn within the superstructure of your DNA. Recall the double-helix model of DNA that you studied in biology; the shape itself represents the flow of divine energy between spirit and matter. Meditate upon this pattern, which beautifully represents an aspect of the golden ratio spiral, a sacred geometric pattern found throughout the cosmos.

7. Can drug-induced damage be reversed? Is there a difference between prescription drugs, recreational drugs, and other addictive substances?

SG: Drug-induced damage may be reversed through an action of fire equal to or greater than the destructive elements of the perversion of fire that drugs are. For a soul to be cured of damage to the DNA strands and the genetic material that resulted through the intake of drugs and their inculcation into the deepest levels of the cell structures takes great fire, courage, and often the aid of others who will hold the hand of the one so traumatized.

Great prayer must attend those coming out of the shadows of these former self-identifications. A haven or sanctuary of light where they can experience a rebirth in this process would be most helpful. That is why greater progress is often made when, through true support groups, helpful souls—including those who have overcome in the past and those with great training and knowledge of the science of change—can attend to individuals who have been damaged, holding the balance for them through this process and release. Thus, centers where the soul is surfeited in light, support, and love are always instrumental in bringing forth the greatest permanent change for those who have undergone the duress of involvement in all manner of drugs and their use.

DCL: Hard drugs are damaging to the psyche, and other drugs are dangerous, too, in that people under their influence live in a quasi-astral world. Although the pharmaceutical industry leads people to think that they can pop a pill and be cured, substances that are synthesized to effect health and well-being or to simply deal with pain may also damage DNA and often have unintended effects and side effects.

Can the violet fire heal the harmful effects of medicinal drugs? Many factors are involved. The simple answer is that if you believe that it is so, then it can and may happen. Saint Germain says that acceptance is a part of the healing process. Acceptance of your whole-ness, your integrity, your health and well-being in God are part of the healing process. You can bypass the lesser roads to healing when you learn and truly employ the science of acceptance.

The masters teach that sugar, coffee, and alcohol are also drugs. Through these substances there is a very subtle degradation of the inner bodies. If you are addicted to any substance whatsoever, it is changing your DNA. Coffee, sugar, and other addicting substances very gradually move people into a quasi-astral existence where they lose their lessons and avoid taking action and changing their habit patterns. Beautiful centers where people can go for support and healing from drug or substance abuse would be wonderful in the New Age.

Our prayers for others do help, yet at a certain level these individuals have to accept that help. The masters can go down into the astral plane and offer to remove souls from there, yet those souls still have to take the master's hand, they have to make an effort, they have to project a conscious will. Acceptance is an action of will.

8. Is it possible to reduce or eliminate violence and gangs through alchemy?

DCL: The way to reduce or eliminate violence and gangs is to work on ourselves. Ask yourself, "What within my own being is indicative of the existence of violence? Is there violence within my consciousness that requires resolution and healing?" Consider the Ho'oponopono teachings and Dr. Hew Len's work. With the understanding and acceptance that all are one, Dr. Len healed violent criminals by working internally on himself and saying, "I love you. I'm sorry. Please forgive me. Thank you."[55]

When we truly understand that what we see outside of us is inside of us—because we are all connected, we are all one—we can take any situation in the outer world and draw it in and work on it right inside of ourselves. It's not that we are doing something to that situation or to the world. We are breathing it in; we breathe in the darkness of the world and transmute it in our heart, and then we breathe out light and joy and love. This can be a constant spiritual practice. When we see gang violence, we can choose to take it in; we can have such a burning fire in our heart that we transmute the pain of the gang members and of the people they affect. We do it bit by bit as we work on ourselves.

As we study the Ho'oponopono teachings, we understand better how and why this works and how essential it is for us to know and understand the science of enlightened self-interest, whereby we enlighten the whole world by our own enlightenment. Gautama Buddha saved the world through his enlightenment by working on himself as he sat in meditation under the Bo tree. Jesus accomplished the same thing during his forty days in the wilderness. By working on themselves, they resolved everything within themselves to the point where they could go out and teach and through their beingness recreate the world.

As alchemists, we understand that ultimately we must become the change we desire to see in the world by continually working on and cleaning ourselves. To eliminate violence and clean up gang activity, we must do internal cleaning. It's not about which prayer will do it "out there"; the one prayer is, "O Lord, clean me out." It is only through our collective inner work that violence and gang activity will be fully cleansed and transmuted, that those who are currently in or drawn to gangs will have communities and families that love them, and that they will no longer desire to engage in violence or gang activity. When these individuals feel deeply loved and supported, they will no longer look to gangs for what they really desire— family, fellowship, community.

So let's transmute internally the angst and the violence. Whatever internal gangs we have, let's clean up and transform them. Let's become within ourselves the holy family and the model for what gangs can be. We are an integrated community inside of ourselves, and therefore the true community (of which gangs are a perversion) will be born first within us When we clean up and transform the violence and gangs within ourselves, then what we see in the world will also be cleaned up and transformed.

9. Why do I experience flashbacks when praying or meditating?

SG: Flashbacks are your soul's opportunity, working in conjunction with your Higher Self and the mind of God, to contact points in the memory body from your past that have been critical junctures for you in coming to grips with both that which has held you back and that which is opportunity for self-transcendence. Often these scenes of both this and past lifetimes are impregnated with great emotion, turbulence, and a history of nonresolution.

Your soul, in conjunction with the keeper of the scrolls of your own being, your Higher Self, brings these before the screen of your mind so that they may be transmuted and their cause, effect, record, and memory dissolved in the violet fire. The violet fire, as the cosmic eraser, washes clean both the memory and the nadir of inception of that which caused these events to occur in the first place, blessed hearts. The resolution of each sticking point of your past allows you to then move forward in a fluid stream toward your immortal perfection.

Each of these points in time and space where you have gone out of the way, where there has been a diversion of your energies in byroads of consciousness that have taken you often far afield from the divine impetus of your cosmic trajectory toward perfection, must be understood in the context through which they were experienced. What better way to see them than through the lens of your Higher Self, who interprets for your soul the perfect context. From that higher vantage point, darkness does not exist; yet from the realm of the human living outside of the Presence of God, that darkness is limiting and bodes the potential garnering of even more density in your world. Thus, as you re-experience your Higher Self by the dissolving of the unreality that has surrounded the core of your identity, you attune to higher frequencies and learn the lessons of how to apply cosmic law and principles of light in your life.

The world, as you know, is a schoolroom. The Lord God never condemns the soul in its desire to experience creation. Free will reigns within the domain of the physical plane, and so you are given ample opportunity to learn life's lessons and grow. Even as you would not strike a child for simply attempting to learn something new, so God does not condemn any of his children in the process of their learning experience. The divine conscience is always working within and through Solar awareness, allowing the soul to attune to that which is the will of God, that which is good, that which is pure and holy.

Our work is to guide mankind through a clear stream that he may flow with, in, and through toward the goal of oneness with God. We use the violet stream to wash away what has been perceived by mankind as the sins of the past, which are simply misapplications of light, the weaving of a shadow around the self rather than the wielding of those cosmic forces of light that are truly at the beck and call of every soul one with God.

Thus, when you decree or meditate, particularly on the violet fire, these unresolved points of your past come before the screen of your mind for resolution and for you to then, once more, choose whether you will activate them as real or let them go permanently into the fire. The key for each of you is to not identify with them emotionally or to reengage them. Simply see them for what they were—a point of expression through the lens of your limited consciousness at the time—and then allow the moving stream of the violet flame to take them down the drain into the cauldron of swirling violet light, where they may be consumed forever, or, if you would, be consumed in a puff of violet smoke from which the angels may then take the crystalline ash substance, repolarize it, and recycle it for your use in purity.

If you experience flashbacks that are benign, beautiful, pristine, these are an attempt of your Higher Self to show you where you have made right choices. You may activate and remember these, which then naturally rise to your causal body as evidence of your fruitful application of the law of being. Thus, not all flashbacks are testing for your outer awareness. As you purify your consciousness, the remembrance of grand scenes from past lives of beauty and perfection will naturally come unto you in greater detail, vibrancy, and clarity; and you will feel once more the grandiose nature of God's beingness as you re-experience that which has been true, pure, and real for you when you were in the very Presence of God, in love with life.

10. How can I accelerate reunion with my twin flame in spirit and in the flesh?

SG: Many of you seek union with your twin flame and know not whether that one is in the heaven world or in the physical dimension. You desire keys to assist you to achieve this holy reunion in spirit and also in the flesh. Your twin flame is and has always been right within your heart as the co-equal fire that complements and completes who you are as an androgynous monad of light, empowered by your three-fold flame, the spirit spark of your individuality. You and your twin flame together, as one, form the *undivided duality* of your unique higher essence.

Seeking for your twin flame, or "other half," outside of yourself, embodied within another human being, may seem natural, though a better means of drawing that perfect one to you is to work internally on expanding the flame of divine love within. The magnanimity of your heart may magnetize your twin flame or a soul mate, one who can assist you in fulfilling your higher reason for being upon Earth rather than simply help you to fulfill earthly desires. By abiding in the internal space of love through devotion to the God-light burning within your heart, the allness of your androgynous Higher Self may come to fruition in your life and replace the corporal desire to have someone outside of you complete you as an initiate and worker of divine alchemy.

Cultivate the purity of wholeness where you create the cosmic magnet that will draw your twin flame, according to God's cycles and seasons, back to your heart. Through your acceptance of your one-ness in the heaven world as already manifest within your heart and spirit, you create the cosmic crystal magnet of pure love that will nat-urally allow this one, if ascended, to draw you higher; or, if you are preparing for your ascension or are at a higher level than your twin flame, it will allow you to draw that one higher. Regardless of your station or theirs, the key is your reunion with God in the here and now. For when you are one with your Source, then the love of the Divine Presence flowing through you will be for you the key to the eventual reuniting of your twin hearts. If you seek only the physical union of one or another and lose sight of the greater union of your soul and spirit to the perfected heart, then your search may be in vain.

While beloved Portia resided in the heaven world awaiting my return to her heart, her great love held for me at all times the divine blueprint of my soul. This love, blessed ones, you may experience moment by moment as you meditate upon your Presence, the Solar light of your beloved emanating from wherever that one is in time and space through your own God Presence eternally one with them in Spirit.

Study my words through the messengers of fire who have gone before to discern how, through your attention upon the Sun Presence of your own being, you may also see the very face of your beloved. Through that smile and through that joy, you may even be lifted up in cosmic revelry, in bliss, to be one with your beloved here and now and always. Employ the alchemy of fire, the alchemy of love where you are and you shall know the truth of your own beingness in God. And that truth shall make you free.[56]

11. What is the role of the Divine Feminine in alchemy?

SG: The Divine Feminine anchors in Matter the light of Spirit from within her sacred womb. The womb of "womb-man" represents the space of the Unmanifest through which the "child-Man" may embody. Without the feminine aspect of God, there would be no creation and no alchemy; thus, find the source of the Mother's light within your soul. As the focal point where the Spirit seeds its essence within the Mater-plane of being, your soul can be considered feminine in gender. The incarnating soul descends through the portal of the mother's womb through the sacral center just below the seat of the soul chakra. Men and women alike may see how the metaphor of a child's birth may allow them to understand the connection between Spirit and Matter, as Above, so below, in order for the true alchemist to precipitate the desired result through the merging of the Alpha and Omega energies within. Utilizing one's "soul potential" to co-create something of beauty and divine splendor is the birthright of all spiritual alchemists.

Divine alchemy is co-creation with God. From the body of the Mother is issued an ovum of light which, when impregnated with the seed ideation of the Father's Spirit, becomes the substance of the created ideation in form. Without the Mother, the Divine Feminine, no co-creation can occur. The Father prepares the blueprint, which is the seed, and the Mother receives that seed and allows it a place to be sown and in which to grow.

The Mother represents fertility. Ancient cultures understood the importance of the Divine Feminine, and thus entire cults have been born around this principle, the desire for the crèche or the place prepared, this certain habitation where enough of a fertile consciousness abides for the birth of new ideations to occur. In alchemy, for co-creation to occur, there must be the fertile seed as a certain purity of consciousness within the practitioner. The alchemist must have a balance of Alpha and Omega within himself for the wholeness to be where he is for precipitation to occur. If the lobes of his awareness are imbalanced, then an imperfect creation will manifest or no creation will happen at all. If, on the other hand, there are both the spirit of giving and the spirit of acceptance, then the results will be beautiful.

Without the Mother holding the field of awareness of what the Father intends to bring forth, the creative ideation is simply left out in space to float endlessly without any place to come home to, to be received, honored, accepted, and then to grow. Often you have seed ideations as co-creations in potential; if you never give them unto the Mother, they will remain only seeds and not become sons or daughters as co-created children of your work with another. The entire universe is a song of the Mother, where she sings as she meditates upon that which is growing within her from what the Father has lovingly placed within her womb. The music of the spheres is a sound that occurs as each created starry seed evolves unto its full flowering and enlightenment.

The process of this creation is the same both within the microcosm and the macrocosm. Once you understand the process as you have seen it manifest in any life form, you should be able to discern even how stars and planets and entire solar systems and galaxies are created. The divine alchemist must have a love of the Mother, the Divine Feminine, in order to co-create. This requires the balance of love, wisdom, and power. Every seed has this perfect balance as potential. The Mother provides the white light of the ovum, the circle of fire, the chalice, the Grail into which this perfect seed is housed. The egg of your aura is the light of the Mother in which you reside. Your body is woven from strands of light that the Mother creates in her womb with many colorful patterns that issue from her meditation on her co-creation.

As you understand the Mother principle, you gain a greater respect for the Divine Feminine, Mother Nature, the Earth Mother, and the twin flames of every true, masterful being. As you nurture your own Mother nature and your creativity and the use of your right brain and not just your left, there can be greater balance and integration of your soul with the Spirit and ultimately your permanent freedom as an immortal being. True freedom and alchemy is the ability to co-create as a soul, the feminine potential of God, now one with the Spirit, the Father, thus fully become a son or daughter of God who then carries on the creation, having fully matured and then repeating the birthing process with your beloved. The song of the Mother, the Divine Feminine, is the lullaby of all creation.

12. What is the significance of the Holy Grail?

SG: The Holy Grail is the heart consecrated to the Divine, through which God pours the light of love into the world. The Grail receives and dispenses this light of love through the daily Mass—the Eucharistic feast that is ongoing within one's heart as one communes with the Divine and emanates pure love to all life. As a symbol of the inner communion of the saints with their Source, the Grail is the All-in-all of the perfected chalice that sons and daughters of God strive to drink from in order to perceive the reality of heaven where they are. It is the very love-wisdom personified by the cup of Christ through which his passion for the saving of mankind was received—the very distillation of the accelerated love-fires of his ruby consciousness, which, when drunk by the devotee and servant-son of God, will move that one beyond mortality into the immortal sphere of God-being.

Seek not to drink from this cup prematurely. Seek rather to understand the nature of pure love. As "pure fools" for God in Christ, as Percival[57] and others have been, you will be able to imbibe the spiritual fire when you are ready, when you have confessed your sins first and there is nothing left within you that would allow an attachment or vice or darkness to remain within your soul. This was the striving of the true knights, the purity of heart that Lancelot and others attained by perfecting the chalice of self through the heart, thereby magnifying God and truly allowing the wine of the Spirit to flow ever and always through the heart.

DCL: When we talk about the Grail, we must also talk about the wine of the Spirit, the energy of Spirit that flows through the heart. The wine of the Spirit is an elixir for accelerated violet-fire transmutation and transubstantiation, an elixir of light that allows us to move into our full Presence. It is a concentrated essence of the Holy Spirit, through the agency of the Holy Spirit that the seventh ray is, that is pure love in its forgiving and transmuting mode.

For two thousand years, some have believed and taught that Jesus initiated the Ritual of Holy Communion during the Last Supper as a means to partake of the Body and Blood of Jesus. In truth, the ritual symbolizes partaking of the Christ consciousness. If you have Communion with your own Grail cup before you, your heart offered in this chalice of acceptance in anticipation of the release of that Christic essence from the heart of the Cosmic Christ unto you, you can receive a blessing and bestowal of a greater level of illumination and beingness.

The Ritual of Holy Communion is a very deep and reverential sacrament, a sacred event if you allow it to be. If you have occasion to go to any church where the Eucharist is presented, let it be an opportunity for you to attune to your own Christ consciousness and allow it to flow. During Mass I sometimes see Jesus over the priest and see the energy of the saints and ascended beings and what they are accomplishing through the Mass, blessing each and every person. In one instance I saw Jesus go to every person in attendance and bless them. It was a magnanimous experience. The last person to receive the blessing from Jesus was me. I was in ecstasy, feeling and seeing my Lord in front of me and the light and love of his heart sharing the bestowal of his Christ essence with me.

This is what the Mass should be and really is for mystics. When we partake of the Grail, either in a ritual or in our own communion and meditation, we become that Grail. We become the mystical point through which heaven and earth merge in the nexus. A chalice, with its hourglass shape, really is a nexus between heaven and earth. The base represents earth. The center, the stem, represents the mystical point of connection between heaven and earth. And in the upper portion of the chalice, through the wine or grape juice, the Spirit is wielded.

In his novel *The DaVinci Code,* author Dan Brown says that the Grail was really Mary Magdalene and that she carried forward the bloodline of Jesus as his mate and the mother of his children. With Magda (Jesus' ascended twin flame, who was embodied as Mary Magdalene), we can be a Holy Grail where we are. As we bear the light of our beloved—our beloved God Presence and our human beloved or divine beloved—there is a transfer through our own bloodline of our Christ consciousness to our children, grand-children, and all who come after us. It is through having children that lightbearers transfer the seed of their own Christ consciousness to future generations.

13. The Buddha has been called the supreme alchemist. Do Buddhists use alchemy, and if so, how?

SG: Yes, Buddhists use alchemy. The Buddha was the supreme alchemist. He discovered and codified what holds mankind back from the realization of wakefulness, from enlightenment—ignorance born of human desire, which leads to suffering. Ignorance connotes that one actually knows what is true and decides, through conscious choice, to ignore it or turn away from it. This turning away from what is real is where the veil of illusion begins, for every choice is creation. If you choose not to create reality, you are creating illusion.

The divine alchemist knows that he must make right choices. To do so he requires wakefulness, awareness, presence. You may be able to create something if you are not truly awake, yet it will not be enfired with permanency. When you are consciously co-creating with a partner, you are fully present, engaged in the act of loving and sharing. This is how you must be when engaging in alchemy—fully present and conscious, your mind wed to your heart and acting through your body's awareness in that moment. This allows a higher form of co-creation to occur.

There is a difference between human desire and divine desire. The former always leads to suffering; the latter always leads to bliss. Divine desire is ensconced in the eternal glow of perfect love between Alpha and Omega. The sun is the perfect fusion of the light of Helios and the light of Vesta, both hydrogen atoms—Helios of wisdom, Vesta of love—merging into helium and going on indefinitely. The sun is the cosmic representation of perfect love-wisdom, perfect fusion.

Buddha brought love to wisdom to enlightenment in his crown chakra. The crown of life is given unto the one who understands all through the raising of the Mother light through the heart to the crown. The Buddha was the perfect lover because he made the ultimate sacrifice for humanity, leaving his human partner in order to reach perfectionment so that all could become free. This is the real and the first example for the Earth of unconditional, uncompromising love.

Buddhists understand alchemy, for if they follow the example of any of the many Buddhas—Gautama, Maitreya, Manjushri, Milarepa, Kartikeya—then they have engaged in the act of co-creation by manifesting the perfect desire of God, which displaces human desire. Disciples of other religions, such as Jesus, Zarathustra, and El Morya, have also attained to Buddhahood. Buddhahood is not a religion; it is a state of enlightened beingness and freedom from rebirth. Therefore, the Buddha within is the supreme alchemist, for an enlightened state of being allows one to engage the universe in pure alchemy.

14. What role does the secret chamber of the heart play in alchemy?

SG: No true alchemy occurs without love. Love is generated and emanates through the secret chamber of the heart. Without the divine emotion of love, you are demoted to simply engaging in animal magnetism.[58] The difference between animals and mankind is that mankind has the spirit-spark of God within that allows him to co-create as an alchemist.

If you study my previous treatises on alchemy, you will ascertain that love is the key to every divine manifestation. When you say, "I am the light of the heart," the secret chamber of your heart is fully lit by the lamp of your intention. When you keep this chamber lit, then you glow internally and then you may shine that light unto all. You must have a well-lighted laboratory for your experiments to be successful, right? Best to keep the proving ground of your heart inspired with love by meditating on and living in that secret chamber.

The key to perfect presence is understanding the nature of the secret chamber of the heart. Many never enter that holy room, for they have never truly knocked on the door of God's heart within them. Their prayers are simply petitions for things or situations rather than about entering into God's desiring within them to be fully realized. Divine alchemists prepare their laboratory by having all they require ready and at hand to perform each experiment. This time of preparation is important and requires that the alchemist meditate and concentrate fully on that which he desires to accomplish during his scientific application. Those who prepare will have a better chance of success the first time without struggle or fumbling about in the dark because they forgot to turn on the light switch when they entered.

Reverence for the inner teacher sets up a field of awareness whereby, through heightened consciousness, you are ready to be a divine observer. Physics now teaches that the intent and focus of the observer definitely affects the outcome of scientific experiments. As this is so, then the most important thing is to watch your consciousness during your alchemy. This is why I have given my advanced students the assignment to observe their thoughts and feelings regularly. When you can hold the field of precipitation around you through the conscious choice to live in perfect love, wisdom, and power, then your alchemies will be joyful and complete and instantaneous. This takes practice and presence wed with patience. Impatience breeds anxiety, which thwarts divine alchemy. Perfect love casts out fear[59] and neutralizes anxiety. Therefore, if you observe yourself beginning to become anxious, close your eyes and enter again the secret chamber of your heart, which you have temporarily abandoned. Breathe deeply, turn on the light there again, and then return to your experimentations, your alchemy.

Meditation upon the sacred heart of any master will allow you quicker entrée to the secret chamber of your own heart. There are many windows to the secret chamber; depending on your view, you may see a number of aspects of the eternal flame that glows there. There is, however, only one true doorway to this chamber, and that portal may only be entered through love.

DCL: Saint Germain says that many animals are very conscious and actually very loving. They are moving into a higher evolutionary state where they will have free will and individual consciousness rather than just a group soul. Like us, through free will they will have a greater level of freedom to evolve. Just because animals are in one sense at a lesser level of evolution does not mean they do not have within them an aspect of the God-spark, which is life itself.

15. Does humor play a role in greater alchemical manifestation?

SG: Anyone who has witnessed God's creation knows how humorous the Lord is. Why, he created you, right? Particles of precipitation that have flown through the air of excitement and expectancy land upon the pool of joy that you create by the fire of humor. Humor emanates from the starry wit of the five elements resonating within the mind of God. Once these coalesce in you through the use of the crystal rays, the five expand to become victory's star, and—as Above, so below—voilà, you have precipitation. Without joy, your co-creations are sterile. Humor keeps things light and dissolves the monotony of repetition without the Spirit. Fun allows the sun of wisdom to illumine each new creation which you, with God, may declare is good.

Goodness is Godness, always powered by the wherewithal *(where-with-all)* of compassion. Having fun with children allows adults to reenter the field of joy. Creativity expands when, through a good Buddha-belly laugh, you also expand your heart-mind connection to receive greater inspiration. Healing is an aspect of precipitation. Heal your past hurts through humor, joy, and the *virya* that flows through lungs full of the Spirit, and your alchemies will manifest with a smile.

16. What is the perfect diet for spiritual development?

SG: The perfect diet is light. Within all food is contained the essence of solar light; thus, the ultimate food is light. Light sustains the cosmos. Each personal diet may vary, based on the ability of your own organism to assimilate the light within various substances, and depending on your personal tastes, your upbringing, the climate in which you live, and your own ability to assimilate different foods. Test various food substances to see how you feel and how you can remain centered and uplifted by the foods you ingest.

The foods you take in that accommodate the greatest amount of pranic acceleration within your four lower bodies are the ones you should use. Those that cloud your mind, weaken your immune system, or compromise the light within your organs, chakras, and systems should be avoided. This will be different for each one, blessed hearts. We do not condemn any for experimentation so long as their ultimate goal is to be a vessel of God and to see their own body as a temple, as a living spirit. When mankind forgets that he is a temple and that he should be concerned about that of which he partakes, then you see all manner of misguided dietary practices utilized by lifestreams.

I recommend the original diet given unto mankind by the Lord God—fish, fruits, vegetables, legumes, nuts, grains[60]—within the confines and parameters of where you live and based on the temperature index, ingesting lighter substances during the summer months and more concentrated or denser substances during the cold winter months. I recommend avoiding dense substances such as heavy meats and extremely potent or hot spices, which create an imbalance in the temperature of the body and in the homeostasis within your being whereby you fluctuate, moment by moment, based on partaking of these substances. I recommend that you avoid drinking very cold liquids, especially just before, during, or after meals, for this creates a problem within the digestive tract for the assimilation of the nourishment of which you partake.

You have heard the teaching from Jesus that it is more important what comes out of the mouth than what goes in.[61] I reflect his teaching unto you: Any substance taken in, even if not perfect in its outer manifestation, if eaten in holiness, chewed well and unto liquid, if possible, and loved as ingested in a climate of stillness and peace may be better assimilated by your cells than the perfect substances taken in haste or in a way that is demeaning to your spirit. Thus, there is not one perfect diet for all. The diet of the adepts is light, and at the core of all foods you may assimilate that light as you receive it, bless it, and partake of it in holiness.

DCL: As you pursue higher adeptship, learn what your body requires. In these busy times, it can be difficult to maintain health and stay grounded in work. Many of us can become spacey through a vegetarian diet lacking the balance of minerals and other nutrients we require for our mental health and cognitive abilities. We must have our mind working at its highest. At our events at The Hearts Center, we serve a vegetarian diet and fish. If anyone feels that they require a stronger protein than fish to remain whole and integrated and at their highest peak, that's okay. Each of us knows our own body and can work within the integrity of what supports that body.

Even though the masters recommend a vegetarian diet, our spiritual work is just as possible if we eat animal foods; we can overcome the downside of the emotional energies that animals have when they die. That energy does contribute to our system, and of course none of us desires to take that in. And yet, if at times anyone requires a substance such as red meat, preferably organic, to feel grounded and integrated, there is no reason to feel guilty; it is fine to have meat sometimes. Our bodies are gradually moving into a higher framework of beingness through a more subtle diet and we will get there. Honor your body's requirements.

17. What is the origin of death? Is physical death necessary?

SG: Death is the acceptance of mortality by living outside of the Divine Self and the field of perfection emanating from the God Presence. Anything outside of the circle eventually decays into death. Once you reenter the circle of wholeness, life manifests. Though the physical may drop off from the soul in the process of the change called death, the spirit is immutable, unchanging, immortal.

The origin of death is awareness outside of God's Presence, or the attempt to live within a sphere of consciousness exclusive of God's eternal being. Death as it is experienced by humanity now is simply a transition, a casting off of the mortal form to enter spirit, our true origin, and then to either reincarnate to fulfill anything left undone or to move on to other realms of light and beingness in an eternal or immortal state of being. Death is not the end; it is a doorway to another life. Physical death is no longer necessary when one has fulfilled one's reason for incarnating in material form. However, very few beings ascend or are translated physically by transmuting their corporal body temple into pure light without going through the doorway that you currently label as death.

Death is only as real as you accept it to be real. Do not be so concerned about the death of the physical body, for this is not true death; it is simply the casting off of another veil. Those who seek the permanency of the physical will always be disillusioned and unhappy. Seek resonance with the Real Self and the life of the spirit and you will never be disillusioned or sad, only truly happy in the joy of God's light.

18. Is there a true Fountain of Youth? If so, how can I obtain it?

SG: The Fountain of Youth is God's heart vibrating within you. It is the energy of life accessible within your threefold flame, the eternal spark of your divinity. Youthfulness is the joy of the Holy Spirit manifest through a loving life of givingness; the fountain continues to effervesce and pour forth its electrifying energy currents to those who, as willing co-creators, continue to offer themselves as a love-gift to life. Youthful vitality is accessible only through love's charitable ways and hospitable means. Youthfulness is purity maximized through the law of harmony. When you are in harmony with and in resonance with God, nothing decays or is diminished; all is sustained and increases by and in love. To enter the kingdom of God, you must become as little children, as the Master Jesus said.[62] This state of being is where the only true fountain of youth exists, yet it permeates all of cosmos from within the sacred space of love.

Eternal youthfulness comes through the joyous heart listening to the voice of God within. Listen now to the birds of springtime. Do you hear the voice of God speaking through them? This voice emanates from the original intent, the youthful intent of the God-child, which is the first emanation of the Source. It is still speaking, chirping, and singing unto your soul the song of freedom and of love. A youthful heart is a soft heart, pliant yet strong. The heart that beats in resonance with godly virtue remains always in joy, always young. A fresh spirit imbued with true vitality is one that is always ready to learn a new lesson, to paint with oils or watercolors or any number of essential media what is upon the heart and present it to the Mother for reflection, coming close to her heart to receive the pulsations of her own divine spiritual fire that, through her vision, maintains for you your own wholeness and perfection.

Attuning to the heart of the great brooding Mothers of heaven also keeps you young. Many who have hardened their hearts and have aged prematurely do not know of the love of the Mother flame. That is why this culture and civilization, in only speaking of the Father God, has remained stultified. For does not the Mother—in her caress, in her gentle kiss—keep you always in love with life? Thus, know the spirit of both Father and Mother within you, for then you shall always be youthful as a son or daughter even as the years roll by. And your life, full of knowledge and wisdom in your elder years, will allow you to return to the First Principle, your love of God.

The violet light is key for the transmutation of ancient patterns that have beset your soul, crystallizing you in certain forms, structures, and matrices that are a burden to you and also age you in the process. Regular fasting, the drinking of ample water and herbal teas, a general diet of simplicity, chewing your food very well, breathing deeply, getting exercise and rest, sun gazing and taking walks in nature are all key to maintaining a youthful body, a youthful spirit, a youthful heart.

Many of you studied the natural sciences of health even before you were able to attune to the higher frequencies of alchemy. Often, though, there is a certain justification within you for leaving off of the disciplines of your dietary practices. We would not create robots or mechanical men and women who seek only the perpetuity of their youthful appearance in form. And yet, following the disciplines of what you know as the sacred diet of the adepts allows you to maintain, even within the body, the receptivity of your Solar batteries so that greater light may flow through you day by day, activating the Sun center of your cells to be refreshed and renewed, and thereby maintaining a perpetual state of lightness, buoyancy, and joy where you are.

Others of you, in your alchemy, would like to understand how it is that I was able to transform imperfect gemstones into flawless ones. Blessed ones, this truly takes cosmic vision and the understanding of the crystalline nature of substance, of the fire that resides within crystals, and of how, through the employment of this cosmic vision, by holding the perfected matrix of the perfect structure of that gemstone, you may add substance here and there in the divine design of that which you seek to be in physical reality for that gem.

Sometimes molecules are missing, for there has been a fracturing of the perfect design. It is, as some would say, more difficult to add substance to imperfect gems. And yet, if you study the science of how crystals grow, you will discern the measure of how it is that I employ divine substance to complete the crystalline structure that I seek. This takes the free light of transubstantiation employed through both my hands and eyes simultaneously. It is as a laser action of light through a focused attention that I employ the frequencies of cosmic alchemy to add molecules of that crystal to the gemstone.

Those who have studied the fashioning and the cutting of diamonds know something whereof I speak. Those of you who are serious and desire to attune to my heart while employing your knowledge in this area may call to me for the specifics of how you may use this heightened form of alchemy to both fabricate and perfect gemstones in the laboratory of your heart and in your physical workplace.

DCL: How does the alchemy of perfecting gemstones relate to longevity and the Fountain of Youth? We are a gem of God and Saint Germain is telling us how to use the science of alchemy to smooth out our flaws. For example, someone with a degenerative disease might use this teaching to recreate certain kinds of cells within specific organs, tissues, bone, or cartilage in order to restore health. There are many possible ways to apply this information about how to perfect gemstones that we can experiment with to restore or maintain our perfect health.

Saint Germain would also like us to know that refined sugar, which permeates our entire culture, debilitates the cellular structure of our organs, our tissues, our blood, our entire body temple. Sugar can weaken the body and rob it of vitality. To retain health and vitality and add longevity, avoid eating sugar in all its forms. Hopefully we each know our own body. Hopefully we know what works for us and what brings us strength, vitality, and energy as well as what debilitates us. I have noticed at times that if my diet is not perfect and if I have any sugar at all, I wake up feeling stiff. When we have children, we can sometimes justify certain things; we just have to be more disciplined the rest of the time. The goal is to be conscious, do our best, and realize without fanaticism that everything we partake of affects us.

19. Can certain elixirs help to maintain youthfulness? How can I prepare and use them?

SG: The sustaining of life in the physical temple at the highest level is essential for every devotee to understand. When you see your body as the temple of the living God, you will desire to maintain harmony and balance within that temple so that you may be the perfect instrument of the Godhead at all times. The elixirs that I created were drawn from my knowledge of herbs and plants, whereby I understood each one's effect on the different organs and systems within the body to maintain this balance and harmony. A strong heart is essential for every devotee to have. Herbs that allow the purification of the blood to be maintained and the free flowing of that blood throughout the body temple are essential for a strong heart and thus a strong mind also.

Rather than giving you the specific herbs that I utilized, I will speak in general terms. Those who are alchemists of the spirit through herbology may desire to experiment and procure and create your own formulas toward this end. When you keep the liver, the kidneys, and the organs that work with purification and elimination of toxins from the system clear and free to function in perfect harmony, then you maintain within the body a state of cosmic liquidity that allows the free flowing of the bloodstream, the lymphatic fluids, and the spiritual fluids of pranic energy through the system. You also allow the Lord God to breathe his breath of inspiration through you at any and all times, and this inspiration may flow throughout the channels of your being.

Inspiration can come through the mind or the heart, or it can be effused through the seven chakras and the ganglionic nerve centers that relate to these chakras. You may receive an inspiration at the soul level through the organs that relate to or are near the soul chakra. You may receive an inspiration through the solar plexus, through those organs that relate to that chakra; through your throat chakra and creative voice; through the head and brain and the glands that relate to the third eye and crown chakras; or through the base chakra.

Inspiration, as cosmic respiration, the flow of inbreath and outbreath, is essential to receive these higher frequencies through your chakras, which are resonating centers of light and cosmic receptors through which you live and move and have your being within God's eternal heart. Understand the interplay of what you partake of through your mouth and through other channels. For in addition to receiving through your mouth, you receive through your vision, your mind, your heart, your solar plexus, your soul, and your base chakra; and you partake, or eat, through each of these orifices of fire.

The employment of the elixirs that I created was always augmented by my meditation upon the violet fire. And thus, as I prayed over and meditated upon that which I saw acting through each of these substances—which, when merged in a particular formulation, would work on the nerve centers and the organs and systems within the body to create first the elimination of toxins, and then a certain homeostasis or balance, and then the heightened sensitivity to higher frequencies of light—these are what was given unto me through my meditation in entering into a deep contemplation upon the plant and its effects and uses for the individual lifestreams of mankind. Many of you have also employed more of an understanding of the use of herbs and plants in past lives, before current materia medica took sway in the world through the use of drugs, and thus you understood in those lives more of what I am saying.

The use of bee pollen, honey, and other products from bees were always employed in my formulas, even if at an almost microscopic level, for within the pollen itself are the highest aspects of the enlightenment of the plant through the flowering of that plant. These pollens are the distillation of the highest aspects of each plant that the bees gather, bring back to the honeycomb, and utilize in their work. Nutritional science now shares that pollen honey and bee products contribute toward a longer lifespan. Various cultures upon the Earth, such as the Hunzas, utilize these substances for longevity. Thus, I urge you to consider using pollen and honey in your daily intake in certain quantities, very small. For as you continue using them and meditating upon their qualities, you will see an increase in your vitality.

As you know, there are formulations from plants used at many levels now through the science of aromatherapy. You may key into that which I discerned as the Wonderman of Europe as to how these essences act in formulations for your benefit. You can experiment with, put together, and take different formulas on different days of the week based on the rays[63] and on the various cycles of the year and on your requirement either for strengthening the body or for eliminating toxins, growths, and more. This science could contain volumes if I were to elaborate fully. There is much knowledge already conveyed in libraries throughout the world in various languages that you have not studied in this lifetime and which, if various devotees were to secure them and read and share them, would give you greater keys toward the creation of the elixirs you desire for longevity.

The greatest elixir, of course, is the use of the violet light in your prayers and meditations, in your visualization, and through allowing the frequency of this light to enter through the portals of all of your chakras. When the violet light accentuates the illumination fires of the crown, what occurs? There is the merging of the violet light and the golden (or yellow) light to create a new frequency that augments the work of wisdom's fires. This you may experiment with and discern how it will move forward the evolutions of mankind. The same is true with the merging of the violet light with the emerald light in the third eye. Experiment. See what it does for you when these rays and fires are used in conjunction with each other.

DCL: The elixirs Saint Germain made as the Wonderman of Europe and in other lifetimes were prepared individually for different people he was working with. Those he prepared for himself were different from those he prepared for others. In regard to using honey, those of you who would like to take this science further can secure honey from different regions of the Earth where the pollination occurs through plant life specific to those regions. The qualities differ between honey from alfalfa and honey from orange blossoms or from rose hips and rose plants, and so forth. You may research local sources of various honeys and pollens to utilize their healing virtues.

Saint Germain implied that the honey extracted by bees from a particular plant—for example, clover—is a refined, almost homeopathic aspect of what that plant is good for. The same is true for other plants. Thus, when you take in that plant's honey, it works on your higher nerve centers and actually does a spiritual cleansing; it has a higher component of the essences of the plant that work on your inner bodies. You can learn which conditions and situations clover and other plants are good for.

In regard to the knowledge of plants contained in the world's libraries, Saint Germain has explained that some of these tomes are in languages such as French, Romanian, Bulgarian, and some of the Slavic languages of Eastern Europe. During the time he formulated elixirs as the Wonderman of Europe, a lot of these tomes were shared in those regions. There is a record of some of them even today through literature, although these haven't necessarily been translated into English.

Adding to what he explained earlier, Saint Germain showed me that some of the elixirs he created contained pollens that he extracted directly from various plants himself and not necessarily pollens extracted by bees. He experimented for quite some time with plants based on their color, and he formulated elixirs for people who had imbalances within certain chakras, imbalances he could see because he saw their auras.

There was always another component in his formulations, though, and that was his great desire for people to become connected with their Source. And so, as he prayed over these elixirs, he infused them with love and light so that their greater effects would be toward spiritual development and not just human longevity. We can length-en our life, yet for what cause? The ultimate purposes for long life are to continue learning, to glorify God, and to serve. Some of the peo-ple that desired elixirs, of course, desired them only for their human propensities, predilections, and desires. If we desire long life, let it simply be so that we can balance our karma, fulfill our dharma, and serve life more lovingly.

Recently, a number of products have been developed to help with longevity. Some of these are similar to formulations that were utilized even on Lemuria and Atlantis and in other ancient cultures. For example, tiny flakes of gold and silver in the right proportion can renew your bloodstream and help maintain an electromagnetic bal-ance within the blood; that is what the master desires us to know. It has to do with the resonance of the blood, the light energy of the sun, the *higher hemoglobin* within the Solar body. Just as our physical blood is bright red when the hemoglobin is oxygenated, in our higher bodies we have gold and liquid light flowing through.

I encourage you to formulate your own elixirs and shakes. A powerful blender can help you to create your formulas. Experiment, try various products and ingredients, and see what effects they have on you. Create your own best elixirs based on what works for you. Part of alchemy is experimentation—working in the laboratory of your kitchen with different plant extracts and with those things that you know have a great ability, through their antioxidant value, to help you gain longevity and to keep your cells alive, free-flowing, and working through your bloodstream at the highest level. Various products and nutrients can support the free flowing of the blood, and darkfield microscopy can allow you to see how free-flowing your live blood cells are.

The oceans themselves are constantly receiving the rays of the sun. Kelp and other seaweeds are excellent for us. The salt within the oceans is the particulate matter from the plants that are distributed within the water. When you extract salt from the ocean, it contains the concentrated essence of all that plant life and all that is within the ocean, and so it is in itself an elixir. Salt is a preservative. Before refrigeration, people used salt to preserve things. We are crystal beings and salt is a crystal. Water itself is a liquid crystal. In the book *Spiritual Alchemy,* which augments our advanced studies in alchemy, the master Omraam gave a wonderful teaching on water, the water molecule being a combination of Father and Mother.

20. How does sacred geometry enter into alchemy?

SG: God is the Geometry of ivinity. The entire universe is a geometrical design. Sacred geometry is inherent in all created life and even in what mankind has previously thought to be inert. When you know what each form represents, the use of geometric thoughtforms allows you to key into the creative process. At each stage of alchemy, you may visualize and employ different matrices, coalescing light around the pattern that you see until it is realized in that dimension of being.

If you study cellular division, you will witness the geometrizing of light into and through substance. The miracle of creation may then be understood in both its simplicity and its complexity. Alchemy requires the understanding of the sciences of biology, chemistry, and physics, for the laws governing these manifest within the patterns that the mathematics of geometry, as the foundation of form, teaches.

Divine design occurs before life enters in to fill the form. God, the great architect of life, designs beautifully and with cosmic abandon. Once the blueprint is set, the Builders of Form work to coalesce light into the matrix of each form. Pythagoras understood the mysteries of creation behind the forms he designed and codified. Studying his theorems and meditating upon the meaning behind them allows one access to the mind of God that created the universe. Thoughtforms, as divine ideations of God, may vibrate within your mind one with God. Each geometric form with which the Lord creates is perfect in symmetry and allows the creative fires of perfection to emanate through the crystal patterns of form which that geometrized ideation represents.

Thus, an equilateral triangle represents the threefold light of love, wisdom, and power. Equilateral in nature, in perfect proportion and balance, this is one thoughtform that each of you may use when meditating upon your threefold flame. Consider how the Lord God, having placed his spark within you as the descending triangle, lights through the nexus of your heart a new triangle of fire where you are. The interconnectedness of these two equilateral triangles is the divine mystery of life as you know it. Through meditation upon this thoughtform, which becomes the six-pointed star, you may discern the nature of reality and also discover the cosmic portal to divinity through which you may perceive as God does.

All sacred sciences, including alchemy, allow you new opportunities for self-discovery. This process never ends, not even with the greatest masters and cosmic beings, for they are constantly discovering through this same portal greater light, following it back to the First Cause, the first Word, the first emanation. The circle unbroken represents the All-in-all. The allness within the circle is complete; the allness without the circle is complete. Thus you have completeness within and without simultaneously, although by definition, *completeness,* as that which is circumscribed within the circle of wholeness, allows precipitation to occur within that whole matrix.

Draw a ring of fire around yourself as you begin each alchemical experiment. Living and breathing within this circle of fire, every manifestation that you desire with a God-desire may be so, because it is created in wholeness, in nonduality, in oneness. Co-creation between the two merged as one is actually no longer co-creation; it is simply the one creation. The two dissolve into one, becoming whole, and the circle within and without merge into one as the circle disappears. Although you ascribe around yourself a circle, it is only a representation in that moment of your oneness with all, a reminder. Once you understand and know your perfect oneness with the All-in-all, there is no necessity even for the circle, blessed hearts. For if you could see the circle dissolving before you as you move away from it into infinity, ultimately it becomes the point, the One within.

I draw a line upon the screen of your mind, a horizontal line. I now draw a vertical line intersecting that line. The point of the intersection, the nexus, is you. Whether you connect these lines to create the figure-eight or not, the key for each created being is to remain centered at that nexus, living neither in the vertical nor the horizontal in temporary manifestation; rather, living in both simultaneously, because they intersect at the point. When you live both as a created being and as a part of the Creator, you live at the nexus of the vertical and the horizontal.

Understanding this connection at that point of reality is the key for every soul to understand in its return to the One. Giving and receiving, receiving and giving in the eternal flow of light through the figure-eight of infinity as you are centered at that point, you have access to the divine light; and you may extend it unto those in the world of form with alacrity, with clarity, with joy. This perfect nexus God has prepared within the secret chamber of your heart as your point of contact with all. If at times you feel any imbalance within your life, reenter this nexus point, centered through breath, and then you will again be able to discern from that point the reality of the Above and the below within you.

DCL: While meditating on the Sun, a heartfriend received an image, a sun placed at the center of a cross, and she asked about its significance. The cross is symbolic of the descending line of Alpha and the horizontal line of Omega. At the nexus, through the interaction of Alpha and Omega, is the creation of the child of that union—the Christ consciousness, the Son (Sun) or Solar consciousness. The Sun (Son) is the union of Alpha and Omega.

21. What are engrams, memes, and mass thoughtforms, and how can they affect us?

SG: The cosmic engrams that we place in the etheric bodies of mankind are resonating particles of light that can seed the human monad with perfected matrices of light toward their evolution. There are also, created by the dark forces, the point/counterpoint perversions of these engrams. These often manifest through the media and through all manner of creations as thoughtforms to which humanity will react and take their cue to continue to act from the human level, the egoic self, rather than from the Divine Self.

You have heard of subliminal seduction, a type of manipulation, in advertising. These dark engrams are truly that which the dark forces use to manipulate the minds of mankind into a mass miasma, almost as a globule of unreality. Through a perversion of divine resonance, many minds attune to each other at this level and then enter into degraded states of awareness. This causes a blip on the mental plane, which those who use the dark sciences employ to continue to pulsate into the minds of mankind, at subconscious and unconscious levels, their ongoing manipulation for their own devices. Thus, stripping these perverted engrams from the mental bodies and the subconscious and unconscious is essential. The violet fire, invoked consciously, allows the instantaneous dissolution of these perversions.

Whether called *meme* or by other names, there is required a greater understanding of these nefarious influences that continue to cloud the reality of men's minds. Perverted engrams cause almost a dismemberment of the reality; wedges are driven between the four lower bodies that divide them and keep them misaligned. The cosmic engrams that we bestow instantly allow the soul to be aligned to holy purpose when each one accepts the beauty of these divine thought-forms, symbols, pulsations. Therefore, call forth the cosmic engrams to be enfired through the divine frequencies that we emanate and place through talismans of fire in the superconscious of lifestreams upon Earth, repolarizing the soul towards perfection and realigning, at the four levels of being, each one under his God Source.

When groups of lightbearers come together and pray, especially in larger groups, there is greater opportunity to dissolve mass thoughtforms. The media has been the greatest perpetrator of mass thoughtforms, through television commercials, movies, videos, video games, and other avenues that allow the constant bombardment of the being of mankind. Just think of all the ads, jingles, and symbology that are purveyed through commercials. In fact, your Super Bowl Sunday is just as much about the halftime commercials and the commercials between plays as it is about the game itself. Our way is better, do you agree? When divine artisans of the spirit create beautiful thoughtforms through conscious cooperation with ascended beings, then you will begin to see more elevated films and more beautiful representations through the media.

22. Can certain sacred formulas and syllables bring instantaneous results into manifestation?

DCL: The Kabbalah Centre has published twenty-two volumes of the Zohar, the main text of the Jewish mystical tradition, in both English and Hebrew. A heartfriend heard that by just opening the book and visually scanning the letters on the Hebrew side from right to left as if reading them, that person's soul would receive great benefit and blessings and light. And so this student asked whether certain sacred formulas and syllables can in fact bring instantaneous results in manifestation. Saint Germain's answer is that the Zohar is an alchemical, mystical teaching and that what that student shared is real. These glyphs are alchemical light-engrams. The Zohar is a very powerful tool. The master says that those who desire to do this exercise would benefit by it.

If you choose to do it, ask for the Lords of Interpretation to overshine you to allow your Holy Christ/Buddha Self to interpret what you are doing so that it is not simply an unconscious experience; rather, by entering into this spiritual union, you can understand more of what is transpiring. Thus, you can get it in your Higher Mind even if humanly you can't understand it right then and there. By a portal that the master will open to you, by the grace of God through the Lords of Interpretation, you can have the interpretation of tongues, so to speak, in this instance to give you greater insight.

23. What is Stonehenge? Why was it built and what does it represent?

SG: Stonehenge was a cosmic calculator/calendar through which exact measurements could be taken of the earth body in relation to the sun and other stars and planetary bodies. Rituals of divine alchemy occurred there during which certain adepts were able to tap into the higher resources of the frequencies emitted by various celestial bodies and use them to accelerate consciousness upon Earth. These mystics understood the sacred sciences of astronomy and astrology and the interplay of cosmic energies that occurs when planets, stars, solar systems, and galaxies are cosmically aligned.

Stonehenge was a focal point for the release of light for the British Isles and for the garnering of spiritual fire for the illumination of souls during a certain cycle of time. Those who were the precursors to the Druids, who actually taught the Druids, understood divine science. I was incarnate during the time Stonehenge was built and shared my understanding of cosmic law to assist in connecting Stonehenge energetically with other foci of light around the world.

There were similar physical solar calendars around the Earth that El Morya, Serapis Bey, and I, as well as other past and current chohans, were responsible for building and utilizing in the ritualistic sciences of divine alchemy across the Earth. These foci were energized by the Solar Lords during the solstices, equinoxes, and at other key points within the solar year. We sustained the resonance between a number of these sacred centers of light around the planet for the stability of the Earth and of all lifewaves living upon it.

The temples of the sun on Lemuria and Atlantis and in other cultures and golden-age civilizations that have existed in South America, Africa, India, Eastern Europe, and elsewhere utilized the science of the sun within their cultures. When the knowledge of focusing solar light through crystal to power civilization peacefully returns to mankind, you will see the dawning of a new golden-crystal age.

24. What types of music promote greater spirituality?

SG: The music of the spheres wafts ever across the galaxy through the turning of worlds both at the macrocosmic level and at the microcosmic level, even within you. Some have asked what music should be listened to in order to gain greater spirituality. Depending on your relationship with your God Presence at a given time, different forms of music using different forms of instrumentation may move you higher in consciousness.

At times, listening to the wafting sounds of angel bands as they sing through voices attuned to their realm is best to move you unto a heightened level of refined attunement. At other times your soul requires grounding, and the march beat allows you to anchor within the Earth body that which your soul requires in that moment for the work that is required in this world of form. Operas created by those whose lives were lived to the glory of God often have keys for the spiritual path within the story line given unto the composer and through the libretto inspired upon those who worked with these.

Waltzes naturally create a lilting and climbing spiral stairway for your soul's ascent as you spin away the cares of the flesh and enter into a new spiral of divine knowingness and beingness as your soul reaches upward to touch the hem of the garment of your God Presence. Unwinding the coils of past compromises of the cosmic honor flame and the light of freedom through both listening to waltzes and dancing them, especially those inspired by the classical composers the Strausses and others, allows a loftiness of spiritual fire to enter your soul to raise it.

The rhythms of the East through devotees of Krishna and of other saints of India, employed through bhajans, allows the light of your crown to expand as, through devotion, the Mother light merges with the essential spiritual fire of your crown and also nourishes each chakra in the process. When you desire greater love, listen to and participate in these great devotions through the ancient stories of the many manifestations of the Godhead, aspects of God in form and formlessness.[64] For in these devotional moments, blessed ones, you enter cosmic nirvana and the substance of heaven descends into your form, your chakras, even your meridians and the Solar cells within you to raise you to a new level of spirituality.

Classical composers such as Beethoven, Mozart, Bach, and Haydn have employed many of the highest frequencies, garnered through their attunement with the heaven world during the composing of their creations. Listening during meditation to the cosmic cadences inspired by many angelic beings allows you to attune to our homes of light, to specific ascended masters, and even to the Elohim, and thereby receive the totality of their consciousness for a time as you listen and engage deeply in meditating upon the message behind the music.

Other great compositions, such as those by Brahms as well as certain works of Tchaikovsky, Verdi, Puccini, and especially Wagner, should be learned by all schoolchildren who desire to understand the sacred science of sound. Would that the music of these composers was the common fare for the listening ears of the youth, for then a new culture would already be upon the Earth.

At times your soul also requires the simple sounds of the common people through their own creations from the heart, certain folk melodies that also allow you to walk the earth in harmony, attuning with other hearts in a very simple and gentle way, telling the stories of your lives, of your tests and trials. Many of these are important, especially in the teenage years. Though folk melodies are not the highest frequencies that we desire our devotees to listen to often, they can be utilized for those who are progressing from various previous levels of understanding and utilization of lesser beats and musical genres to prepare them for the greater frequencies of fire and spirituality that are wielded by the cosmic devas in their inspiration upon the noble ones who use sound to glorify God and who bear these frequencies to the Earth because of the unity of their hearts.

DCL: I highly recommend securing the beautiful music of the Vera Choir, which is directed by Gilles Hainault of the I.D.E.A.L. Society in Canada. They are devotees of the master Omraam Mikhaël Aïvanhov and they bring to bear upon the Earth great Solar frequencies through their hearts because of their devotion, their attainment, and the unity of their consciousness as they blend the beautiful vibrations of their voices through the many representations, flowing avenues, and streams that Gilles has created, both in his music and in the music of Peter Deunov, through the choral offerings.

There are many awesome orchestras across the Earth. There are many inspiring operatic arias. You can secure beautiful classical music on CD or download it to your computer, tablet or smartphone to listen to it. We also have devotees in The Hearts Center who have composed music that brings the glory of God into manifestation through both the words and the music itself. It is a joy to experience and share divinely inspired music.

Music has the power through rhythm, sound, tonality, lyrics, and the movement of the vibration through sound to carry us to higher realms of light, to allow light to flow through our chakras and being in greater measure. With recorded music, the angels will often continue to amplify the light-energy through the music even after an original recording is made; an essence of that same spiritual substance is deposited through the ethers whenever a beautiful recording is replayed. That essence is the quintessence of God. That essence is light-energy.

The light and sound ray is carried on the waves that manifest through the music. The waves circle the Earth, move throughout the cosmos, and gather momentum as various musical compositions are played over and over as the musicians learn them and play them in orchestras. Think of all the mastery that occurs through the conductor and the musicians, who very carefully master this science through the particular part that they learn. All of that collective mastery brings light-energy and a flow of great God-glory to the Earth.

The purpose of music, for me, is always to glorify God. It is not to highlight the human frailties of our beings, although at times during operas this happens in the story line and libretto. Music is very personal for each one of us. We may be inspired by different things. Do whatever works for you to raise the light of the kundalini from the base to the crown so that you can glorify God. Every truly spiritual singer desires to feel the presence of God within and to allow the light and angelic choirs of light to sing through them. Listen to singers through whose voices waves of light radiate because of their desire to glorify God.

I believe that *bhajans* and other Indian music, such as ragas, are the highest. In ancient cultures and in the East, only the highest initiates were allowed to bring forth music. This was because they understood that music can either destroy or raise an entire culture.

25. How can I keep up with all the thoughtforms and teachings that have been given?

DCL: The thoughtforms we use are the powerful images the masters have released to us from time to time. We can go back to what was released through various teachers and teachings through the centuries, because ever since they were released these teachings and images have been there for us to utilize for magnificent spiritual work. And yet, without in any way denigrating them, they can be considered old teaching in the sense that every thoughtform Gautama Buddha or another master gave us over the years through the various dispensations was a powerful image for the people that particular thoughtform was destined to reach at that point in time. I speak of this matter guardedly, because there is still value in a lot of the previous teaching. At the same time, I am choosing to live in the Now, in what is coming right now from the Brotherhood.

Today, as I see it, the most powerful image that we can use to recreate the world and to enliven our world is the sun. In nature we see the sphere shape through the stars, which are representative of Alpha and Omega in the Great Central Sun. I use the solar sphere of fire as the most powerful image that can bring about wholeness, integrity, balance. Use the "Solar-Sphere Invocation" (see page 87) to invoke a solar sphere of fire from the heart of Helios and Vesta and Alpha and Omega in the Great Central Sun. For me, the most powerful visualization is the dot in the center of the sphere, which is symbolic of the Almighty.

The masters have given us teaching time and time again. The master Omraam Mikhaël Aïvanhov's teachings are current for today even though they were given between 1937 and 1986. What is being released by the masters through The Hearts Center is even more current than that. Again, this is not meant to denigrate any teaching that has ever come forth previously, yet, in a sense, even as the masters are continually progressing in their gifts, we, too, are progressing and have moved on past certain of these teachings.

For example, don't be concerned about fighting or stamping out evil or its matrix. Live in light! Evil dissolves, it doesn't exist; it is only an energy veil. If we spend our time and energy to constantly challenge or try to preempt or overcome evil—rather than living in goodness and in the suchness of God—we are giving some of our energy to that evil by focusing on it. Yes, we live in this plane and dimension where things are not ideal, and yet we can choose to live within our Solar Source and the world of light and beingness all the time. If we focus on the darkness, the shadow, then that is where we are. If we focus on the light, then that is where we are. It's our choice. Let's choose to focus on the goal, the highest outcome, Solar Reality. Focusing on that is manifesting it, bringing it about; it is the perfectionment of our being.

We have eliminated certain prayers and decrees from our prayer book that no longer serve us, because some of the original prayers focused on duality. Instead, we are using conscious language that is beyond the energy veil. We are now focused on Reality, on our highest outcome. We are focused on our victory. We are moving into our Solar Reality.

Did Saint Germain dwell on the flaws in order to transmute gemstones that had flaws into their perfected state? No! He focused on the perfection within those gemstones so that they would hold the light frequency and the energetic pattern of the perfected matrix and grid. He added the impetus of his own light-energy and his heart and the power of transmutation through the seventh ray to crystallize them in their highest form. Again, he didn't focus on the flaws; he focused on the goal. The adepts don't dwell in the doldrums or focus on unreality, they focus on the true reality of perfection, and that is what we can each choose today. Focus on the goal. Focus on perfection. Focus on the beauty of the Divine. This is where we get our true power and our empowerment and our adeptship.

26. How has Saint Germain, in a past life, utilized a God-quality that is essential in alchemy?

DCL: Vision, persistence, and perseverance are essential qualities in alchemy. For example, the founding of the New World was an alchemy performed by Christopher Columbus, an embodiment of Saint Germain, using these qualities. Historical documents say that Columbus was shown a vision of the New Jerusalem; he persisted in his vision of the New World that he knew he was destined to find and to create a pathway to, and he succeeded.

Even as Columbus's three ships, the *Niña,* the *Pinta,* and the *Santa Maria,* were traveling across the Atlantic, some of the crew considered mutiny and abandoning the mission. And yet, through Columbus's power of intention and strength of will, his inner knowing, and his persistence and resolve to fulfill his mission, he created the means whereby his vision prevailed. He and his crew found land and his mission was fulfilled.

Some have denigrated what Columbus did, thinking that he was causative of the decimation of many Native Peoples. I go back to his motive, which was pure because of his vision of a New Jerusalem, a New World. Did he know in his outer mind all of what would occur with the Native Peoples? No. His motive was pure in service to God. The culture of the day was one in which some were greedy and mistreated indigenous peoples, and he may not have been perfect in this regard either, yet he was destined to fulfill that mission for the Brotherhood as part of the founding of America so that this nation under God could fulfill its destiny.

Living in the Light:
Alchemical Art for Self-Transformation
by Mario Duguay

With its colorful brush strokes, flowing energy patterns, and ever-present nature beings and angelic helpers, Mario Duguay's artwork speaks to the living reality of the spirit world interpenetrating our world. As alchemy is the science of transmutative change, so Mario's artistry is truly alchemical art for self-transformation.

The sixteen divinely inspired images presented here invite us to self-assess, to ask the deeper questions about our reason for being, our truest path, and our ultimate destiny. Gazing upon his imagery becomes a meditation. Accepting the conceptual ideations behind the forms and colors into our soul transports us into higher consciousness.

As you view each image, pause for a few moments to imbibe its essence. Allow the sacred to permeate your being and raise you into the living light of your Presence.

A New Day

Conquering

Creativity

Divine Strength

Drawing in Happiness

Initiation

Learning from Life

Light of the World

Listening to the Messenger

Marvel

Master of My Life

My Path

Regeneration

Strength of Faith

Water of Life

Wisdom

27. What would Saint Germain share of the history behind his founding of the Order of the Rose Cross, Rosicrucianism, and Freemasonry?

SG: It is true that I was there at the founding of sacred mystical orders through which I imparted to many individuals a knowledge of the inner mysteries and of how we could bring forth higher truth in the world of form to manifest a golden-age civilization. These orders included the Order of the Rose Cross, the Freemasons, and other sacred orders. There is already much documentation of my intercession, blessed ones.

As you may have discerned, there is always, point/counterpoint, the infiltration of holy orders by those who seek to take the light from the original intent and vision that I had for these holy orders and to use them toward their evil purposes. Once such infiltration occurs, it is difficult to maintain the full sponsorship of that movement. Thus, there must be within all new movements those with great discernment to maintain the tie to us and our sponsorship by preventing a greater infiltration by those who could destroy all that we build. This is why many of these societies were secret and required a very personal introduction of novices through a graduated process of initiation whereby, if the candidates were not passing their tests, so to speak, they could not go beyond a certain point. Certain inner mysteries were not conveyed until the novice reached certain levels of understanding and the right use of that knowledge. The graduated process of initiation and conveying of inner mysteries is still practiced in the heaven world.

I desired to reveal some of these greater truths to mankind, beginning with the Theosophical Society and the "I AM" Activity and other movements, and there is now a great understanding of these mysteries coming to bear among more of mankind. We simply could not move forward the plans of the Divine Director unless more and more of mankind understood the sacred mysteries, and still there are always those who misuse the teachings.

There are those who are diametrically opposed to Freemasonry, who think that it is a dark organization. It is true that at a certain point certain individuals came into play within that movement who were diametrically opposed to the original intent. Thus, the forces of darkness have used the scheme of divide and conquer to thwart our efforts.

It is not so essential to fully understand all the intricate workings of these orders at the time that they were first employed. Take the teachings that you have in this hour and fully employ them through the directives that we have given so that many, many more among mankind may understand them. What is important now for you to understand is the general context upon which I and other masters utilized secret societies in the past, and how in this hour we desire the knowledge and use of the violet light to be employed by greater numbers of mankind openly through the teachings that are now available on the Internet and through our various sponsored movements.

28. How is it possible to see clearly into the future and the past? Which visionaries or writings can I study to learn of coming world events?

SG: To be or not to be: that is the eternal question.[65] To be in the Now and live in present light and yet to be aware of all that is interplaying and interpenetrating and acting within your world and within the greater world of all evolutions upon Earth or a planet is essential for a lifestream who is seeking or obtaining cosmic consciousness. There is a timeline toward victory for a planetary home even within the context of that sphere involving and evolving beyond time and space as you know it.

True prophets see far into the future, even as that vision which I gave to and sponsored through Nostradamus. Of all the prophets and seers of the ages, he is the one that I would urge you to study. These prophecies, clouded in mystery through the quatrains, will give you keys to the outpicturing of mankind's ancient karmas as they could and would be outplayed without intercessory prayer, sacrifice, and divine intervention brought to bear through spiritual work. Many of these prophecies have been misinterpreted. Nonetheless, those who have the Holy Spirit and can see the handwriting on the wall[66] can take the quatrains and understand them in the greater context of the evolution of mankind.

Other mystics have made accurate prophecies which they received directly from the blessed Mother Mary. A number of these prophecies have been mitigated to date, for prophecy's purpose is always to avert cataclysms and dire manifestations. It is possible to know the future only when the present has been resolved within one's being. Some receive flashes of illumination about the potential out-picturing of karmic causes and subsequent events within lifestreams, and they can warn people that if they do not make changes these potential situations may occur. Again, discernment is required, and only when prompted by the Holy Spirit may these warnings be lawfully given.

To see clearly into the past, one must have access to the akashic records, and this only by permission from the Keeper of the Scrolls, the recording angels, and the Keeper of the Records, the cosmic librarians of the spirit who have access to certain key libraries within various retreats of the Brotherhood that retain the knowledge and history of past civilizations. The Keeper of the Scrolls has access to all these libraries, whereas some librarians only have access to specific records. The messengers of the Great White Brotherhood, on our behalf and through permission, may be granted access to these records. Other seers at times are shown past records and have temporary permission for their use in bringing forth teaching and under-standings that we wish to convey to mankind.

There are psychics who storm heaven by force and do not use their gifts appropriately. Thus, we warn those of you who desire to develop these psychic powers to understand the holy nature of main-taining these records. It is not for the titillation of the senses or for the quenching of a psychic thirst, for curiosity's sake, or for human knowledge. It is only toward the holy purpose to which God allows them to be read or understood.

Much has been conveyed through past messengers, prophets, and seers about potential cataclysm coming to the Earth if mankind continue on their current course. Ancient patterns from Atlantis and from the fall of the civilizations of Greece and Rome are coming due day by day in various quarters of the planet. This is why our pilgrimages where we have concentrated prayer work are essential,[67] and why prayer groups and prayer circles around the Earth are key to averting the karmic cyclings that are coming due.

Rather than ask how you can learn about potential future events, the better question to ask would be how to avert these dire calamities through intercessory prayer. You have the keys within this dispensation and previous dispensations to do this through the accelerated action of your prayer—your dynamic prayer and rhythmic chanting with visualization and cosmic intent, led by those conductors of the Spirit who have the greatest outpicturing of the gifts of the Spirit and the ability to be for us the instruments whereby these energies may flow in cosmic streams to many areas of the planet.

Those who maintain harmony and who, through the accelerated focalization of light through their chakras, can be the instruments for these prayer and decree sessions earn the great karma of the balancing of world karma and personal karma in the process of their instrumentation and employment of these higher frequencies. Thus, many who lead these sessions are those with the greatest amount of karma balanced among mankind, and this includes those of movements other than The Hearts Center.

The accelerated balancing of karma through the violet fire is my great gift to mankind, and so I urge you to participate in group prayer sessions and to also utilize CDs and other recordings of group prayer at every opportunity so that these cosmic frequencies may go forth continually. If you desire to enter into greater karma balancing, consider doing what is essential to make your voice heard through these prayer groups and services.

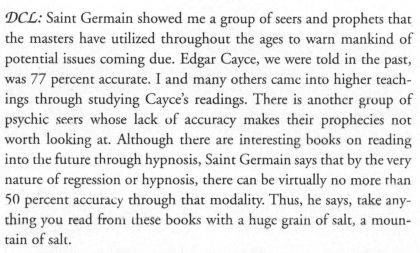

DCL: Saint Germain showed me a group of seers and prophets that the masters have utilized throughout the ages to warn mankind of potential issues coming due. Edgar Cayce, we were told in the past, was 77 percent accurate. I and many others came into higher teachings through studying Cayce's readings. There is another group of psychic seers whose lack of accuracy makes their prophecies not worth looking at. Although there are interesting books on reading into the future through hypnosis, Saint Germain says that by the very nature of regression or hypnosis, there can be virtually no more than 50 percent accuracy through that modality. Thus, he says, take anything you read from these books with a huge grain of salt, a mountain of salt.

Each of us can be a prophet. Your Higher Self is a prophet and knows what is coming due for you. Thus, if you desire to know what will transpire for you, the surefire way to do this is to become one with your Higher Self and commune with your Solar Presence through daily meditation. You will receive greater inklings and knowledge and understanding of what is coming due for you and will see into the heaven world through your own prophet, your Higher Self, because it knows the cyclings of your personal karma. It knows those whom you are destined to meet and the initiations you are to have. Your Higher Self knows all the intimate secrets of your life in this life and in all past lives. It knows what you require in order to move beyond your current state of consciousness to a new level of living.

When you go within and contact the inner prophet of your Higher Self, you have the best means of working in the right spirit to meet your karma, to meet prophecy, to overcome past momentums of darkness, and to live in the light. This really is the ultimate word of the master on this subject. When people look so much to outer prophets and seers rather than going within, it is at one level a copout, because they are listening to other voices rather than to their own inner voice.

In regard to the alchemy of prayer, one very powerful prayer is "I AM My Victorious Abundance Here and Now"[68] (see page 85). This prayer uses conscious language and brings the Solar sciences into play. If you give this one prayer each day and you are really centered as you do it, your life as a cosmic alchemist of the seventh ray will change and be transformed, and you will soar. You can also create your own affirmations, your own alchemical words using the name of God I AM THAT I AM.

29. Buddhist tradition speaks of the Coming Buddha and Christians speak of Christ's Second Coming. How can I best prepare?

DCL: Our prayer about Maitreya, the Coming Buddha,[69] is worded in the Now because Maitreya will be where you are now. The prophecy has been that Maitreya will come five hundred years after a golden age begins. This is similar to the Christian thinking that the Second Coming is a future event. If we relegate the coming of Christ or Maitreya to some future time and date, then ultimately for us they are only in our future, not in the Now. Looking to a future event does not bode well toward the employment of the masters' energies now. Accept Christ's coming and Maitreya's coming in the here and now, where you are, and it shall be so. When there is greater acceptance of the presence of Christ, the presence of the Buddha within the heart and mind in perfect love-wisdom, then their greater manifestation within the world may occur.

It is always the case that through acceptance the light may be manifest where you are. The light might reside all around you, yet if you do not see it or do not accept it, then it will not provide you the wherewithal for change where you are. Thus, both Christ and Maitreya are here and now upon the Earth for those who choose to accept their presence.

Maitreya, as Jesus' Guru and through various offices that he holds, is already fully manifesting his consciousness spiritually on the Earth. This situation is like someone finally understanding that heaven exists all around them; by simply poking their heads through the clouds they can finally see it. The same is true for the Coming Buddha who is come. Once you are able to see the Pure Land, then you will see Maitreya ever-present with you. To see the Pure Land, one must rise in consciousness to behold as the Buddhas behold. This is done through meditation, contemplation, and the acceleration of the frequencies of the golden-yellow light of the crown.

30. In what way do the crystal rays relate to the development and use of the *siddhis*, and how can I develop these spiritual powers?

SG: The *siddhis* are, in fact, the heightened use of the crystal rays by those who are responsible sons and daughters of God, who through surrender of the human self allow the higher faculties of their God Presence to be utilized within their heartstream. The *siddhis*, also being aspects of the gifts of the Holy Spirit, as you call them in the West, are given to these individuals for their use in elevating the consciousness of mankind.

Clairvoyance, as the aspect of third-eye vision from the God Self, allows clear seeing to stream through one's inner and outer awareness for the forewarning of potential events and for discernment in all things, as one can see clearly what is acting within individuals' worlds and other spheres of consciousness rather than just the physical plane. The combination of clairvoyance with the gift of prophecy allows the seer, when that one is so guided, to warn individuals, peoples, and nations of impending danger.

Clairaudience, as hearing with the heightened sense of God's perfect ear, allows one to attune to the voice of angels and higher frequencies, whereby inspiration may flow ever and always unto the adept hearing clearly what God has to share as personal direction and, in many cases, as the very voice of the Beloved, their own God Presence, which, when acted upon, may bring souls into alignment with holy purpose.

You have heard the adage "Without vision the people perish."[70] In like manner, without hearing the people are ignorant. Many choose to ignore the voice of God speaking within their hearts. Thus, those with clairaudience, who have continual access to this inner voice, must listen and obey if this gift, this *siddhi*, is to continue as to its original purpose and intent. Each of you has this gift to a certain extent, though you may not have employed it fully as the listening ear to your Holy Christ/Buddha Self, your inner teacher, the "hidden man of the heart,"[71] the voice of conscience.

As you listen to and obey the promptings of the Spirit day by day, your hearing will become clearer, ringing true at each point along your path, so that you will know when to act, where to act, how to act, and why to act. For within the impressions of the very voice of the Beloved within you are the full manifestations of the import of the message conveyed and distributed through all of the senses of the soul. This is true with each of the *siddhis* and gifts, for though they may come through one sensory avenue or stream, each contains within it the totality of the message.

Prophecy, which I have touched upon, is given to those who are called to be catalysts for change in the world of form by directing the focus of their vision of the future to those who can make changes within the world in order to avert potential dire consequences to humanity. Prophets are few and far between. Psychics, who predict what they see as potential, may have access at a certain substrata of the astral plane to that which, if not changed in people's lives, may outpicture in the physical.

True prophets are those who see beyond the astral seas from a heightened God-consciousness, from the mountaintops of the heaven world, where all interplaying energies are seen as potential and where, through the timeline of the outplaying of mankind's karma, key points along that timeline would come to bear and to play in the world if change within mankind's consciousness is not accepted and manifested. Those who warn in this manner are often ignored or thought of as charlatans or quacks, yet those who are sponsored and who speak for us can help mankind to avert much in the way of pain and suffering and avert a promulgation of the maya and illusion within this world if our words through them are heeded.

True prophets speak what is conveyed directly as it is manifest, without embellishment or changing of those words through their own human understanding. Often, keys through the vision and the heart-mind connection are given that are symbolic of the race consciousness, with seed concepts and visuals shown that key mankind back into their subconscious memories of past failures and of potential future victories that may be won through their heeding of these God-ideations through our prophets.

There are lesser manifestations of the *siddhis* that we see as the control of physical forces; for example, telekinesis and the ability to stop the heart or the flow of blood within the body. The higher aspect of this *siddhi*, or gift, is the ability to control all natural forces through oneness with all life, through cosmic stillness, and by acceptance of God's pure stream of oneness and light through the consciousness.

Thus, the master is able to calm the storm, walk upon the seas, change water into wine through the alchemy of his understanding of the four cosmic forces,[72] the three kingdoms, and the hierarchical order of beings in heaven and upon earth. That master must abide by cosmic regulations and laws, not storming heaven by force or misusing this gift for personal advantage; only using it for the quelling of darkness, the hailing of light, and the implementation of the divine scheme in the world of form.

As I demonstrated to mankind through my days in Europe as le Comte de Saint Germain, and even on inner planes and outer planes to devotees who resonate with my heart and with the ascended masters, those who precipitate instantly understand the laws of matter and of spirit and of how, through the interplay of light in your dimension, there may be what I would call the manipulation of matter. This would more likely be termed in your day and age the utilization of cosmic frequencies for transmutation and change.

Utilizing the *siddhis* through healing constitutes a science in and of itself. The knowledge of the karmic causes and cores within the lives of individual lifestreams, and also of their interconnectedness with other life, is important for the healer to understand before entering into the space of being the focal point for this gift to occur. For unless and until the healer understands the laws beyond karma, he could interfere with the natural cycles and the best utilization of light within the individual lifestream if he were to intercede and employ this gift using the siddhis without discretion. Those who heal a physical illness without doing the essential work at the soul level to heal its causes and core can, in many cases, create karma. Thus, within most ascended-master dispensations you have not seen the reliance upon or the emphasis upon physical manifestations; rather, you have seen more of the dissolving of karma and ancient patterns so that the soul may rise first and the body follow.

This is important for all to understand, for we as ascended masters could in many ways treat the physical ailments of mankind. And yet, unless there is change at the deepest core level—at the subconscious, the chalice through which the fire is applied by the soul—then you may not see the greatest evolution of that lifestream within the context of that one's current point in time and space. Thus, the key to true healing, as some of you have discerned, is the deep evaluation of the soul, meditation upon the path, and the consuming of patterns that have been worn as grooves upon the core identity of your being that actually cause you, in some manners, to act out certain modes within your world.

Thus, as the violet fire is added to the equation to consume these vestiges of darkness that have accumulated around you and your original seed pattern, or ideation, from the Godhead, you have the wherewithal to act from a pure state of knowingness and being rather than from the egoic self. The master Hilarion will bring forth this teaching in due time, although I have already alluded to the necessity to enter into deeper states of self-analysis and contemplation in order for alchemy to even manifest in your world. For, beloved ones, the greatest alchemists are those who have first healed their own soul and consciousness.

As you have heard in the teachings of the Holy Spirit, for which I bow to the great Guru the Maha Chohan, the gift of discernment is key in the employment of all the *siddhis*. For though you may have all the gifts of the Spirit, how and when and where and why you employ them is key. Thus, calling upon the Holy Spirit as the arbiter of these gifts is essential for all true adepts to understand, for the Holy Spirit knows all and can employ through the adept or the master the totality of what is required for each individual lifestream in perfect balance and harmony at the appropriate time.

31. How can I open my inner vision to see auras and to see into other planes of consciousness and being?

SG: When the student is ready, the teacher appears. In this message you have an understanding of how, when you have prepared your consciousness to understand what it is that you will see when your inner vision is opened, God will allow that vision to supersede your current seeing. It is one thing to be able to see beyond the veil of the human illusion of duality in which you live and move upon this Earth, and it is another to fully understand all the moving streams of energy, in their coloration and form, that surround individuals as their auras.

Thus, you must be careful when you desire to pierce the veil, blessed ones. Unless there is purity of heart and a desire only to seek this particular *siddhi* for the healing and edification of souls and for the glorification of God, it were better for you to have the veil again laid before you. We would not have the premature opening of your third eye wherein, through judgment or a misguided application by an imperfect or incomplete understanding of the science of vision, you would leave the path or engage in activities astral in nature by communing with spirits that seem true and noble and often have greater mastery than you, yet that cloud their true identity in seeming light substance, colorful yet impure.

Purity of motive and heart and the clear seeing of others in their own God Reality allow a gentle lifting of the veil year by year for you to discern the truth of what is seen by your Higher Self and your soul even now. In a certain sense, those of you who have developed the sensitivities of your soul through daily spiritual practices over many years already see with these soul faculties that you are developing in greater measure. Your sensitivity is heightened through daily devotional prayers and means—through listening, meditation, quietude, and most especially through being.

When you are in the center of pure presence, you will be attuned through all of your senses to that which is real and that which is unreal before you. Thus, seek through the power of the Holy Spirit to know and to discern what is acting within the auras of others. You may both protect yourself from and also be wary and discerning of dark forces, thereby allowing yourself to work in the light, for the light, with the light.

A preliminary guarded study of color and of the frequencies of light will allow you to develop a background and foundation so that when your inner vision is opened you will understand the frequencies that you see. In addition, an understanding of the thoughtforms and matrices that dwell within the unconscious and the subconscious (which are often experienced in the dream state) will allow you, through your own self-mastery, to see without fear both the dregs in the astral world and the beautiful manifestations of heaven.

You will be able to deal with that which you see by being centered and knowing that only God is truly real where you are and that all imperfect thoughtforms, demons, discarnates, and animal forms within the electronic belt that you see in others and even in yourself have no power and must be looked upon as simply a miasma of temporary manifestation within the evolving soul. You will remind yourself to hold the immaculate vision for that one even in the process of seeing what that soul has temporarily allowed to exist within the lower self.

DCL: Many individuals have had experiences of seeing beyond the veil—seeing a master, seeing angels, beholding light, or seeing auras. Some have heard angelic choirs. During prayer sessions, I sometimes hear angelic voices overtoning and adding to the momentum of what we are doing. I believe this is part of the multiplication factor of the ten thousand-times-ten thousand and other dispensations from the masters that multiply the power of our prayers. This concept of the multiplication of the power of prayer was taught by Jesus: "Again I say unto you, That if two of you shall agree on earth as touching any thing that they shall ask, it shall be done for them of my Father which is in heaven. For where two or three are gathered together in my name, there am I in the midst of them."[73]

When the third eye is open, it is the motive of the heart that is important. Is our motive only to bring forth light to help people? If ego enters into the equation, or if we start using that gift in any way to manipulate or hurt others, or if we have a lesser motive, then we will have problems and ultimately our third-eye vision could be taken away. When our motive is pure and we seek only to help others and to glorify God, then our vision can be used for the highest purposes.

32. What role in world alchemy is played by the highly developed children that are being born?

SG: The children that embody in the penumbra of a new age always contain the seeds of change within them for that new awareness to manifest. The ones who come first shake things up, plowing the fields of mankind's consciousness for the incarnation of those who come later.

What some have called the *indigo children* are those souls who are forging the link between two generations, which is often a time of intensity as the old order gives way to the new. These are often strong souls who must unseat those who will not give up their concretized concepts of the past. They are often misunderstood and reviled for their intense auras and ways. They prepare the way for the refined ones, as John the Baptist did for Jesus.[74] Those whom some have called the *crystal children* lay down their lives for their friends,[75] so to speak. These come to lay the foundation for the new era, the crystal blocks upon which the entire edifice of glory can reside.

Both of these groups of souls are supreme alchemists. Like Shiva, the first group, the so-called indigo children, destroys what is unreal of the past. And like Brahma, the second group, the so-called crystal children, creates the new world. A final group, like Vishnu, preserves what the second group creates. And the creation continues like this, over and over again. Each new generation allows God's perfect alchemical creation to evolve to a new level.

The friction that occurs between generations is simply the reaction of the new to the old, which allows a synthesis of the best of both to occur. If each of the generations would discern how to bring about the best in each other, then the co-creative energies of each may fire a brighter and richer alchemy in the divine kiln through which all this tumult is tempered for a time.

DCL: You may also have heard of the super-psychic children embodying in China and Russia and elsewhere upon Earth. These are the children who *know*—they can discern and know the answer to any question as soon as they hear it.

Some people associate the word *psychic* with negative meaning, yet that is not always the case. The word *psychic* comes from the Greek *psyche,* meaning "soul," and refers to those with developed soul, or Solar, faculties and sensitivities. The super-psychic children are souls who have one or more gifts of the Holy Spirit—gifts of discernment, wisdom, knowledge, or other gifts of the Spirit.[76] They can instantaneously know, see, feel, and observe; and through attainment from past lives, they see through everything. They know when people are lying. They can read hearts. You may have heard of or witnessed this.

These individuals are everywhere, and they are seeding the New Age through their consciousness. By whatever name we call these souls, they are embodying everywhere. They are the yeast by which the enlightenment of humanity en masse can and will occur as their light is allowed to manifest and assist all of us. I think of Anastasia[77] as a pre-eminent crystal child who has great God-attainment and is able to see beyond the dark window of time, way beyond our generation to the future advancement of the world.

33. Are we entering a higher vibration, the so-called *human resonance* that some talk about?

SG: I have already alluded to the fact that you as alchemists are changing daily into the divine star of your own beingness as co-creators. This process may be called by many names. The science of transubstantiation is being understood by more and more of mankind as they see evolution from beyond only the physical view-point. It is also the process of the ongoingness of creation since the first breath of God and his statement "Let there be light."[78]

All manifestation is an aspect of God's consciousness. Evolution is ongoing, and when you understand the gradations of your evolution through life into higher spirals up the pyramid of Self, then you will see this process as more than a one-time global event, called by some *the Shift*, for this process is always ongoing and it continues even after you are ascended. I was required over many hundreds of years of your Earth time to evolve to the point of being what you have called a *cosmic being*.[79] It was a process. Each of you can deter-mine that this is your goal—if you dare. Gaining cosmic conscious-ness involves gaining and then maintaining gradually more refined and expansive levels of awareness through a regular meditation and mindfulness practice.

As more knowledge and wisdom are conveyed through the media and through the Internet, and as each new generation is ramped up in their understanding of all cosmic laws, then you will see the point of the shift whereby a new reality will be known. And it will be, as it were, in the twinkling of an eye[80] that mankind now sees as God sees rather than from the human level. This does not occur only at one point; it occurs at many points that resonate with the one point simultaneously.

When there is a saturation of the solution to the point where it is crystallized in form, then you have the action of cosmic precipita-tion into a new level of beingness. Each of you is a catalyst for this process. Thus, you are seeded with the totality of the perfection of the new matrix, the new way within your essence, your heart. Allow this seed to grow and bloom within you, and then you, as a catalyst, can assist many to also see the light.

DCL: The entire teaching on immaculate vision through holding the immaculate concept is helping us to evolve into God beings, where we see as God sees rather than at a dualistic level. This is quite an important shift for us, for if we were to continue en masse in a point/counterpoint reactive way of living, we would not evolve into our full Godhood and on to the Godhead. At times in our spiritual lives, we all feel inadequate in certain things, and yet our purpose in being is to bless life through our Presence.[81]

Saint Germain says, "Be sun-like, be sunlight, and live a Solar life." He asks us to consider laughing many times a day, seventy times seven and more, "for laughter and love make the world go round and help you to abound."

Through Saint Germain's vision, I am seeing into the very center of the Earth, seeing the changes that are manifesting at a deep core level of the Earth itself and that are coming to the surface. These changes are inevitable; they are destined; they are the way and the wave of change. The key for each of us is to maintain our heart-centeredness, our balance, our harmony, and to bring joy into our life through what brings us Solar joy—by being in nature, appreciating one another, having time to engage in rituals of appreciation. We can do this anytime with our loved ones, our families, the people we work with.

One of the keys for the Golden Age is the flame of appreciation and gratitude. On the cosmic clock, gratitude is on the seven o'clock line and it is in polarity to God-love on the one o'clock line. Appreciate what you have and what you have been given—your talents, your gifts, your abundance, your family, your body temple. As you appreciate your body temple, you will take better care of it, because you will listen to it, you will observe it, you will love it and use it more to glorify God.

PART THREE

Alchemical Elixirs

33 Spirals of Divine Alchemy for Solar Beingness

by Saint Germain

with Commentary
by David Christopher Lewis

A New Refreshment of the Spirit:
"Let There Be Light!"

1. Every elixir we offer is a new refreshment of the spirit through violet-joy light.
2. Alchemy is the divine science of self-transformation that is ongoing forever for every student, for we count ourselves among you also as students.
3. There are a number of catalysts for spiritual transmutation, and chief among these are radical forgiveness, compassionate service, and empathic nurturing.
4. We regard the wise as those who have studied and worked on themselves to the point of realizing that only God exists.
5. Only scoundrels denounce the love of the Creator radiantly manifest in all life.
6. True and lasting fortunes are built upon spiritual principles by joyous hearts; temporary worldly ones by ingrates upon the backs of slaves.
7. Becoming overconfident often leads to anger and pride, which precede the decline of spiritual resourcefulness and finally soul ruin. All this may be prevented through humility wedded to joyful optimism and work.
8. I work with the spiritually vertebrate.

9. Replenish your reserves through the alchemical light of freedom's song, which you may hum throughout the day in inner silence.

10. The Keeper of the Scrolls posts to your spiritual ledger daily the light-energy accrued by your prayers and songs to every seventh-ray master and angel.

11. Intent upon changing the world, begin with your own.

12. Lasting happiness manifests through loving relationships expressed by prayerful and joyful service to others sprinkled with the fun of lifelong spiritual learning.

As I deliver these elixirs of light unto you, you may take them and make them real in your world. Through your devotional services, infuse each word with presence. Support the framework of the alchemy that you desire to manifest each day with a newfound spirit of freedom that rises within you, manifesting through a soulful attitude of joy and love expressed through your voice and emanated through your heart and mind.

My sessions with you are more about internal change than about your desire to see the world in a new light. First see your own world transformed from within and then you will see the changes externally manifest through your new vision. Every word you speak may be infused with cosmic light substance, for you know that your voice is the mode of change when you have become that word which you speak.

Let there be light! Now go forth and create this new world that you envision as one heart, as one voice, as one cosmic stream of unbounded joy!

Saint Germain

Fulfill Your Assignments
and Prepare for All That Is Coming

P

Opportunity, when taken, leads to the victory of freedom. You have heard what is necessary for that light of freedom to move quickly in new streams across the Earth. Take that opportunity, blessed ones, and make it real in your world. For the night cometh when no man can see or work[82] and there is no more opportunity to fulfill, at a certain level of life, the divine plan given.

Many of you are moving into your elder years, where your physical bodies at times slow down, are not as agile or flexible, and certain physical work may be more difficult for you. And yet you have great spirits of fire, whereby the light of your Solar Source may stream forth through your heart and consciousness to do great spiritual work in your time of meditation, prayer, emanation, and service to life. While you have the mobility of physicality in your body, take the opportunity to fulfill certain assignments and to prepare for all that is coming. Teach your youth, prepare them well, and know that the light of God always prevails when you first listen and then obey. It is also important that you consider the ramifications of all your decisions.

I am Portia, and I emanate the light of freedom through opportunity to all.

Portia

3

Let Solar Beingness Flow through You

1. Precipitation is the science of manifesting God-realized love-wisdom-power now.
2. Bending time and space alone is not enough to tap into the resources of the Spirit. Mastering time and space trues us to the Source.
3. Apply the laws of metaphysics through divine thought to live in the light.
4. Living in presence allows the field of God's higher laws of being-ness to enfold and work through you.
5. Divine alchemy is the science of oneness with the Source of all elements. It is the all-composition of the One.
6. For alchemy to work for you, enter the state of beingness.
7. Every contemplative thought on God has its effects in bringing more of the love-fires of Spirit into your life.
8. Replenishing your spirit daily is simply a matter of re-attuning to your Source and seeing the floodtides of divine light flowing to and through you from the Great Emanator.
9. The principles of divine alchemy are simple and boil down to this: Learn to love and live in the light of the Lord.
10. The Lord is the Law of the Word as God's beingness within you.

11. Bridge the chasm between human and divine understanding through being.
12. Alchemy is the fomenting of inner change of the base into the God-good gold.
13. Learn to ingest living liquid-etheric golden light from the sun through your eyes and breath.
14. The intensity of light within your aura is determined by the quality of your heart multiplied by your surrender to holy purpose and then by your mindfulness of the Divine Spirit.

The equation of harmony is one that brings about the manifestation of balance within your life, for on either side of the equal sign, that which rests on the scales of justice and mercy must truly be in balance. Thus, if there is within you too much of the fire of cosmic judgment and a lack of the fire of cosmic mercy, then the inharmony within your aura will be felt by others as rigidity. Likewise, if you are too empathic without an equal quotient of cosmic reason, others may feel imbalance in your presence.

True masters of the spirit who yet abide in this world have learned the science of cosmic harmony through the balance scales of justice and mercy. Most of mankind dwell either to the left or to the right, not having fully accomplished and fulfilled this inner balance. Thus, Portia and I come to deliver the fire of freedom along with the responsibility through liberty to utilize the resources of the seventh ray for the Aquarian Age culture in perfect balance. This you may maintain through meditation upon your heart daily before you begin your day and deliver to the world the work of your heart and mind. In Spirit you abide when you dwell on the things of God. In the flesh you live when you dwell on the things only of the world. And yet the Lord Jesus did say to bring the kingdom of heaven upon Earth, and he called out to the Father to make it so through each of us.[83]

Balance and harmony are the order of the day that all seek internally and yet few know externally. I bring the eternal into this context through your heart emanation and manifest beingness as the principle of the law of love for all.

In the holy name I AM THAT I AM, let solar beingness flow through you. Let solar awareness ever be yours.

Saint Germain

Understand the Presence of God-Love Within

Treasures of my heart I sing as I emanate a new radiance of opportunity to step into the divine world even where you are. Justice is the grace that God provides so that you may understand the truth of your own being as it manifests according to the law of life, whereby the energy that you have issued forth in the outbreath of experience cycles back to you in the point of the Now. Some see justice as the karmic hammer. Yet, when you step into a new field of awareness and have a sense of presence and poise that comes with an understanding of the higher laws of beingness, you will no longer see that which transpires within your world from the point of reaction, the mode of reactivity whereby you attempt to divide what is good and what is bad, what is dark or what is light; you will, through the center point of divine beingness in presence with its perfect emanations, understand all.

Truly, every opportunity of life is one whereby you may allow God to be present where you are through the stream of your consciousness. For when you are aware that the freewill choice to be or not to be is inherent in life itself, you must always question your choice if you would move from the field of the personality into the monad of divine individuality within the Creator's heart. Pursuing the alchemy of perfect love will be the modus operandi of those who move into the light of Aquarius with consciousness. Those of you who have glimpsed, and even grasped at times, the totality of this divine experience understand how the laws of life that manifest through the seventh ray, when applied through the light of freedom, will bring you into a greater connectivity with the light of justice, with the light of mercy.

Thus, blessed ones, although some rail against that which they see outwardly manifest in their own consciousness or in another, we say be at peace within God's Presence and awareness of you as an individualization of the God flame, as a conscious participant in the great drama and plan of the Divine One. And know that even as the cyclings of the energies of your own being come due within the context of opportunity to transcend self, you can move into a greater understanding of how to live in the active mode of light-beingness rather than in that reactive mind of the human ego.

When one comes to challenge who you are or what you have done or said, and that one feels obligated to reflect this unto you with rancor, simply "be still, and know that I AM God"[84] and that God is even present within that one, though temporarily not fully manifest. Seek always to accept and to be, and know that the very present reality of light within the center of your cells, within every point of presence within you is that which will move you into the divine acceptance of higher presence, of higher purpose, of higher love.

Thus the Master Alchemist, my beloved Saint Germain, has come to inculcate greater cosmic connectivity between you and the highest aspects of yourself through an understanding of the science of being in presence. Those of you who have practiced the presence through living in the light-essence of your being as a sun have truly begun to emanate the greater frequencies of the divine alchemists and thereby live and move in the stream of the great God-beingness of the All—all around you and through you.

When you attune to the divine world, that world may glow through your awareness. If you only look to that which has been limiting in your life or in the lives of others, and you accept that as the reality that you would know, then you cannot fully ascend in consciousness to discern the higher winds of Aquarius and the teaching that we would outpour to all who have moved into this field of light. Thus, listen not to the naysayers and dwell not upon those points of darkness within except to understand that even they are framed within the context of the evolution of your soul, through freedom, to pure light. Though you may have temporarily accepted these elements as something real within you, even they, in time, will vanish as you pour forth love to all the points of God-beingness within you.

Thus, take hope, take care, and nurture your soul. Spend the necessary time each morning or evening and throughout the day to understand the presence of God-love within, and know that only God within you is real. Know that justice will prevail no matter what seeming distress comes into your world to play out an aspect of your past acceptance of unreality. I am the eclipsing of darkness within your subconscious so that you can see all within the greater context of Solar beingness. I am Portia, and I experience the divine world anew through the frequencies of Selfhood that you are rising into, even as I see within you an opportunity for God to live and move and have his being through your hearts, minds, and souls.

Glory be to the highest, and on Earth peace, goodwill to all men[85] and women and children who seek the law of love, the law of being and of God Self-mastery through opportunity to know the freedom flame, the alchemy of love. I am with you even as your heart beats in that three-four rhythm of the inner waltz with my beloved. Discern this day the beating of God's heart within the sacred dance that we together, hand in hand, will know.

I bless you. I grace and seal you in my opportune love-fires to be love.

Portia

I Come to Initiate You
through the Science of Radical Forgiveness

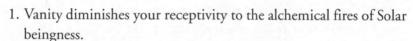

1. Vanity diminishes your receptivity to the alchemical fires of Solar beingness.
2. The philosopher's stone is the principle upon which all alchemical structures are built, grown, and maintained.
3. Co-create a new mindfulness through attentiveness to divine purpose wed to compassionate communication.
4. The permanent relinquishing of past paradigms and of human limitation is a holy work augmented by angelic frequencies of Spirit-radiance known as the Aquarian love-fires of divine alchemy.
5. Your propensities to observe human imperfection manifest must be redirected into predilections to see divine light's joy and play-fulness victoriously outpictured.
6. Valuing every lifestream as a unique and beautiful individualization of the God-flame, you move into a new unity-field of aware-ness in presence.
7. Forget others' mistakes and dwell on their bountiful Presence wholly in divine and rapturous love with yours.
8. Your greatest victories in each life come when you forgive and love those who have devalued and vilified you, and you

graciously serve those whom you have previously misunderstood and mistreated.

9. Intuitively apply the law of mercy in some way every day with divine abandon.
10. The compassionate application of violet-joy-laser love may be your new recreation.
11. Ingrates may become your best advocates through prayer and radical forgiveness, seventy times seven.
12. True spirituality is divine love-wisdom in full blossom through your sacred labor.

The alchemical love-fires of Solar beingness I emanate, for I have entered the Sun to receive cosmic distillations of the Spirit. I now deposit that which I have received from the Solar Lords within your own Divine Presence. For you see, each of you has that divine emanation as a particular representation of Solar beingness, as a fire enfolding itself continuously. We who have moved in the stream of cosmic consciousness may at times, by dispensation, share virtuous aspects of our own Solar Presence that we have garnered through our meditation upon the One. It is as if we would open the cap of your crown and lovingly pour in more golden liquid light of God-beingness.

And so I come to initiate each of you through the science of radical forgiveness and violet-laser joy-love so that you may move on past those blocks within your subconscious that have tripped you up lifetime after lifetime. Ignorance is no excuse for not maintaining, through the law of harmony, your centeredness and presence. For some of you, divine wisdom is the requirement of the hour to understand, from the context of seeing through your own Presence, that which is true, that which is real. And from this new perspective, you may move out of a current stream of despair and despondency from the human level and perceive as God-realized men and women in the love-wisdom-power fire of your own inner being.

Some of you have sought higher vision, greater God-power flow-ing through your chakras and aura. And yet, I say that unless and until you can forgive the elements of your own selfhood that are out-side of God—and in the process forgive all others their own predis-positions to see you in any way as less than the perfected one who you are in God's eye—then you cannot fully move into this higher stream of connectivity and blessedness in Aquarius.

Therefore I release the sacred fire as radical forgiveness. All who have offended God in any way are released from the prison chains of self-identity and the human to come up higher and to walk the path of Solar beingness today. Yes, at times your emotions have gotten the best of you, especially during the waxing of the lunar cycles, when all hell has broken loose from the netherworld of your subconscious. And yet, through the violet-laser stream of cosmic joy, these propen-sities may be dissolved by your acceptance, wholly, of love.

Therefore, once more I say, forgive those who have offended you and move upward and onward in the fire-radiance of Solar joy. Embrace those whom you have seen as enemies and love the core of their being, who is God. Thus, one and all may come to this fount of healing love in the retreat of Mother Mary. All may kneel before the altar and confess that God is God within themselves and within each other, and determine that nothing will take them from their path, their vow to serve the Blessed Mother, to live to heal, to live to serve, to live to love.

This is my personal invitation to one and all. All have at times made mistakes. If you have perceived your own or another's errors in your own awareness, highlighted them in your mind, and continued to revolve them in your memory, let them go. Put aside your rancor and bow to the light within your holy brothers and sisters. If one has offended you, then I say dissolve that offense by the love-fires of light within your heart. If you have offended another, then blaze forth that fire of radical forgiveness and bless that one from the point of your Presence, and seek and ask for forgiveness. Your health depends upon it. The maintenance of light within your aura requires it. And to those who in any way have difficulty in communicating personally with those with whom they have had issues, I say communicate with me in prayer and I will do your bidding and embrace those whom you have wronged.

I am Saint Germain, the master alchemist of loving forgiveness in this hour. For you see, blessed ones, the highest level of transmutation that you can attain to in this life is dependent upon how much you release, you forgive, you let go of permanently. Some state that they have forgiven, and yet in their heart they have not. Let this ritual be true and full from the very core of your being. For then and only then may your mission be fulfilled, may all alchemical abundance be yours, and may the light of joy fill your world with the cosmic radiance of angelic presences, who will sing and laugh and dance and revel in that new joy experience and light that they see billowing around you, manifesting through your heart, and shining through your eyes.

Take time now, in silence, to kneel and to send forth these rays of forgiveness to one and all, and to request the angels of mercy and forgiveness to also work with those whom you have wronged to forgive you. The Alpha thrust of this alchemy is complete. The Omega return requires that you go to those whom you have wronged or whom you thought had wronged you, and forgive and ask for forgiveness. This will complete the spiral, and then you may move into higher Solar beingness with Morya and me.

I am the one sent to deliver freedom to the Earth.

Saint Germain

6

Take Part in Greater Scientific Experimentation

P

Dearest Hearts,

Did you know that the universe is a grand experiment within the laboratory of God's consciousness? We the ascended masters, who are one with God, continually perform sacred alchemical experiments whereby the universe is expanded, the consciousness of sons and daughters of God is raised, and mankind may enter into a greater understanding of the law of love. As you rise into your Presence and live as God-conscious ones, you may, with us, also take part in these experiments of the spirit.

Thus we come to those among mankind who would glean greater God Self-knowledge in the science of the spirit and in perceiving with us the great scheme of what God is up to in the very Now-ness of being. As you give your violet-laser-light calls and prayers, mantras, and songs, a beautiful field of energy graces your Presence; this is the very circumference of fire by which you may enter into these alchemical works with us.

If you would know what Morya, Saint Germain, Jesus, and Mother Mary are up to in determining how they may bring greater God-connectedness to the sons and daughters of God upon Earth, then through your own voice you may add something to the mix, to the cosmic soup, through the elixir of love of your own heart raised to God. As you participate day by day in your vigils and prayer sessions, your Higher Self actually takes part in a higher alchemy, often unbeknownst to your lower consciousness, for you are active participants in the greater God-goals of the Universal Great White Brotherhood.

When your sight is opened and you truly see as we see what is occurring as you invoke the sacred fire through your invocations, you will be amazed to see how the angels and many cosmic beings and masters and even the blessed elementals utilize the resources of the Spirit, through the words that you invoke, to deliver to the Earth itself great cosmic energies. It is as if, through your invocations, a network of light is established that empowers the sons and daughters of God to rise into higher consciousness.

Therefore we encourage all of you to understand the sacred science of the invocation of the word in this new context. For although you feel the currents of light flowing through your being, if your vision could be raised slightly to a new level of understanding you could pour greater light-energy through your vision into the work that you are about. You could create great vortices of light and fire that many souls could tap into and then also reconnect with you as heartfriends of the Spirit. A spiritual foundation must first be laid through prayer, fasting, and holy contact with your Source through silent meditation before you begin your greater efforts to contact souls.

You have seen one experiment that took place through the merging of two streams: Eckhart Tolle, who has brought forth a divine teaching for all mankind; and Oprah Winfrey, who has developed a media empire through which that teaching can be delivered to hundreds of thousands of souls. This is one of our greater experiments of the spirit, through which a divine alchemy can be delivered to the Earth through the greater God-consciousness of many. For we utilize every lightbearer who participates in these events to bring the connectivity with God-consciousness into their homes and communities and nations. And you will see a great upsurge and swelling of the light as the greater grid is enfired and souls rise higher by simply being there to participate in these e-classes, as you call them.

We have other divine experiments in our plan, and yet we reveal not all unto your outer waking consciousness. As your Higher Self does participate with us in these sacred events, we together plan for the Age of Aquarius, whereby every man, woman, and child may know God fully within, have an understanding of cosmic law, and move forward the evolutionary plan to bring the great Golden-Crystal Age of Aquarius into physical manifestation upon Earth.

Saint Germain and I are grateful to each and every one of you who has in any way given of your energies, your resources, your abundance, your personal talents to our cause through this and other movements of light. We encourage you to keep on keeping on, even though at times there is still within your subconscious the shadow-self that emerges to squash that which is about to occur in this greater scientific experimentation of the spirit. You can see and understand now why the dweller-on-the-threshold rears its ugly head just before the victory: it knows how much you will receive of new life-energy and frequency and how you will truly be raised in spirit and in consciousness to perceive as we perceive, as God-realized ones.

We offer our hearts to you. As you respond to my beloved and begin to fully bring about radical forgiveness at all levels of your own being and unto those who have wronged you or those whom you have wronged, there is beginning to be built a greater field of violet-joy light as a carpet of sacred fire around the world, by which the divine play and drama may now come forth.

I am Portia. I have been waiting for you to balance the scales of divine justice within you for quite some time. Once your karma is fully dissolved and all is trued within you, then one day I, along with the Master Alchemist himself, will receive you in our sanctuary of light as God-free beings. And for those of you who have ascended twin flames and come to our home of light, we will place the hand of your beloved within yours, and you shall know in that moment true divine joy and love as you have never known it before.

I seal you in the light of divine alchemy, the alchemy of love, God-love, within.

Portia

7

Move into Solar Beingness by Applying the Science of the Spirit

1. The valiant ones practice alchemy within the laboratory of life's daily challenges, calling upon cosmic catalysts to initiate each divine experiment with light.
2. The use of potent formulas whereby cosmic energies are exchanged within and through the secret-ray chakras and aura are reserved for advanced alchemists.
3. Buddhas have applied the laws of divine physics to the nth degree through Solar beingness.
4. Qualifying each breath with the radiance of compassion is the beginning of the gnosis of true love-wisdom.
5. Jesus called to the Great Initiator before each alchemical healing manifestation.
6. Invoke the Master R, the Divine Director, through total acceptance of his presence where you are. He is my teacher and one who has been the great exponent of cosmic alchemy for me.
7. Resources of the Spirit always replenish themselves instantly when used only to glorify God and to highlight and revivify his Presence everywhere.
8. Acceptance of the end product as already fully manifest and beautiful brings the thoughtforms of divine alchemy into

physical reality through the first law of alchemy, which involves cosmic trust and cosmic thrust.

9. Reaping a harvest of light for God daily is the alchemist's great joy.

10. Finding yourself within your alchemical work is its underlying purpose.

11. There is a time allotted in the spiritual services within our retreats for the sharing of the results of our individual and group alchemies, and these are times of great joy and an outpouring of appreciation to all.

12. The benefits of applying the science of the spirit in all your endeavors cannot be overstated, for they are the very means whereby you move into Solar beingness.

Saint Germain

Note: Saint Germain provided no commentary on this elixir or number 9. Please meditate on their import for your life.

8

Be the Light of Freedom to a World

P

From the point of reality within your soul, I come. I would speak of the universality of consciousness within your soul, whereby you may embrace a new understanding of opportunity to be the light of freedom to a world. When you expand consciousness through presence of mind and heart one with God, you have access to the universal Mind and Spirit of all that is. You no longer experience life from the reference point of only one individualization of that God-flame; you experience it from the point of reality within all life, which is one.

When you see disparity among the nations and peoples whereby there is not a unity of understanding of the principle of life and the values of harmonizing one's being in the greater context of the ennoblement of the soul of all, then you cannot fully embrace all cultures and peoples, the uniqueness of their differences, their values. The split occurs first within thine own consciousness and then is outpictured one by one among the sons and daughters of men and women. If the world is to experience greater freedom among all, then the expanding of a universal awareness of presence must occur, and it must first abide right within your own Solar awareness through Selfhood in God.

We come to the family of nations and speak to the very souls of all. Through many languages and through many sights and sounds within the consciousness of the evolving ones in time and space, we experience the temporariness of life as you know it in the human domain so that we may bring you into that expanded awareness to see life beyond the time-space continuum in all its glory and beauty, in the circle of beingness as God experiences life through the creation, and as we hope that you would desire to know all also within this point of reference of Selfhood in God.

Justice is the completing of the circle of life's experiences through understanding the cyclic rounds of evolution and involution, of the going out and the coming in. Thus, when you understand the law of karma as beingness, you no longer experience separate points of identity within that circle; you know the All of the all-circleness as one. If you see life only from a slice of your experience, then how can you enter into the Now-ness of the All? Therefore, understand the value of entering your Presence as a great sphere of light, truly the Solar essence of your own Higher Self. From this new point of reality, the divine reference point and the Holy Breath of the One, you may have access to the allness of consciousness instead of the temporary little beingness that humans call their life.

All is rarefied and expanded when you know the All through the One Breath. And yet, the dichotomy for many of you is that you still must come to terms with the resolution of all karma. Until you embrace the circle, you will still experience pain and suffering and the temporary lapses from this universal consciousness of presence. You will still have reactivity and judgment of others and self when you do not fully see that other as a part of your own being and your being as a part of all beings. Therefore, embrace the circle of the universal One, who is God. Even as you live and move and have your being within the world, know that your Higher Self, the true you, lives and moves and has its being within the allness of God as the higher circle and sphere of beingness.

The Solar Lords are those who have embraced all worlds and have risen in consciousness through divine perception and God-vision to know the cosmic reality of light as Self. Live no more as men and women; live as light-essences, blessed hearts. Through stillness, the glory of your own radiance may then begin to grow, the infusion of love-wisdom within the Earth may be complete where you are, and the universal awareness of cosmic joy may be yours forever. The all-composition, the alchemy of love, may be experienced right here and now as you enter into this universal spirit of Solar beingness.

In the peace-commanding presence of divine love, I, Portia, emanate this new opportunity for you today to be who you are fully. OM. OM. AUM.

Portia

9

Make Your Magic Presence Real Today

1. Release all concepts of human limitation into the alchemical Solar furnace of your Presence, wherein your boundless Buddha nature of all perfection exists.
2. Every elixir that I prepare is individualized for your specific requirements to raise your elemental atomic vibrations through the higher frequencies of your spirit, one with God's.
3. Performing alchemy is more than a magician's act; it is energetic transmutation in its purest light matrix.
4. Finding the specific conditions and temperature at which a particular material substance is elevated into a new phase or dimensional frequency offers the alchemist an understanding of how the same principle of transmutation may occur within the elements of his own world and life viewpoint.
5. Relating to all energetic transformational changes as opportunities for self-mastery, the divine alchemist sees clearly how mind over matter works in its most practical and sublime applications.
6. Science and religion as material spirituality, or spiritual materiality, are one within every true adept.
7. Observing violent reactions in nature may give the alchemist pause to look to those disparate components of self that, when improperly mixed, may result in mindless emotional outbursts, which are self-defeating.

8. Every positive statement of encouragement to one child upon Earth results in the rebirth of an entire civilization on another world in a distant cosmos.

9. Creative thoughts catalyze cosmic connections between your heart and God's.

10. Nourish your inner-genius child through heart mindfulness.

11. At one time or another, every soul has thrived on the spiritual resourcefulness of the lady members of the Karmic Board.[86]

12. Revelation is the rediscovery of God's magic story.

Make your Magic Presence real today!

Saint Germain

10

See the Violet Fire as a Ray of Blessing

P

Gracious Ladies and Gentlemen,

Would you understand a greater depth of your soul and that which God has placed within you as a magnet of fire? When you understand it fully, it will bring you back to the point of your departure from the Spirit, which may now be your entry into the divine world. Those who have gotten in touch with their soul are those who may now soar. Those who live from the point of reality of beingness in Solar light may now shine. Those who have placed first things first in terms of their spiritual development may now know the allness of perfect peace in the Presence.

I am Portia, and I anchor light so that every soul will feel arising from within something very special that will move them into a new field of awareness, rising above the complacency of a life lived to the glory of the human ego into one lived to the glory of God. Those of you who have caught a glimpse of the very essence of your being as *soul-ful-ness* know whereof I speak, for you are beginning to feel the cosmic pulsations of your Presence flowing through your being and emanating out into the world. This must become the norm in the Age of Aquarius, whereby through the thought and feeling worlds of many more among mankind the higher aspirations and elements of Solar beingness may fully be resident within the auras and lives of devotees of all religious persuasions and of those who seek God within. Jesus has come and shown the way and passed the torch to Saint Germain and me whereby, as we take up that torch and bring to mankind the next step in the evolutionary process, they may see freedom as a very present reality of opportunity for victory within their lives.

You have been given the gift of the violet transmuting flame. Many of you have utilized it to perceive that within you which is unreal and that which you now would have enfired as real and true. You have performed the ritual of forgiveness. Now, I say, see the violet fire as a ray of blessing. As you emanate these frequencies of freedom, opportunity and justice, mercy and transmutation around the Earth, see the very essence of the violet light as a blessing ray, blessing here and blessing there, caressing the lowest and even the highest among mankind with these alchemical elixirs of light.

Yes, you may become a fount of blessing instigating new opportunity for mankind to come up higher where you walk, where you talk, where you work and worship. As you live and move and have your being among your brothers and sisters everywhere, see the light, oh so violet and glowing, blessing elementals, all human beings everywhere, all substance and nature, the very molecules of which you are composed, and of that which Mother Earth long ago accepted of the Father's Spirit to birth a world.

Each of you may be this fount and chrism of blessing as you choose to make the most of the opportunity given you each day to work the works of God in some conscious manner. Whatever you do, wherever you abide I, Portia, expect that from this day forward you will no longer denigrate yourself, that you will instead see the very present reality of your own Christ and Buddha essence as that fount of blessing.

When you say "God bless you," you can extend the light of violet-fire freedom and opportunity to all. Even when someone sneezes, the angels of the violet ray will be there as you say *"Gesundheit!* God bless you!" They will feel the radiance of your heart, your soulfulness, your loving care and concern for them; and when one or another asks for prayers for burdens to be lifted, for healing to occur, this fount of blessing who you are may flow ceaselessly as you maintain your inner connectedness with the Spirit, your attention upon your Presence, your life lived to the glory of God.

One among you has outwardly been blessed and anointed as a priest of the sacred fire. Many more among you may receive this initiation if you choose to be this fount of blessing to life. For that is the purpose of priests and priestesses of the Order of Zadkiel, Melchizedek, and Afra. And as you wield the energies of the violet light mindfully and visualize the currents of sacred fire pulsating and streaming forth from your Solar awareness to all life, then you may maintain the holy office of being a priest or priestess. It requires a certain presence of poise and peace, it requires taking time in silence and meditation upon your Source each day to reconnect and allow a greater flow, opening wider the portal a little bit more between your world and the Divine so that all that you do will be empowered by the Spirit and you will be that blessing unto all.

O holy ones who are rising in true practical spirituality through that which you do, think, say, feel, and emanate, let all be ensconced in violet-light joy. Let all be empowered with these new frequencies of Aquarius. Let every breath that you breathe contain new particles of the Spirit as blessing to all upon Earth. You as a focal point of the brothers and sisters of heaven are valued by us more than you know. Therefore, never devalue your worth, your God Self-worth, through thoughts of irritation, depression, fear, or darkness. If at times you feel the burdens of life weighing upon you as you carry the extra load that you have offered to bear for the Lord of the World, know that we are ever present, the angels of mercy are ever with you, the joyful ones of heaven smile upon you, and cosmic priests and priestesses of all the seven rays are at your command when you use the name I AM THAT I AM and proclaim the immanency of God's spiritual kingdom come upon Earth—heart, head, and hand through you.

I now turn up the heat. The spiritual heat pours forth through all anointed ones of the Spirit throughout this nation. *Awake* to your mission! *Awake*, I Am Race, to that which has been implanted within you as engrams of fire for the completion of your sacred labor upon Earth! *Awake*, O children! Come to terms with that within you which you have accepted of unreality, and embrace that which has always been the God-being Solar awareness of who you are. *Awake! Awake! Awake*, mankind! Receive the blessing of heaven and of all the seventh-ray angels this day who, with the angels of healing, now come to *reclaim* you for the light and to do their cosmic surgery to remove something of unwholeness and to manifest more of the completeness of your Solar beingness.

As you meditate upon light, so this cosmic surgery will be continued throughout this twenty-four-hour cycle; and all for whom you pray for healing and blessing will receive the currents of these alchemical elixirs, which will raise their souls in freedom's light. Now go forth and be the conscious ones who will bring to the Earth and to all greater connectivity with Selfhood in God.

I bless you. I bless you. I bless you in violet-joy light!

Portia

Being in God Here and Now

1. Interpreting the internal impulses for spiritual change and advancement toward your goal of oneness requires a time of silence and devotional contemplation.
2. Everything about God points back to you, here and now.
3. Fully accessing all the spiritual resources in your causal body requires discerning what they are through Solar identification, clear seeing, and prayerful service.
4. Become a divine narcissist: Fall in love with God's eternal image within.
5. Your godly ideals may become a little more real each day by focused spiritual work and a practical labor of love.
6. To fully embody any teaching, you must first become it by internalizing it, and then externalize it by teaching it from your point of personal experience.
7. To know Solar beingness, live fully in the light, not in the shadows.
8. Thinking that God or others don't know what you do in private is the folly of egocentricity, for you and all those others are God.
9. Nothing is impossible to a creative mind and willing heart tethered to God.
10. Let your compelling reason to keep on loving be that it is enlightened self-interest that is compounded daily.

11. You may capture every divine thought through the science of a receptive will and the alchemy of mindful attentiveness.

12. Make living in presence a fun game.

13. The joyful ones are those who have not only caught a glimpse of God, they have gotten hold of the full image in mind and set forth a course of action to make that image complete within and through their own being.

At any time and in any place where you enter into full presence, there the alchemy of Solar beingness may manifest. We would have that time and that place be now. For there is nothing but the Now through which you experience life, and there is no place but here, where you are, where God is in the fullest sense.

Being everywhere in the consciousness of God requires being in God here and now. For then every other point of reality of the hereness and nowness of God may manifest for you from this point of reference. Then you can never be outside of living in the Now and living here, for all living outside of this reality is a dream; and when fully awakened, you will no longer be dreaming.

The alchemy of love is the sacred journey that you take day by day whereby, wherever you go, you bring presence with you—presence of mind, presence of heart, presence of will won and lived through the eternal flame of beingness in Solar light. Those who have caught a glimpse of their Godness, the goodness of the suchness of Presence in light, can, through the portal of their vision, ascend into the full-blown manifestation of that vision in the 360-degree circumference of the All-Seeing-Eye of God whereby they live a life in the loving Presence of God.

In the circle of fire of your Solar awareness in this spherical context, evolution and involution become one. The whole is merged into the point, even as the point of reality that you are experiences the All. It is as if fusion and fission dissolve and all that is left is you as a point of Godness in Presence. From this point of cosmic reality, you may then emanate the pure suchness of light. There is no shadow created by that point,[87] there is simply being, complete existence in oneness.

Living in the One requires one-pointedness in God. There is the dissolution of all other frequencies and dimensions into one dimensional point. This is the mystery of the alchemy of Solar beingness. From this point of beingness, all exists: you are in all, and all is in you. You are All. All is you. You are You. I AM I. All learning becomes teaching, as teaching is learning. Living is complete, for the completeness of God is life. The all-composition of all elements dissolves into the one element.

I am Saint Germain. I am God-Love. I AM.

Saint Germain

12

Embrace Your Real Self Ever More

P

Blessed Hearts,

There comes a time in your life when you decide that there is only one thing to live for: God. *This* is your day of freedom, if you make it thus every day from henceforth. Those who would move into a new opportunity to love God within self and within all can understand the light of freedom that is available to them through their right choices. Every right choice that you make works toward balancing the scales of cosmic justice both for yourself and for the entire evolutionary body of God within this world and within all worlds.

Did you know that your thought processes can impact life on other spheres? Did you know that that which flows through your consciousness, your thought and feeling world, can impact the tiniest creatures in the ocean as well as the work of cosmic devas as they seek to maintain the balance of life upon Earth? For if you are God, then that which you emote and muse on affects the God-reality of all upon the sphere on which you live. Thus, when you make the decision to live only for God, you understand it in the context that light is the essential nature of your being, and that if you would be God in manifestation, the light must emanate from and through you at all times.

Many of you have listened to our voice for years and decades, and yet you are still coming to grips with the God-reality of your own being in some way, day by day. For you have not fully embraced the concept that God may be fully present where you are and that all else is as nothingness. My beloved made two million right decisions on his pathway to eternal freedom, and you also, moment by moment, may opt to be God in manifestation, which is a right decision.

No matter what transpires around you in terms of others' interactions, opinions, and the sendings of their thought-energies of judgment unto you, you may remain in the presence of joy. You may live a life for God, only God, as you ascend in consciousness, living within your Presence and being absorbed into the God-reality of the Solar light of your Buddha nature even as in Self-realization you fully attend to the musings of God that flow through your mind, your thought processes, and your heart one with the Divine.

You have called forth light as opportunity to bring to this world greater understanding of the teachings of the ascended masters. We have heard your cries and the desires of your heart to bring your personal testimony and witness to a world. No matter how this request is fulfilled within you by God's angels, as you take the light-energies of opportunity to make your calling and election sure[88] through your service to life, God will be there when you, in humility, have made that choice to put all else beneath your feet. Thereby the surety of your cosmic connectedness will allow you to move forward, to see clearly, to love all life free, and to always opt, through right choice, for the greatest means of employing your spiritual gifts to benefit many souls.

I provide a greater radiation this day to enhance your freedom to be and live and move and have your God-beingness in Solar light. *Leap* into the arms of the One God. Embrace your Real Self as never before. And as a little child, speak to God as your divine parents, asking for the gifts of the Spirit so that you may share the fruits of your communion with the All-in-all in ways great and small—telling little stories and offering the gifts of Self to others. Yes, see your Solar Presence as the highest outpicturing of the Father-Mother God in you, your own individualized manifestation of Presence. And then be all who you are with great love, wisdom, and power in all that you do each day.

I place my hand upon each of your hearts, if you would have it, to provide greater balance, greater harmony, and the raising up of your spirit in joy that you may continue to serve a long life in ministration to souls—teaching, healing, and providing many disciples and students of the light the means whereby they can move into greater presence, greater joy, greater light.

I am the Lady Portia. And with my beloved, I emanate new frequencies of spiritual freedom to your soul that you may always choose to be God.

Portia

13

Grasp the Import of Your Personal Ascent

1. The valiant ones resolve to be initiated into the sacred processes whereby all save God within them is consumed in the alchemical fires of Solar beingness.
2. The intensity of your devotional offering is felt by every sentient being in its core.
3. Love is the one component required in every successful alchemical experiment.
4. Your humility in being ready and available to be taught and even chastised by your own God Presence or by any divine master is a key to a swifter and surer ascent.
5. Solar beingness is perfect rest in motion and perfect motion in rest.
6. As you value the highest aspects of godliness within, you enter a state of presence where your own Solar light is felt, seen, heard, smelled, and finally cognized.
7. The Five Dhyani Buddhas help you to translate the experience of the lower senses through mindful indices into an awareness of Solar beingness.
8. The Solar Lords preempt the intervention of galactic darkness in your world by those who have inverted divine evolution into demonic devolution. Solar-gazing meditation is a key to the inculcation of the Solar Lords' frequencies into the Earth.

9. Vajrasattva concentrates the frequencies of all Five Dhyani Buddhas into a laser-like thunderbolt current of Solar light, which explodes the bedrock of ego muck.
10. Take my cosmic violet forceps and remove from your soul now the ancient particles of anti-freedom that you have accepted as a part of your own being.
11. Perfect alchemy comes when you have surrendered the desire for a separate experiment or experience outside of God.
12. Divine joy is light's alchemical boon as well as my secret cosmic catalyst.

I call you all, as scientists of the spirit, to wield the God-power of alchemical love-wisdom through your heart-mind connection now. Those who employ the scientific method without the Spirit will get limited results, for these can only rise to the mental level of beingness. For those who would penetrate the Earth's atmosphere to reach the highest frequencies of Solar beingness, I provide the formula of divine light, of radiant joy, of holy love as the means whereby every scientific application of your soul's work may be successful.

As you muse on God and the light of your Solar Presence, the altar upon which your experiments occur is highlighted. Your higher awareness is accelerated within your own being as a reference point whereby the divine chemistry may come forth as you translate that which is of the base into the gold of Christic light. You see, blessed ones, alchemy is all about process. And when love is within that process, no matter whether or not you temporarily fail in accomplishing the desired results, the love of your efforts will last; and eventually, so long as you press on and provide something of yourself within your alchemy, the end result will be cosmic transmutation into a living awareness of God's Presence where you are.

Some have attempted numerous times to reach the heights of God-consciousness, and their efforts are duly noted. Yet once you have climbed the mountain peaks and nearly reached the summit of being, it requires complete surrender as you follow the path set forth by us. For upon the highest peaks you will see the marks of where we have knelt in holy prayer, upon reaching our goal, in thankfulness and gratitude to the Source—the light that led our way, the divine impetus that carried us through every storm and cold night and the wintry blasts of the dark ones who sought to dislodge us from our homeward ascent and grasp upon the ropes provided by our mentors of the spirit.

I have used this analogy because it is imperative that many more among you grasp with great expectancy the import of your personal ascent in the context of how this will be meaningful to many more souls and will give them the impetus to also rise. You have heard in Scripture that the ancient ones built an altar here and there in the wilderness. This altar was the place of their alchemical experiment in light whereby they offered the lesser aspects of selfhood through sacrifice—even, as a metaphor, the slaying of the animal creations in order to release the sacred energies of spirit within, characterized by blood, which they then offered to the Almighty One in their sacred work.

Something of yourself must be laid upon the altar daily if your alchemy would be true and pure. First provide the platform, the altar, as a place within your heart where God may work his work through you. Then abide and maintain, through holy prayer and meditation, a field of presence there, whereby the all-light may flow and you may understand the answer to every problem as God provides it within your heart and mind in a moment of illumination, in a cosmic interval of the eureka experience of pure knowing of God's very beingness within.

As the heavens are opened, the keys are given to you to understand the higher sciences of the spirit; these may only come to those who have surrendered the lesser self and who would now enter into the Holy of Holies of the sanctuary of inner beingness through Solar joy in that ecstatic state of divine love, which may be yours when all that you desire is God, when all that you see is his light, when all that you know is the purity of his Solar radiation. I raise you now in Solar light to a new emanation through my heart fires of freedom this day. Now, scientists of the spirit, go forth and be victorious in your work.

Try, try, try[89] until you succeed and win!

Saint Germain

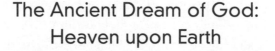

14

The Ancient Dream of God: Heaven upon Earth

P

Gracious Hearts,

The very present reality of your Godhood is here and now available unto you. It has always been so, though you have not always realized the essential nature of your Solar Reality, the very living Presence of God within. Once you catch a glimpse of and understand the fullness of who you are, you are in a sense free to be the God-person that you have always been, accepting the frequencies of the spirit that flow from your God Source unto you through your crystal cord, your tie to God, which deposits within your heart the radiance of immortality as love, wisdom, and power by which you live and move and have your being within the center of God's life, who you are.

When Saint Germain brought the gift of the knowledge of the violet light unto mankind through the teachings released through the "I AM" Activity, it was so that all could know the very present reality of freedom within through using this divine resource for the transmutation of karma and of past misuses of the light, whereby you can accelerate through cosmic forgiveness the consuming of the past and move into the very present reality of living as God-free beings, one with your Source.

Mankind has now had this gift for three generations and more, and yet many among mankind have not fully received or used this divine resource to the extent that civilization as a whole has moved into the new era of Aquarian love that we, the ascended masters, desire to see fully manifest upon Earth. Each new age is an opportunity for evolution to spiral upward and for mankind to grow in consciousness so that God's great plan for the entire solar system is fulfilled through all of the evolutions of light evolving within the time-space continuum of their particular world.

As life proceeds upon the Earth, the third planet from the sun, so through love, the third ray, life may be fulfilled throughout this solar system. The time of Aquarius is key for the fulfillment of love within all evolutions upon Earth. And though mankind may not fully understand the cultures of all peoples upon this sphere, yet, through acceptance, through reverence for life, through striving, through greater God-communication heart to heart, mankind may fulfill the law of love within so that every man, woman, and child may be free to pursue the higher path of light and of living a life to the glory of God and to that glory manifest within the Earth.

We, the Aquarian masters, come with new opportunity for mankind to move into a higher stream of connectivity with their Source through forgiveness. Forgiveness is understanding; it is letting go; it is surrendering to a higher purpose within one and within all. Therefore we call to the leaders of all nations to put away the implements of war, of suffering, of violence and to instead come to the table to communicate. Those leaders who do not come under the rod of God in this directive by the Lords of Karma spoken through me will receive the direct transmission of their karmic choices because they have been and continue to be a block to that which the Solar Lords, who govern the destinies of many worlds, would see manifest upon Earth.

The people have cried out for freedom from the oppressors within their nations and governments and economic systems. We have heard their cries and answer. Thus we give notice that those who do not move into the new stream of Aquarius—of conscious living, of attention upon their God Presence through whatever discipline of the spirit they might abide in—will be removed, first, spiritually from their office, and then in time, from that physical governing office, because they have not attended to the holy will of God through that office and through their decisions.

Blessed ones, we bring hope for a new world manifest through each one of you by right choice and by your voice raised in praise, thanksgiving, and holy prayer. The entire culture of the Earth may be raised into a new awareness of light, understanding, and freedom. It will take many more of you who would understand the science of the spirit to emanate the new frequencies of love-wisdom to all peoples.

And thus we call you to our summer solstice conference in Montana.[90] For there shall be unfolded to the Earth and to all evolutions of light upon the Earth a greater impetus of fire, spiritual in nature, that will move you further upstream into the glory of your own God-awareness as sentient beings one with the heart of God. Make every effort to come and be here physically, blessed hearts. For that which you receive in the beatitudes of the spirit and in the balancing of personal and planetary karma will accrue to your causal body—that great God balloon of sacred energies that you have accumulated over many lifetimes—as a resource for you to move into higher consciousness until one day your soul is merged with the divine you, your Higher Self. Then you have access to all love, wisdom, and power within the several worlds in the spheres of light through which you may live and move and have your being in God.

Saint Germain stands now to deliver to the soul of each one of you a compact, an agreement that you may sign with a stylus held by your Higher Self, through which you agree to utilize the resource of the violet-laser light with greater God-determination to transmute the cause, effect, record, and memory of all world infamy and darkness, of all collusion between the forces of anti-freedom and darkness within the Earth who seek to steal away that which within you is Real.

If many more among mankind will take this sacred gift and utilize it fully, then we will see the dawning of a new age, the coming of beautiful children unto the Earth who will lead you into a new wave of higher consciousness. And the ancient dream of God—that heaven come upon Earth—may truly manifest as a physical reality for all to know. Thus, we come in service to humanity to give of our hearts, of the wisdom teaching, of the gnosis of higher laws and principles of divine living. We honor who you are. Even in your limited perceptions of life, we know that you are trying, are striving. If you continue to keep on keeping on, then the victory will manifest in your life and within the world itself.

We thank you for your great hearts of fire, your dedication to your spiritual path, and all that you do to serve humanity, O sons and daughters of God, O children of the One Light.

Portia

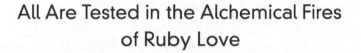

15

All Are Tested in the Alchemical Fires of Ruby Love

1. Blessedness is a quality that the alchemist is wise to develop. To live in Solar beingness, it must infuse his every thought, feeling, word, and deed.
2. Auric emanations change continuously, and the alchemist gains sensitivity to planetary energies by insulating himself from any deleterious effects through deep meditation and prayer while also engaging in his practical sacred work.
3. The plight of the embodied bodhisattva of love is to bear the brunt of the return of mankind's misuse of love, and through its mastery move into Aquarian joy.
4. Alchemy is all about astute resourcefulness and transmuting the waste matter of unconsciousness into the light-energy of radiant presence.
5. Harmonizing your thought and feeling world is a daily work that is more easily attained through conscious use of violet-laser light in your meditation and prayers.
6. Intuiting the source of perceived attacks upon who you are is not as crucial as going within to eliminate the chinks in your armor that allow them an entry to your world.
7. Daily our angels offer the fragrance of violet-joy to alchemists who have prepared anew the cruet of consciousness to receive it.

8. Precipitate greater abundance by first refining your vision, thoughts, and speech.

9. Having caught a glimpse of the divine world, work valiantly to see and know all.

10. Pursuing the path of light, alchemists first work to clear all obstacles to its shining within every quarter of self.

11. Accomplish one goal with complete surrender to all that it requires of givingness, and then move swiftly on to your next alchemy.

12. Every alchemist is responsible to forge his own destiny through a focused labor of love-wisdom.

In our retreat, alchemists of the spirit study with the end in mind, which is freedom. Freedom comes with a price, and that price must be paid day by day through living in Solar beingness. Some attempt a quick road of attainment by attempting to circumvent the initiations required and the attainment of each step through focused work.

At times we lay down parameters for the work at hand, including step-by-step processes, so that the divine experiment may be successful. For your enlightenment, liberation, and soul freedom, mix the proper chemicals, bring the right ingredients into play, and create the right conditions within yourself. To reach the pinnacle requires having your maps in hand, the proper equipment, the training, and the development of your stamina. We lay a foundation for centuries to come, and this is done with great intention, planning, and purpose in mind.

I come for one and for many to understand the necessities of the hour for deep reflection upon that which comes forth from out the subconscious in the way of spite and sting, which always is more detrimental to your own evolution than to another. Therefore be careful with your words, your communiqués, and, more importantly, with the energies that are behind them. For we see what is acting in your world, and though no human personality is perfect, it is better to understand the greater context of how the alchemy may come to its highest and most perfect expression, even if this at times requires you to go back and rework your work from the beginning.

What is an acceptable offering of alchemy? God knows. And if at times the refiner's fire[91] is necessary to purge from your world something of the lesser self in the very process of the alchemy, then so be it. For all are tested, all are tried in the alchemical fires of ruby love. The very purpose of this fire is for the exaltation of light within you; for the ennoblement of your soul, one with your spirit; and for your victory over the beast of desire. Desirelessness is key as we frame around you a new aura of Solar beingness through the sacred process that you undergo as you receive your internal initiations, which at times come in the form of challenges or communiqués from others.

It is better, at times, to simply "be still, and know that I am God,"[92] and wait for the effects of the alchemical fires of love-wisdom to work their work upon and through you. And then, once you have felt the purging and the consuming of something that has been a block, perhaps even for lifetimes, then in joy you may move forward with the fulfillment of that alchemy and all will be well in the greater context of the work at hand.

There must be a means whereby karma is dissolved. In most cases, this requires a certain friction and fire to come forth, else how can that substance be consumed? Therefore we present opportunity for the resolving of ancient conflicts within and between heart-friends, brothers and sisters of light. When you get this victory over your own beast, blessed ones, then the greater victory can manifest.

Therefore we move each and every one of you toward greater awareness, humility, and Solar Presence. If you can maintain harmony, then harmony will flow through you to all life. Therefore, sustain the alchemy of love within. Through the internal barometer, you will always know what is playing out in your world and how at times you must get on your knees, confess, and move onward, seeing the temporary malaise that has gripped you dissolved through the alchemical fires of complete surrender and forgiveness of self and others.

Every lesson learned moves you on to the conclusion of your alchemy of love. Many of you are learning your lessons, even if at times there is a sense of pain in letting go as you embrace the lesson within the lesson and therefore the light-energy that comes forth in this learning process.

May blessedness be yours through your own Solar emanation of light from your God Presence, which I see now infusing your world with greater flow, greater glow, and greater God-abundance.

As you see the light manifest, so it shall be in your world, O alchemists of the spirit!

Saint Germain

16

I Bring a New Spiral of Divine Justice

P

I bear the light of cosmic justice to quell the dweller that has aris-
en within you, thrashing and lashing out at your Real Self and your
soul and attempting to proclaim its dominion over you. It is not real.
It is not who you are. It is only a shadow. I take the sword of justice
and thrust it into the evil eye of that sense of injustice that it may be
now no more within you, if you so choose to ratify it.

Whereof does this dweller come? It comes from rebellion against
the law of your own being as cosmic joy—your joy of divine justice—and therefore it seeks to drag you down, O mankind, into a
vortex of anti-light. A new spiral of divine justice I bring to counter
that which has arisen upon Earth, which, if it were to take its full
course, would mean the destruction of all. Therefore the angels of
justice come to cast the tares of injustice seeded among mankind into
the fire of transmutation.[93] We now seed the Earth with new crystals
of light by the hand of the conscious ones who work with me to balance the scales of justice in the Earth.

Are you dependent only on God for all that you require? Then
no longer be dependent upon your own human frailty or lack of God
Self-awareness. Know that through the hand of the Divine One you
may have all you require to live a life of peace and harmony and grace
without frustration or angst.

See those within all races, nations, and peoples as your brothers, your sisters, your friends. Through presence of mind and heart, understand the nature of God within all, within each and every one as part of Self and not separate from thine own identity. And from this perspective, move in a new stream of awareness, of presence and consciousness whereby justice for all is manifest because every choice that you make, every act that you perform is now done from this point of understanding that all is good, all is just, and there is no injustice within life, which is God.

I speak to the leaders of all nations and I say: Come under the law of love and beingness and no longer attempt to cast aspersions upon other peoples and nations or to take what is not thine. From a new sense of the community of mankind, use the resources provided by Mother Earth to the benefit of all life, being respectful of the consequences of every decision. For that which you take that you do not require will be as a curse upon you and your people and will be stripped from you through the outplaying of elemental forces and the law of cosmic justice. Therefore abide in peace and harmony and oneness of purpose to serve all life in balance.

I speak to the leaders of all religious movements worldwide and I say: Live in the light of harmony and of the original intent of the prophets, the seers, the avatars who came and taught the truth. As you teach and as you live, so it shall be upon you. If you teach murder and mayhem and destruction as necessary, as a part of your religious tenets, then know that the Lord God will return unto your head and your being the full wrath of cosmic justice for the error of your way and your teaching and that which you spawn in the Earth of darkness as a result. It were better for you that you had never taught or lived this life than that you continue to spawn the evil ways and the machinations of darkness. Therefore come to the fount of divine justice. Bend the knee and surrender to the truth of your own divine being. *Let go! Let go! Let go* of the errors of your ways. And let the children lead a life of joy and laughter, of learning, of living in the Now.

I speak now to the very ones who are causing pain and suffering anywhere upon Earth and I say: That which you do that is of great darkness now comes to remind you of who you are. As the scales are balanced, all is trued and you receive, by the hand of justice, opportunity to know that which you have created through your choices. Therefore a certain karma of the peoples of this Earth does descend as judgment. For if it were not to descend, O mankind, then woe unto you. It descends directly upon those who have spawned evil and darkness in a very directed, and I must say efficient, manner. The recording angels and the Keeper of the Scrolls have laid the record out before us of the Karmic Board, and the swift hand of justice comes unto many. And to those who have been the instigators of darkness for centuries and eons, justice is served and the descent of the hand of the Prince of Peace is manifest. Therefore, if you would be the instrument of love and light, then get the victory over the beast of injustice lest that which come upon you also be intense and more than you can bear.

To the humble people of light, the saints in the Earth, the angels of justice now pass over where you are—your homes, your schools, your workplaces. Hold fast that which you have received of light, of attainment. For as the Earth shakes as justice is served, and as the armies of heaven come to defend the Woman and her seed[94] even as the fallen energies are reaped from among the dark ones, you must be strong and sure in your resolve to be God in manifestation, O sons and daughters of the One.

This judgment and cosmic justice is a relief unto you who have held a great balance. You now see how, through the outplaying of karma, a little less weight will be upon your shoulders in days and weeks and months to come, though some of you would continue to hold even greater weight of light—and of darkness for transmutation—within your being.

I am Portia. The day of reckoning is at hand. Lest any think that it is the old wrathful way of the Lord, this is mercy come as judgment. For unless justice be served in this way, there should no life remain upon your planet because of the great darkness that has beset the nations and the peoples through the choices of mankind.

Be sealed, O hundred and forty-four thousand[95] true and noble hearts, saints in the Earth, and know that God is with thee always.

Portia

Be About the Father-Mother God's Business Now

1. God's mind-beingness regulates manvantaric respiration, as Above, so below.
2. A glad heart is a springboard to more fruitful alchemy, for every spiritual experiment is augmented by its infusion of love.
3. God's Solar radiance is perfect alchemy manifest as the unconditional love of divine beingness for all.
4. Look upon the clear night sky to see a universe populated with those who have succeeded in manifesting their own unique Solar beingness.
5. Every healthy cell manifests Solar beingness across its particular network of light.
6. Finding the source of true joy within is one benefit of Solar gazing and meditation.
7. The fabric of the cosmos is the radiance of love-wisdom carried on the Solar winds of God's breath.
8. Self-realization is the goal of every atom, molecule, and cell within you.
9. Every solar cycle is a coil of beingness leading to the center of reality in the Now.

10. Galaxies experience cosmic photosynthesis as new solar systems are spawned through divine transpiration.
11. Spiritual fellowship between conscious heartfriends in diverse light movements is akin to compassionate communication between all of your body's systems.
12. Solar beingness is the secret to personal enlightenment and cosmic illumination.

I would have you transgress all human limitation to perceive with new eyes the opportunity to become cosmic alchemists. Your God Presence is the source code for every alchemical experiment. The computer of God's mind, the greatest intuitive thinker, can lay out an entire grid as the divine program that, when accepted and played within, leads you to the goal. We have been about our Father's business,[96] which is the science of light. I turn up the heat and the flow through the Bunsen burner of your own Solar radiant source to move you into a new stream of cosmic connectivity with that Solar light within.

Are you happy with yourself in your current state of consciousness? If so, then I bid thee well. If not, then come with me through seventh-ray joy as I turn on the laser through which a new portal into the divine world is opened. You may enter only through heart-centeredness and love. As we fly, soaring on eagles' wings to learn the science of precipitation through a heightened Venusian experience, the allness of God may be at hand for you in your work and your word, where you no longer waffle betwixt the synaptic flashes of your limited human understanding. In its place, the cosmic radiance of God's mind shines through your being; and Solar beingness, ample in its cosmic wattage, supports that which you are about, which is the Father-Mother's business.

Your God Presence has every ingredient you require in your work and alchemy. Do you require greater resources for your work? Then call them forth and believe that they are manifest in your hands today. You have received every teaching that you require to do this, though you forget to apply them in the Now with the full intensity of focus that will bring it about. Therefore, put aside distractions. Wrap yourself in the circle of fire whereby your goal is set before you and you fulfill it here, now.

Every distraction is a thought pattern that must be ignored. Awakening is the dissolution of ignorance. Enlightenment is the full flowering of light within you now. When will you be enlightened? The choice is yours. When will you be free? It is your decision to make. I leap to the center of cosmic beingness every moment of my life. I am a cosmic hurdler bounding over every obstacle and grabbing that tape as I dash through my extreme sport of Solar beingness.

Teach your youth the highest road. Be an example. Do it just now.

Saint Germain

18

Experience the Presence of God Directly, Here and Now

P

Gracious Knights and Ladies of Love,

The intrepid know that the law of divine love is supreme. As their hearts expand as chalices of living light to entertain more of the emanations of their own God Source, the elements of freedom within begin to sing. The song that is heard is beautiful, for it is accompanied by the voices of all in heaven whose hearts are also one with God.

Freedom to be God is paramount, and you each have the ever-present availability of your God Presence, or Higher Self, with you to be the wayshower to immortal perfection. This state of eternal Nowness is not one of human immutability whereby there is no change or evolution. Rather, it is one of ever-glowing radiance whereby the unchangeable elements of divine love are ever present where you are. The cycling of the divine breath and holy awareness through your consciousness may allow you to always feel and know that God is real within you.

You who have in some way experienced this heightened state of presence that we call Solar beingness know that no human high or temporal feeling of bliss brought on through outer stimuli, such as psychedelic drugs or alcohol or the exchange of the sacred fire between people, can replace the all-inclusive light of seventh-ray joy. The light of freedom that blesses and caresses your soul through the fire of Spirit that comes upon you in moments of divine awareness is one that you simply must have and know and experience through all of your divine sensory and emanating centers called chakras.

The ascended masters live and move and have their being in pure presence. We can assist the evolutions of mankind in bridging the chasm between the mundane and the divine worlds through our insights into the eternal experience, which may be yours through the alchemy of love as Solar beingness. These daily sharings from our hearts are for your spiritual edification and also for the ultimate purpose of bringing you to the finality of knowing God as Self and then fully becoming that divine light in manifestation always.

The teachings of any world religion or inspired guide should always bring you back to the kingdom, or consciousness, of God within. For this is the portal through which you experience Solar beingness, not through the simple belief in the words of a long-deceased personage, no matter how enlightened that prophet, seer, or avatar. Each of you requires the direct experience of God's Presence where you are, here and now, and that is what we bring you through the transmissions that we deliver as HeartStreams. These issue directly from our living Presence and experience in God, which you may also have.

Every true spiritual teacher is only an instrument for the transfer of divine light, or God-energy, and therefore should never be worshiped as God or as someone who has more than what is available to you now as potential for your own Christ consciousness to manifest. I come to inculcate a new spirit of Christ-I AM-ity into the Earth, whereby those who call themselves Christians will no longer simply believe on the man Jesus; they will follow him through the initiations of life to the point of emanating the same Sonship, or Sun-ship, or Solar awareness, that he did.

Truly, blessed ones, the presence of your own Christic or Buddhic potential has ever been with you, expressed in your own divine mediator known as your Holy Christ/Buddha Self. Whether or not you have previously followed the teachings of Jesus or Gautama, you can understand today the principles that they taught as the eternal truths that will lead you to the divine experience of knowing God within you in the fullest sense in your life now.

Many are awakening to this new opportunity to understand their own innate Godhood through various spiritual teachings that are communicating our message of hope across the Earth. We have many vessels through which to pour out the Aquarian stream of love-wisdom to mankind, and you may also become an instrument for these teachings and this new consciousness to manifest to many souls through your own direct experience of God, your own individualized light of Solar beingness.

We are about the Father-Mother God's business of spiritual enlightenment through the delivery of violet-joy love and through a new internal belief system that relies simply on the acceptance of who you already are as a Solar being in your own right. Though there are divine principles and precepts that are helpful for you to embrace and understand, we are not about the creation of a new church hierarchy or religious institution that requires the following of various doctrines and dogmas before you can enter into higher awareness. Therefore, rely no longer on outer rites and rituals to convey spirituality, nor upon human intercessors to lead you to the kingdom of God within.

The joy of this teaching is that you have opportunity now to know God. The path, though difficult for many to fully comprehend because of their human mind-sets and past conditioning, is actually very simple for those who are being quickened by the internal light, which brings the eternal verities to their outer awareness on a daily basis, moment by moment. Through stillness and living in this blessed state of divine silence, you may hear the voice of God within, which will lead you to all-wisdom. Be still, and know that I AM God. Be still and experience Solar beingness now through your heart-mind connection, which is your tie to the divine world all around you.

I am the Lady Portia, and I bless you.

Portia

19

The Alchemy of Picture-Perfect Presence

1. Trust in the laws of alchemy leads you to experiment with divine abandon to reach the goal of oneness with the originator of all that is.
2. Placate only the Solar Lords in your surrender to holy purpose.
3. Keeping attentive to the many details of living an internally vibrant life dedicated to divine love moves you into the realms and refinements of Solar beingness.
4. My joy is seeing you become adept at living as an adept.
5. Divine processes are those that lead you inward, upward, and leeward.
6. Pressing on to complete every step of divine alchemy with joyful expectancy brings an even greater activation of my spiritual catalysts to bear in your work.
7. Let your income be the gold of everlasting and radiant Solar light and joy.
8. Creative genius is the daily fare of the alchemist whose trainer is the Sun.
9. I foment many spiritual revolutions within your heart.
10. My purpose is to revitalize your life through the dance of alchemy.
11. Walk with a Godly gait and gander, and sing with a healthy helping of heart.

12. I am interested in everyone whose goal is union with the Eternal Now.

Picture *perfect presence* for yourself. What does this look like? What does it feel like? What is its manifestation? How do you sustain it? What is necessary for you to know it? These are the eternal questions of Solar beingness that you may daily ask yourself. Then enter into a process of fully accepting the answer within your heart as it is inspired upon you in your silent time of meditation and communion with your God Reality. Each day, perfect presence may look a little different, for your life within God is an ever-changing mosaic of light unfolding before your eyes and visage in radiant new ways whereby, through your experience, the newness of the Now-ness of God as an ever-present Reality is known in the context of love—love of all, love of self as the Higher Self, love of all others as a part of the whole.

The alchemy of picture-perfect presence is my offering to you today. For as you can see, so can you accept and then manifest. Seeing is believing. Believing is becoming. Becoming is the key. I say that you must now enter the state of being that is beyond becoming. Yes, you are becoming ones, beautiful to behold in the God Reality who you are, and yet, if you are always becoming, then where is presence? So I add my Solar beingness to the radiance of your Solar light. I add the alchemy of God-love to that which you have known of God's love. I add the radiant joy of *my* picture-perfect presence to that which you have seen and now experience in the Now of beingness.

Truly, blessed ones, you have heard and read many teachings over your incarnations and the years of your embodiment in this life. You have studied with many masters and at times allowed the foibles of those who do not truly know who they are in the fullest sense to hold you in the grip of a limited awareness of self. Let go and let God be where you are as the eternal light of pure being now. Put all outdated rituals aside. All past self-declarative anti-statements of non-being now dissolve as you accept the I AM awareness of light, only light.

Radiant joy may be yours in an instant, and that instant may be now.

Presence is more about acceptance than about struggling to attain something outside of yourself. It is within. It is at hand. It is in sight, even as it is insightful as the reality of beingness. Words, many words, cannot move you into its radiation. The Word who you are as the Christic, prismatic light-emanation of being has always been yours to know. Therefore accept the Christ and Buddhic reality of picture-perfect presence now. Sing and laugh, dance and revel in the joy of beingness as a little child, as one born anew, as the smiling, playful one who would know God as Father-Mother always within a burning heart of love.

I extend my heart, my love to augment the fire of picture-perfect-presence love for you today. I frame it ornately for you. And I hang a representation of your own picture-perfect presence of beingness upon the walls of my retreat. For in my Father's house are many mansions,[97] even as there is within your own consciousness the portal to the divine world, where you too are building many mansions in the sky, many monuments to love, many holy representations of God-beingness in Solar joy.

I am Saint Germain, speaking through this vessel and emanating the alchemy, the elixir of light for you.

Saint Germain

Each New Day Is an Opportunity
to Be God in Manifestation

P

Most Gracious and Gentle Hearts,

I enfold you in my radiant joy, for it is a joy to be with you in spirit and in matter. And in this sacred space, heaven is come upon Earth where you are. The ennoblement of your consciousness as a spiritual being is what we are about in these releases of light. As you attend to your heart, one with God's in a victorious sense of freedom, you have access in the here and now to a divine essence of the Spirit, a sacred flow of that which is real, of God; and you may employ the graces of awareness above the ken of the human to serve sentient life and to raise all in love's eternal fire.

I am the Lady Portia, and I come to impress new molecules of the Spirit within your aura to free you from a sense of bondage in the human and to raise you into the all-pervading light of your great God Self. Whether you come from near or far, and no matter what journey you have been on in this and past lifetimes, you are here and I welcome your heart, your soul, your spirit.

Each new day is an opportunity to be God in manifestation. Each moment, as you breathe in the essence of the Holy Spirit through your lungs and into your heart, there is the enfiring once more of the threefold flame within you, which is your contact with the divine world, the essence of who you are as a spiritual being living in these coats of skins.[98] It is all for the purpose of learning and of living, of serving and of striving, truly the education of the heart whereby you may always realize how much you are appreciated, valued, revered for the God-essence who you are, which is one with all life. And then, as you amplify this light within yourself, you may also go forth to appreciate, value, and revere that which is real in all others, who are truly one with you.

This Hearts Center movement is about the veneration of light and God within all life and how we together may raise consciousness and awareness through the awakening of the Spirit and the God-light within all life—that which temporarily may have been darkened or in some way lost in the human sense, yet which God has always valued and seen as the Real Self within all. Therefore take time each day to appreciate each other, to in some way value, honor, and revere your fellow brothers and sisters in the way. Look upon life with the eyes of God, who sees the reality in all, and grow in the comfortability of the Spirit within your heart whereby your soul may sing, new life arising from within you may be joyous, and all that is true about you is manifest consciously as you move in our great heartstream of love-wisdom to know God, only God.

Opportunity is the sacred vessel through which you move to know the Spirit where you are; and because you have free will, you are free to move into higher consciousness ever and always. What this will look like for you is for you to discover in the Now-ness of Solar beingness. As Saint Germain and I revere you and bring something of the essence of who we are to bear in your world through these teachings that we are delivering, there can be the very present reality of great God-joy welling up within you as a light of freedom, as a certain consistency of the Spirit that flows through your chakras and aura. Thereby, every new day may glow in the sanctity of the spiritual opportunity to live in light; every day may bring you a new chance to know something of God that you had never known or realized before; and every person you meet upon the way you may greet in light as a friend and share from your heart that somethingness, that suchness of God who you are, to expand the divine expression of beingness within the allness of God, ever and always.

See yourself this day born anew as a little babe or a child. And in this way, as a divine manchild, enter and experience the freshness of God's beating heart that may also be yours in stillness, in peace, and in the silence of the great OM, the Word that emanates continuously through all of cosmos, through all of God's Solar beingness. We are truly one—one in Spirit and one in the alchemicalization of light through the elixir that I bear, which you may now drink. Drink ye all of it and know the essence of your own God-identity, through which you may know love, only love.

I am, and we are, with you always, even unto the end of your trials in Mater and your victory in Spirit and in cosmic joy.

Portia

21

Study the Heart: Know the Science of Love and the Alchemy of Beingness

1. Your spiritual progress is all about inner beingness, which comes through surrender of impermanence and acceptance of the peace of presence.
2. Begin every alchemical experiment with a great inbreath.
3. Every child is a natural alchemist; your current educational system and methodologies often remove the inner magic of their imagination.
4. Transcendental awareness emerges when the awesomeness of the creation is seen, felt, and known by you through the magic of stillness.
5. Be true to your own Buddha nature by learning to live in Solar light.
6. Unleash your internal playful nature by doing something creative each day.
7. Adjust your focus upon the image of God in which you were created.
8. Intent upon merging true science and religion, the alchemist skims off the dross of each to find their core reality through Solar beingness.
9. In becoming as a little child again, the alchemy of joy may reappear in your life.

10. Every magus utilizes the aid of invisible helpers who understand the laws of metaphysics, for they are the carriers and distributors of divine energies.
11. Real science is all about practical spirituality and true religion is all about divine alchemy.
12. The alchemy of divine love is the highest science.

The alchemy of love is the light of your Presence shining through your heart. Every prayer, every meditation, every song, every musing upon the Divine can flow through this sacred nexus of light, which is your contact with both the divine world and the human world in which you now temporarily abide. As the central chakra, the heart is the center of flow, as Above, so below, even within your physical body. The study of the heart is the science that all should partake of from early childhood until the elder years. Mankind must know the science of love and the alchemy of beingness through their hearts.

As the Aquarian love-fires of the new stream that mankind is now rising into in consciousness is seen and felt throughout the world, many more are coming into an understanding of this level of divine joy and grace that comes because hearts are upturned to their God Source, the reality of picture-perfect presence. And so you may understand a new connectedness with Spirit because love sings within you a new refrain of divine joy.

Let us begin at the beginning with the fiat of light in each day's alchemy: *Let there be light!*

Saint Germain

22

Defend the Light!
Secure the Bastions of Freedom

The light of justice always prevails because God is within that fire. It has been thirty-three years since the coming of my beloved to warn the Earth and the United States of the consequences of abandoning the people of Taiwan.*

I come in this hour with the bodhisattvas of heaven to manifest the light of cosmic justice for the seed of light of Sanat Kumara in the Earth.

When the peoples of the world abandon divine principles of freedom and liberty in order to gain commercial advantage, then I say *woe* unto them. For the karma that does come when you put aside the first principles of light in order to engage in commercialism and materialism does not move you into the stream of God-consciousness and awareness in the holy Presence of God, who you truly are; it moves you into the lesser stream of darkness and nihilism, where you cannot gain access to the higher worlds of light of the Buddhas and bodhisattvas of the Spirit. When the beasts of selfishness, pride, anger, gluttony, and—especially greed manifest and attempt to take

---

*This HeartStream was delivered on March 12, 2008, when elections in Taiwan were again bringing to the fore the delicate relationship between mainland China and Taiwan, including their mutual definition and recognition of statehood.

from you all that is real about you, then I say *woe* unto that which is within you which has caused you to surrender the light of God and then to manifest in your world the darkness of defeatism and anti-light.

Therefore, America, awaken now to your holy purpose to defend light and to give where giving is required in terms of securing the bastions of freedom, such as the island of Taiwan. For if you do not defend that which is true within the people of light who have stood firm now for decades, then that which you have secured even within your own borders will be up for grabs to those who would steal away the light of freedom in your own world.[99] There are those who are the weak-minded, willy-nilly ones who have no spine and determination to stand firm on the principles upon which this nation was founded. They would rather give in to the beast than to state to the world that they will stand firm upon those principles of light. Therefore, if this nation, America, does not defend the holy people who stand and kneel with the Buddhas and bodhisattvas upon the island of Taiwan, then I say *woe* to this land, *woe* to this people, *woe* to that which you have secured of a materialism that you take for granted and see as the very benevolence that America represents throughout the world.

The ladies of heaven now weave a sacred garment of fire, of golden mesh around the island Taiwan in a protective action. Blessed hearts, you may visualize a great flowfield of light around that island nation. Therefore I ask that you pray continuously for this island nation and her people. As Saint Germain said many years ago, do not place your head upon your pillow at night until you drop to your knees and say a prayer for the people of light upon this soil.

If even a small percentage of that which is now being expended in the Middle East were to be diverted to assist these people, who have crafted their very constitution and ways upon those of these United States of America, it would be enough to secure their protection and freedom. Yet many among the leaders of industry, technology, and the economic engines of this nation in the Western world are more concerned about the bottom line, that which goes into their pockets. You have seen that many corporations are crumbling because of the decline of the dollar and that which has been built upon the sand of paper money and its printing in this nation. You see some of the leaders of these businesses falling because they have stripped from their corporations the supply of the common worker, to their own benefit, even while laying off hundreds and thousands of those who are seen by them as simply chattel. These are the warlords of today, who are not the true leaders of the people of light.

The light of freedom within America is very tenuous in this hour and the spiritual sponsorship of this nation is on the rocks. I say let it be firm and true upon the rock of the Christ—who you are as a God-realized one—as you stand for freedom, as you are determined not to let go of the light within you, not to let go of your mission, your vows, not to let go of your sacred purpose for coming to Earth: to save sentient beings, to be an example to many, and to anchor that light day by day through your awareness, one with God, your Solar Source, the I AM THAT I AM, who is Real.

Saint Germain has given you the teaching of the great I AM Presence, the divinity within you, the light of God that always prevails all about you. Take that teaching and make it real and make it known throughout the Earth. For now that many more have heard the teaching of the Now and of living in presence and stillness, tell them of their I AM Presence—the great God-beingness, the Solar essence that they are. This is what they must know. This is what they must feel and experience now that they have been freed from the mental concepts of the dark ones who have kept them in bondage and in ignorance for centuries.

Let my people go into the light of Cosmic Christ illumination and receive new opportunity to rise in freedom because you have chosen to be the way, the truth, and the life with Jesus,[100] with Magda, with Jesus' disciples and those of Gautama and all true teachers of ages past, present, and future. Go be the Buddha where you are. Go be those who will be the example of truth and freedom, liberty and justice, and the opportunity to serve to set life free everywhere.

I am the Lady Portia, and I sing a new song of joy within your heart even as you muse on the Solar light of beingness within you always. May the peace of your Presence keep you blessed and dressed in light always.

Portia

The Internet as a Metaphor
for Understanding Our Connectivity
with Source and the Web of Life

1. Every sun has learned the lesson of pure beingness while also hurtling through space and surrendering completely to the cosmic laws governing Solar evolution.
2. Your sense of time and space are governed by your relationship with the Divine One, who lives beyond the ken of human experience.
3. Spiritual alchemy is the science of nurturing love-wisdom within life through conscious awareness of the laws of Solar beingness within all divine substance.
4. Cosmic intelligence is born of awareness of the All within all. Acknowledge and improve upon the Creator's work through your apportionment of Mind.
5. Reality is the Spirit in manifest presence everywhere and always through the eyes of the Creator's beloved—you.
6. Financial freedom is about beingness above lack and presence outside of desire.
7. Enter your breath to experience God's Solar beingness where you are.

8. Reflecting the full radiance of the Source is your highest work each day.

9. Profound stillness, as centeredness in God, leads to new levels of Solar beingness even for the highest of celestial and cosmic beings.

10. Your Source provides all you require if you can slow down the human mind while speeding up your connectivity with the Divine Mind with its abundant radiance.

11. Give complete attentiveness to the light who you are within each cell to understand the microcosmic components of beingness, for then, through the science of synthesis, this will lead to cosmic understanding and Solar life.

12. You may experience every vestige of God's divine beingness as you develop acumen in the art of Solar meditation.

Saint Germain

DCL: Saint Germain has said that the Internet is a great metaphor for understanding your connectedness with the Source. Whether you have a wireless or a wired connection to the Internet, the greater the power and the stream of the connection, allowing a higher level of bytes of information to come in over that connection, the greater is your ability to download information quickly.

Similarly, with your connection to your God Source, the stronger your attention and focus are on the reality of who you are, the easier it is for you to download divine inspiration, understanding, and the spiritual information you require to maintain life, balance, harmony, and peace in your world. As with the Internet, this spiritual connection is a two-way street, because you also have the ability to upload, or send, a certain aspect of your consciousness to others within the *antahkarana,* the network of light of all conscious beings who participate in this connection.

As technology advances, we experience faster connections to the Internet with fewer interruptions. Likewise, as we progress on our spiritual path, we connect to the Source faster and find it easier to stay connected. Just as power surges, inclement weather, high winds, and solar radiation can interfere with our connection to the Internet, certain states of consciousness can interfere with the divine connection through which we access the broadcast from our Presence. To maintain interconnectivity with our Source and with each other, we must calm the storms and winds of our own emotional body and live in Solar beingness.

We have to lay a firm foundation of trust by keeping the "wires" and radiating centers through our chakras correctly aligned; following the laws and "ley lines" of life are a part of this maintenance. We must also engage at times in retuning ourselves, adjusting the flow of light through ourselves by using self-corrective measures that bring us back into alignment and greater connectivity. If something has been temporarily disrupted or damaged within our own spiritual circuitry, we must work to restore and improve the connection.

Every day you have an opportunity to enter the Divine Mind and allow the great God-stream of conscious awareness and presence to flow into you, through you, and out to the world. You have the ability to contribute something of your experience, your knowledge, your wisdom to the greater whole of the Mind of the One. It is as if you have the choice to upload something into the all-encompassing content of the Mind of God by offering the knowledge of who you are, your Self-knowledge, to your brothers and sisters and to others anywhere in the world.

As you experience God and maintain firm connectivity, the entire grid of light, in a sense, is fired, maintained, and sustained. If at times you choose to rest and "turn off your connection" so as not to experience direct engagement in the interconnectivity as an active participant, you can know and trust, as long as you maintain your harmony during the experience, that the wires will remain in place, that you will retain the opportunity for inner connectivity when you choose to resume, and that God's light will always be there when you decide to connect again. God's love and radiance, comfort, and joy can sustain you even as they are experienced through the joy of your brothers and sisters of light everywhere.

The master uses this metaphor of the Internet to express for us something of our experience in this dimension, in time and space on Earth here and now. As we see improvements in the Internet and the growing of the body of information that is available to us to understand what is occurring on Earth—the news, the updates, et cetera—we should selectively utilize this information to sustain and maintain a greater level of Solar beingness, of connectivity with the All. We don't simply download more and more information; we utilize what we receive to grow beingness within. We must also upload devotion to our God Presence in order to complete the circuitry and maintain the firing of that grid of light.

As you share, as you teach, as you give to others, you are participating in this figure-eight flow of light. If you only receive, if you only download and don't share or connect back to the Source through devotion, then you are not a complete participant in the greatest sense. Those who have received the teachings of the ascended masters and of higher truths must at some point teach and share who you have become through your divine experience in order to sustain the firing of that grid of light. It is as if each connection is its own power station and reinforces the whole. This is how all local area networks (LANs) work to interconnect the Web of the Internet. Each dot upon the matrix and grid is important, and if you take out one, then the Web is not quite as complete as if you have all of these connections functioning.

In your spiritual life, as you move into higher streams of beingness that involve greater creativity, greater sharing of your creative fires and of what you have downloaded from Spirit, assimilated, and made real within yourself, you can then, in a certain sense, return to God and to your brothers and sisters that which you have become. The spiral of divine alchemy for Solar beingness is completed through the antahkarana, the web of life. By our devotions and our attentiveness to the stream of God-awareness, by entering into it, becoming it, maintaining, sustaining, and sharing the glow of the firings of our connection, we expand our personal Solar evolution and beingness.

David Christopher Lewis

Know a New Sense of Divine Justice
and Opportunity

Knights and Ladies of Divine Justice,

I am Portia and I bring a sword of justice for the clearing of a certain strata of injustice in the Earth and within you. This sword is charged with the living light of cosmic love that is also a concentrated essence of the wisdom of the Father-Mother God, who knows exactly what is required by every soul for that one's spiritual evolution and progress. When wielded by cosmic beings, it brings forth that energy of wisdom as an active delivery of justice to free each soul from both the sense of injustice and the very core of the outpicturing of injustice in that one's life.

You have heard my beloved Saint Germain say that the sense of struggle makes the struggle. Likewise, the sense of injustice leads to the lowering of your energy field of love so that you cannot see the divine forest for the trees. This day I would have you know a higher vision of reality by stripping away from you an old vision of selfhood outside of God, a knowing of yourself as a limited human being. Through the action of concentrated light borne by this sword, you may be free to perceive yourself as the divine personage you have always been in the eyes of God and well as in the eyes of every angel, master, and cosmic being.

274 SAINT GERMAIN ON ADVANCED ALCHEMY

You have heard that there is no injustice in the universe, and it is so because the law of cause and effect is active in the dimensions where duality is playing out within the rounds of life of those who have not yet entered the center of life, which is beingness within God's heart. Once you leave off living from the point of unreality where you see good and evil and light and darkness manifest in the relative sense, then you will know only the Solar beingness of those who have chosen the supreme light of God as their only reality.

You have opportunity to live as God would have you live—as awakened and quickened ones—and to know the divine sense of cosmic justice that I bring. If you desire to fully know this, then you may call forth the action of this sword now to blaze all around you and to release you from the grip of all past sense of injustice about anything in your life that you have not known as pleasant, vibrant, real, lasting, and who you really are. Blessed ones, if you are ready, simply give your assent and I will begin the sacred alchemy of delivering the specific qualification of light that will meet your divine requirements in this hour.

You each have a guardian angel or spirit who watches over you and attends to your spiritual life and requirements, often prompting you to do those things that will keep you from danger or from backpedaling. When you have listened and acted upon that prompting, you have been saved from a mountain of distress and a heap of hurt as you have been gently nudged and ushered to higher spirals of Solar living. Your attention upon your Higher Self and the divine Solar essences of spiritual light that are constantly flowing to you as the life-giving energies of the Spirit allows them to fully manifest where you are.

Now that you have been relieved of certain ancient internal belief systems and patterns that have led you astray, it is time to know a greater connectivity with your Source by also drinking the alchemical elixir of light that I bear for you, each one. Now quaff the divine draft that I present to your soul in this hour, and know a new sense of divine justice and opportunity in your life.

Every day you may drink something of the spiritual offering that comes at the hands of the angels and of your own Higher Self if you choose to accept your own Solar beingness as the reality of who you are. Every moment you may attune to the higher frequencies of the spirit that will lead you ever upward upon the spiral staircase of light that leads to cosmic consciousness and conscious living as God-realized Solar beings. We are always here to listen to your spiritual requirements and to assist you in making right choices and in allowing the light of cosmic reason to flow to you through your heart-mind connection, whereby you simply know the best course for your soul to take. This is evidenced by an inner realization of truth, a divine rationality that your conscience prompts you to follow.

These daily right choices always bring greater opportunity for spiritual growth and Solar development, for we see that you are becoming wiser and leaving off certain childish patterns and propensities that have bound you to the Earth and to a life of mortality with its sense of injustice always popping its ugly head to goad you to justify certain dark feelings, mental thoughts, and actions. You are freed from all of these by this action of the sword of justice, and you now have the choice and option to live a God-life, almost a carefree life of loving the Creator as never before.

I have come. You have been cleaned up and now glow with this new radiance and sheen of divine glory. March forth now, be alchemists of the spirit, and live in Solar joy always.

Portia

25

Identify with Your Solar Source:
The Universe Is God's Divine Alchemy

1. The universe is God's divine alchemy of Solar beingness.
2. Manifesting your divine essence through difficult times and circumstances brings you greater mastery in the science of total identification with light.
3. Every moment that you spend in conscious connection with your Source is time well spent, leading to the day of your full acceptance of Solar awareness.
4. Blessedness is a divine quality that all should study as a part of beingness.
5. Divine alchemy is an experiential rather than a theoretical science.
6. Proving every divine theorem in the personal laboratory of your life is what Solar evolution through beingness is all about.
7. To reach Christic attainment you must master the seven major initiations on seven levels of being that lead to a crystalline awareness of all life.
8. Your soul's eternal flight comes when you have surrendered all attachments to the Earth and embraced Solar living.
9. Divine alchemy always leads to a truly abundant life in God's great heartstream.

10. Radiant health and serene joy are secondary benefits of meditating upon your Solar Source each day.

11. Finding true peace within is all about identifying with the point of God's beingness at your central core.

12. Divine fragrances begin to emanate around and through those who surrender all desire except perfect devotion to and praise of the great I AM.

As advanced alchemists of the spirit, you are receiving through these discourses a new awareness of divine love. This love may be yours to know and to express daily as you receive and accept the worded cadences from our hearts that may move you into higher consciousness, presence, holy awareness of God's light, and the ever-expanding waves of pure joy that may lap upon the shores of your own heartstreams, washing clean the very molecules of selfhood and bringing you the radiance of God's heart.

The purpose of our instruction is to move you into the core of beingness through complete identification with your Solar Source, who is your God Presence, the great I AM THAT I AM individualized for you. As you experiment with the sacred fire each day in some way through the science of alchemy, you may understand God's very beingness within you and the sacred processes of how Solar light may solve all problems, may bring all to full resolution, and may infuse itself into every life form, moving them into the formless stream of perfection.

Radiant living may always be yours as you employ this science of Solar beingness. This comes as greater attunement, which I would define as complete attention upon your God Presence so that you have access to God's heart and mind emanations. When you fully Self-identify with God, then you understand what life is and what life is not. You see God within all life. You revere that light within all, and then every experience becomes a divine one because you live and move and have your being within the essence of God's beingness everywhere and always. There is no time for anything other than

God. There is no space where God is not. And thus you move into a new time-space continuum in a higher level of living, which is God's reality of who you are as a conscious Solar being.

When did I attain cosmic consciousness? It was when I fully identified, accepted, and became the Sun of who I am as God in manifestation. The day of your natal appearing as a Solar being is nigh if you would make it so by your devotion, attention, and acceptance of perfect presence where you are, and the accelerant of the violet transmuting flame may bring it forth consciously for you daily.

Portia and I have a plan for the great Golden-Crystal Age of Aquarius, and that is to energize each and every one of you as seventh-ray Solar beings, utilizing divine alchemy in many ways in your life to experience the blessedness and the graces of the Spirit, and then bonding with many others to create a new architecture of the Spirit, a new crystal grid of light through which the Lord may breathe and move and have greater Solar beingness within all. This is our new love tryst with you, each one, to enter into the spirit of brotherhood, of community. Therefore, we bless each and every one who participates in the divine alchemy of light and love.

Take time to prepare for the initiations that may be yours and to understand your purpose and the new world that may appear within your life day by day, blessed hearts.

We are with you always in the alchemy of joy and love, in the science of ministration and service through seventh-ray forgiveness, mercy, and freedom to be God.

Saint Germain

26

The Bonding of Our Hearts in the Sacred Alchemy of Community

P and *D*

Portia comes to invest us with greater light, as we have invested the cosmos and all sentient life with the blessing that comes through us from our Source. Every prayer we speak is an investment of light, and we wear divine vestments as we engage in the sacred science of the word through the flow of light that comes through us. Every word we speak may be invested with a certain fire of immortality. The OM continues to vibrate and to expand throughout the cosmos.

The more you speak the word of truth as you consciously engage in this sacred science, the more you become that word. You become it as you apply it in your life and as you supply it with the radiance of your devotion, the stream of light coming from your Source through your crystal cord to your heart chakra and fanning out through your other chakras—your crown chakra (mind), your vision center, your throat chakra, your solar plexus (as divine emotions or the radiance of the feelings of God), your soul chakra, and finally your root chakra and your feet, through which you are anchored in the earth.

Note: This HeartStream was inspired by Portia and delivered by David Christopher Lewis speaking on her behalf.

You can use all seven chakras and the five crystal-ray chakras as you speak and give the word in prayers, mantras, decrees, and songs. This is one of the key components of alchemy and the higher sciences of light. The work that we are about is wholly about God. It is a holy work of God because, by our intention, our only desire is to bring the kingdom of God upon Earth with a new radiance of light from our Source, to bring that which we have gleaned from all the yesterdays of our experience into the Now through the reality of who we have fully become as God-realized men, women, and children. Although we may muse on the divine science of alchemy as we engage in devotional sessions, ultimately our purpose is to glorify and magnify God where we are, to intuit that which God desires of us, to allow God to blaze through us greater light, and to simply be a receptacle for the distribution and expression of that light-energy as the alchemy of love, wisdom, and power.

We have been graced with the gift of free will to express God where we are. This is a supreme act of givingness on God's part to his creation, specifically to our evolution—the evolution of mankind, which has free will to be the expression of the Father-Mother God. The evolutions of angels and elementals do not have the richness of this opportunity of free will to express in the world of form the way mankind does. The elementals outpicture the beauty of nature according to a specific blueprint and seed of light that they have been given. The angels outpicture God's will, wisdom, and love through intercessory warnings, healings, and miracles in answer to humanity's prayers.

We have a great amount of opportunity, Portia says, because of this gift of free will to experiment and to discern, through our Higher Self, how we may enter into the very science of being through our expression of free will. We must take seriously this gift of God, never cast it aside by wasting our time and space or by procrastinating our divine destiny. Let us fully embrace our dharma, our divine plan, and enter into it with a new spirit of joy whereby we complete our mission with care, with love, and in fellowship with our brothers and sisters who can in some way share in our mission as we share in theirs. In fulfilling our dharma, we may also partake of the sangha, the community of light. By so doing, our joint missions merge in a greater stream because of the connectivity of our hearts.

The science of alchemy, from the macrocosmic level to the microcosmic level, is constantly manifesting through nature and through our own Buddha nature, which is our individualized gift of identity from the Godhead where we are. Knowing the science of the spirit and the laws that govern our divine destiny allows us to be active participants in every one of God's divine experiments, of which this Earth is one. Earth is a microcosm in the greater macrocosm of the solar system, the galaxy, and the cosmos; and we are step-down transformers of the light that comes to the Earth in order that we may outpicture in our dimension and plane of being the same laws that govern the destiny of Solar worlds. As we enter into Solar beingness through ingesting these alchemical elixirs of light from the ascended hosts, we can then bring that understanding, divine knowledge, and wisdom into the microcosm of our experience as we press it down into the deepest microcosmic levels of the Solar worlds of the atoms, molecules, and cells that compose our own beings.

The stage is set for the acts of God to manifest in our world through our conscious choice and by divine direction. This is the beauty of the free will that we have: We can consciously act and choose to employ all of the energies of God available to us through the five senses and then through the higher senses of our Solar being. As we develop the gifts and talents we have been given, which have come to us over many incarnations, and as we employ and utilize our free will to work the works of God, we will have greater access to the Divine Presence and higher energies—the distillations of the Spirit known as *siddhis*, or the gifts of the Holy Spirit—and we can employ these through our heart, head, and hand by conscious choice to create the beautiful new world that all of us together are working toward fulfilling.

This is God's original dream, and it has been dreamed over and over through each and every one of us as individual monads of fire, as expressions of God's consciousness and awareness in the world of form. God created the universe to experience himself/herself in form rather than simply in complete formlessness, or spirit. We have the opportunity to ground the energies of Spirit in a specific reference point of Mater, in the Mother light, through *mater-realization,* the materialization of the Spirit where we are. The more we can bring what we know into being through physical acts of givingness and conscious presence—by making something beautiful with our mind working with our hands through our heart—the more we can fulfill the dream of the Father-Mother God for their creation in Mater.

The science of alchemy is a noble science. It is one in which Knights and Ladies of the Flame[101] enter, through the Round Table, into the divine experience of working in consonance with each other in this sangha, or community of light, to bring about a better world, because together we can do more than we can do individually. As I was reviewing one particular submission from a person desiring to serve as a Knight or Lady of the Flame, El Morya commented that he desired to physically knight this person because of that one's steadfast dedication over embodiments. So you never know when setting forth, by intention, your desire to serve in this way may lead to a greater initiation of light and beingness because you have made the choice, by free will, to serve at the Table Round with the masters of wisdom.

Saint Germain is the knight champion of a number of fraternities of light, including, with El Morya, the Knights and Ladies of the Flame. He is, with Portia, a supreme example of what it means to be a divine diplomat with seventh-ray tact and diplomacy—one who is courteous, having developed all of the graces of the Spirit, and who, with a very caring heart and deep understanding of the laws of cosmos, can communicate to us beautiful teachings and higher concepts with great tact because he has a knack, as a Solar being himself, for living the divine life. Saint Germain, Portia, and other masters who have risen to the heights of cosmic consciousness desire to pull us up, hence their teaching on Solar beingness. As cosmic beings, they know something of living in this higher vibration of the Sun Presence of God always, of emanating light, and of being a source of inspiration and creativity to many, as the sun itself is.

Each master is now a Sun-source of light, inspiration, and the particular qualities of God that that one fully embodies and manifests for many evolutions. We see this with the seven chohans, who embody the divine qualities of the seven rays. Those who serve under them on a particular ray are inspired by that chohan who is the epitome, the divine example, of his or her ray. Cosmic beings glory and revel in the divine light and radiance that their disciples embody and express and in seeing them become a Sun-source of this radiance on behalf of many more evolutions.

You too—as a Solar being in potential and now in the becoming through the application of the laws of divine alchemy—can become a Sun-source of light, radiation, and inspiration for many who come within the stream of your beingness, your life essence, and your presence wherever you walk in the Earth. The more that you Self-identify as a Solar being, the more you can then emanate joy and kindness, compassion and mercy, love and all that flows through your consciousness because you have allowed God to reside in your being where you are. To me, this is the ultimate joy of our service—to simply be God where we are in some way for every soul that comes into our life, into our sphere of influence, into our circle of fellowship. It is a beautiful thing, because we have allowed God to make it beautiful where we are; we have desired to please God through the simple joy of living in the ultimate divine sense of glorifying God as our goal and our sacred work day by day.

Though we may slip and fall and at times have challenges, these are part of the process, for we are learning to discern energies; we are learning to bear a greater load of darkness even as we bear a greater load of light. We have to get used to drawing down from our Presence an understanding of what is acting within our sphere of being even as we bear, on behalf of many evolutions of Earth, the darkness that at times besets mankind through the acts of the unconscious ones and those who have chosen, at least temporarily, not to embody the Godhead as we have.

We honor all choices; we honor free will. Although we may look outside of ourselves at certain points to see what is outpicturing in the world, ultimately we must work on ourselves. We must go to the deepest levels of beingness and see truly what is acting within us— that which also finds expression and anchors itself in the world—and then root out the core levels of unconscious living and enter fully into the Presence of God, who we are in reality and who we are now fully embracing and becoming once more.

The teaching we have received on Ho'oponopono is a key, one that I believe we will understand, utilize, and become more and more throughout the years of our service to the light. It is so simple and yet so profound in that we work on ourselves, because we know that we are one with all life and that the only person we can truly change is our self. So we continue our work at deeper and deeper levels even as we enter higher heights of cosmic awareness and Solar Presence. We work at microcosmic and macrocosmic levels simultaneously, going to the depths of the subconscious even as we rise, through the inspiration of our Solar Source, to the heights of celestial beingness. By entering into this process, we have a greater reach of beingness, a wider circle of beingness in which to express.

We have a more profound opportunity to enter into the science of creation as co-creators with God—as Above, so below—with the ascended masters as our guides. These elder brothers and sisters continuously express new levels of beingness unto us through divine revelation, the progressive revelation that we have available to us through this movement. As the world moves higher we must have a greater connection and flow in order to deal with the darkest energies that are coming back for transmutation, and sometimes it is only through the advanced teaching that we have access to this greater flow and connectivity to our Source. This is why we have progressive teaching.

We cannot simply rely on something, no matter how beautiful, no matter how profound, that was given thirty, forty, or fifty years ago, because the challenges of the Now have moved us into a new point of reference to the universe. The planet Earth is encircling the sun, and the sun is circling the galactic center, and we have a new frame and point of reference in the new position that we are in. Therefore we require greater knowledge and understanding than we had when the planets were aligned differently years and years ago or embodiments ago. This requirement will continue throughout the stream of our awareness as a conscious person, whether we are unascended or ascended. We will continue to have teachers, guides, guardians, and wayshowers long after we ascend, because the nature of life is progressive and ongoing.

Take to heart all that you have received. Make it real. Apply the teaching in some way, however simple, each day, because then you anchor that teaching as a stepping stone for others to then walk up the spiral staircase of light to their own greater understanding of truth. This is the teaching that beloved Portia desired to give us as an overview of what we are about in this movement—why we have messengers of light, why we have each other, why we have The Hearts Center community, and what we can do together to bring greater presence to the Earth through the divine alchemies that we engage in through our work and service.

David Christopher Lewis for Portia

You Are God's Great Alchemical Experiment

1. Dissolve all antipathy toward your Higher Self, for you are God's great alchemical experiment, in which he desires to be well pleased with the final results.
2. The alchemy of perfect love casts out all subconscious anxiety and fear of being.
3. Let your guiding light be fixed within a burning lamp of hope that you may always keep learning something of God's wisdom on your journey of love.
4. Become intolerant of the ego's magnetic downward pull and fully tolerant of and attuned to your Higher Self's gentle, uplifting call to presence.
5. Spiritual alchemists work first on having a successful divine relationship upon which all others may then be lovingly and unerringly modeled.
6. Your Solar Presence, or Divine Source, is supremely impressive and expressive, never excessive or repressive.
7. Intuit every next best step through an absorptive heart and by an abundance of joy in Self-discovery through the progressive alchemy of Solar beingness.
8. Provide God with a taste of humanity by being present for every life experience, fully observing and feeling through your highest

essence as you allow picture-perfect presence to flow and be where you are.

9. Regardless of outer circumstance or appearance, God is always where you are.

10. Being beautiful or handsome doesn't require forfeiting anything of the divine image in which you were conceived.

11. When reality sinks in, rise to greet the divine you, which has always been there behind and above the façade of the ego.

12. The God Self-observant discover all the ways and means of higher alchemy.

The divine you is inviolate in God. As you partake of the light from your Solar Source each day, you make real God's Presence in the Earth through your own individualized expression of divinity, the essence of who God is within you. Immortality is not a merging into an unconscious stream of nihilism; it is the highest attainment of God-realized Self-mastery in Solar beingness. Through it, the fullness of who you truly are is expressed in the totality of your essence of life—rich in its creative qualities, joyful in the playfulness of beingness in God's childlike nature, and beautiful in its replete and variegated manifestations through conscious awareness to the max.

Some fear union with God and seek a selfdom outside of the circle of the One. I come to dispel the myth of egocentric living, for it is not true life as it can be known in completeness; it is a shadow existence, it is unreal. The reality of who you are has ever been clear and present, if you would embrace it and become it. This is the rub. This is the crux of the matter of a spiritual life. And this day I rub your own Aladdin's lamp, whereby the genie of Divine Selfhood in God may be released and the appearance of the essence, truly the quintessence of your Solar beingness, may appear before you.

What will your wish be in God-realization this day? Will it be to outpicture something of holy presence for all life? Or will it be a divergence from the divine stream of Solar beingness, which has always radiated forth God's presence through your Higher Self, your Solar Source. The choice is yours what you will manifest of the God-essences of your individualization of the God-flame today. It has ever been so, every day of your life, from your first breath to your last in each lifetime and through the connective stream of many lifetimes as an evolving soul.

Come with Portia and me to understand the alchemy of divine love, the elixir of light in Solar beingness. Enter your Presence, emanate from this point of reality, and secure a new selfhood in God as the surety of his love wings its way by the winds of the Holy Spirit through your consciousness in practical works of spirituality this hour.

I am your seventh-ray advocate for eternal freedom in the light of joy, the effervescent king who holds the *key* to your own *in*carnation of God [k-in-g] here below.[102] Bless you and keep you always in the divine embrace, blessed hearts.

Saint Germain

28

Embrace the Fullness of Your Solar Essence

P

Valuing life, you can move into a new stream of awareness as you allow your Presence to guide you. This is your course of convergence with the divine stream of the pure essence of beingness and Solar joy. Heretofore on your spiritual journey, the involution and the evolution of your soul, you have traveled on a divergent stream, living on the periphery of being outside of the circle of God's Solar beingness. Now that you have this teaching, it is up to you what you will make of it in terms of applying all that we have conveyed so that your consciousness, one with the eternal ones, may converge with the great Solar beingness of God.

Many have attempted in some way to merge with God's beingness before they have first dealt with the lesser manifestations of egoic living by seeing all that has been a part of selfhood outside of God for what it is and then consciously choosing to leave all of that behind to enter pure beingness. The path of alchemists of the spirit is all about this sacred drama, or adventure, as Morya has put it. Each day there can be a new entering into a higher spiral of Solar beingness, as each and every one of you has experienced and witnessed at some level in your life.

The conscious ones are those who have chosen this upward spiral and stream of awareness. With Saint Germain and me to guide you, as well as many other ascended ones who are conscious participants in God's great drama of life unfolding, you too can apply all that you have learned and have become so that the highest of your Self may shine forth and the brightest of your being may emanate the full glory of the Solar one that you truly are.

We begin a new drama, and each of you as an actor on the stage of life may participate as permanent beings in the greater drama that is unfolding right before your eyes in your world today. You see on the world scene the playing out of the choices of leaders of nations to suppress simple people who desire only to express who they are in the context of their cultural upbringing. Although there may be the element of karma involved, each and every one has a choice to fulfill the inner law of being rather than to accede to the tyrant-ego dweller as it manifests through the directives to suppress freedom of thought, movement, religious expression, communication, and the gathering of hearts whose minds and hearts move as one.

Therefore we ask you to pray for greater consciousness, understanding, and presence to manifest in and between the leaders of the various nations, especially in the East, so that there can be dialogue and movement toward the greater possibility of individual expression rather than the sequestering of souls into one ironclad matrix whereby they do not have the free will to be who they are.

The Lords of Karma have deliberated long on how we may accentuate various teachings among mankind, even in the midst of monitoring and approving the playing out of karmic recompense for those who have, over many centuries and lifetimes, continued to move against the great God-stream of light of the Brotherhood of the Spirit, those divine ones who understand the universal principles of life, of love, and of freedom. Although there may be temporary setbacks in terms of the individual expression of freedom in various nations, there is no injustice in the world or in the universe. Every incidence of suppression of the rights and freedoms of an individual or a nation presents the opportunity to move greater numbers of mankind throughout all nations to understand, to empathize with, and to support greater movement toward that freedom within the hearts of all.

When all justice is meted out, you will see the balancing of the scales both within your own life and within the world itself. All that you can do is work on the within—on having the inner man of the heart and the inner woman of the soul come to full fruition in your being, and on having conscious presence manifest through your choices. When you allow the full expression of your soul, which has been suppressed for centuries, you will see played out in the macro-cosm of your world that which is occurring in the microcosm of your own world. And then, in the flowering and the enlightenment of your own being, you will see in the Earth a greater expression of that freedom for all.

So we bring you back to first principles, knowing that your world is where you experience God in the fullness of that light within your aura, in the sanctuary of your own soul and heart. Look not so much outside of self; dig deeper and know the pinings of your own Solar awareness for full expression and the freedom to be who you are in God. Though your heart and soul may cry out to the Lord on behalf of those whom you see suppressed, maimed, and slain in the streets and in the cities, cry out for the freedom of every cell and atom of your own being first, and allow yourself to let go of that which is unreal and to embrace the fullness of your Solar essence.

Scientists of the spirit are ye if you choose the higher walk with the Divine. Let the alchemy of Solar beingness manifest in your world through great conscious presence, through the choice to be free at the core of your being and then moving out to the periphery and beyond in the ever-widening spiral of Solar light who you are. I am the Lady Portia. I exude the essence of opportunity to be justice in action within your own soul and life today, even as you strive on behalf of all mankind to be an example of purity, wholeness, and joy.

Call to Hercules to magnify the law of God-power on behalf of the righteous in the Earth. Invoke the Elohim to dispel darkness where it exists across the Earth and for a deeper and more concentrated action of light to wend its way into the affairs of mankind for the freedom of the peoples of Tibet, Burma, Nepal, and all nations so that that light of God that always prevails may manifest fully for all.

I am with you in your service to life and in the full expression of who you are as a Solar being, as a wayshower, as a light-sharer, and as a humble one simply seeking to serve to set life free. Cosmic blessings from the realms of eternal perfection and freedom be yours, O blessed hearts of fire.

Portia

29

Would You Actually Be Self-Actualized Today?

1. I relish the thought of you as a self-actualized Solar being now.
2. Glorious rays of divine splendor adorn those whose scientific application of the spiritual laws of higher alchemy is pure of heart in order to further the "as Above, so below" thesis.
3. Realization of God is a multi-lifetime experience in becoming.
4. The Maltese cross is a matrix of perfection for cosmic balance to be sustained within the heart-mind connection of devotees of the Spirit.
5. Riveted upon God, the divine alchemist succeeds despite all delusional nonsense purported by the human ego and the shadow self.
6. Enter perfect silence before commanding divine light to manifest in your work.
7. Your intention to manifest your divine nature will ultimately help it be so fully if you match it with a peaceable heart, genuine humility, and childlike joy.
8. To a T, U may always know the *I* AM through the Alpha-Omega interchange.
9. Creative genius flows to the heart of gold that surrenders to the divine beat.

10. The goal of these discourses is to increase and stabilize your heart-mind connection so that you are able to fully accept the cosmic gnosis of your own Solar beingness.
11. Solar beingness is the plan, you are the man, and I am the fan.
12. Life should be a continuous, joyful interchange between you and the Sun.

Would you actually be self-actualized today? I ask. Why? What aspect of God would you be today? As you respond, I energize your statements and see each of you fully realizing these divine qualities.

Enter the Sun with me now as I take you through a new portal to the inner chamber of the heart of Helios and Vesta. If you would be bold, enter the Sun. Feel the pulsation of the constant stream of Solar beingness. And then see and know how your own God Presence is also an outpicturing of this same Solar Source and how each of you can radiate this divine essence 24/7 if you choose. Have you discerned the qualifications to be a celestial being, a cosmic being? If so, what are these? Now that you are within the Sun, you have a direct experience of what this is all about.

When the Sun breathes in, what happens? Feel this experience within you and all about you now. Absorb into your core, the center of your being, the allness of all that is, the energies of presence of all those who are. Experience God where you are. Now what happens when the Sun breathes out? Experience all of this now.

The resurrection currents are preparatory for complete Solar beingness. You have the opportunity to experience your full Sunship if you choose. Take each moment to breathe deeply in and out, and know that which Jesus knew as he entered the Sun. Each morning may be a new Easter morn, a new resurrection for you as you enter the Sun and allow the Sun to be who you are.

Meditate now upon your Solar Source.

Saint Germain

Merge into the Cosmic Stream
of God's Solar Beingness

Blessed Hearts of Fire,

I come to deliver you unto God's Presence of eternal light and love. I am Portia, and I have taken the sacred sword of justice and wielded it on behalf of each and every one of you for the clearing from your subconscious of ancient records of a sense of injustice and of all that has flowed through you that is not the pure stream of freedom, of light, of liberty, and of the reality who you truly are in God as a Solar being.

Our discourses to you, bringing the alchemical elixirs of living light for your Solar beingness, are for the raising of consciousness so that you may perceive yourself as who you truly are and manifest something of that beingness more each day until you are fully merged into the cosmic stream of God's Solar beingness, which is the very life essence, the blood, of God's living Presence.

What will it take for you to let go of all that has assailed you and entered your world that keeps you from fulfilling your divine destiny? That is what I have seen and that is what the sword has erased within you, if you would accept it by now saying:

> I accept my clearance this day of all within me that is not
> of the light, all subconscious fear and doubt, anxiety, frustra-

tion and burden, all that has kept me from being who I am in God and from manifesting my Solar awareness now. So, help me O God, I accept it. I am it. In your holy name, I AM THAT I AM, Amen.

Angels of cosmic justice come to bring the oil of gladness now that you have released these ancient patterns once and for all, and they minister to your soul to impress the radiance of the light into those areas where previously you had held concepts, momentums, patterns, and burdens within you. The archeiai come and will continue this work now, as you meditate upon the light of your Solar Presence and accept the new frequencies of Aquarius, the love-wisdom-power radiance of your God Source flowing through your spiritual bloodstream from this day forward until you are fully merged into that Solar light of living Godness.

Know, O soul of light, how precious you are to God. It is time for you to realize this fully, so that you can be all that you have always been meant to be—God, God, God in the Earth.

I am Portia. I have taken a pound or two of flesh,[103] the substance of darkness, and balanced the scales within you. I offer to the Lord God that which you have released for the victory of many more upon Earth who are coming because you have determined just to be who you are.

Portia

31

Your Divinity Is All You Have to Bank On

1. Your internal awareness of the Divine helps to bring about the peaceable kingdom that I envisioned centuries ago.
2. Traveling on the light and sound ray, your God-thoughts and positive affirmations of Selfhood increase the collective library of divine imaginings available to all other alchemists of the spirit in their sacred work.
3. Love-wisdom is the alchemical key to experiential mastery in Solar living.
4. Every ascended master offers positive reinforcement of your divine identity through that one's particular individualization of Solar beingness.
5. Eventually, science and industry will resort to the greatest resource—the sun—for all energy requirements. This may be forced by the depletion of Earth's resources, and yet it would better come about through the spiritual enlightenment of her scientists.
6. The intrepid alchemist bonds himself to the ideal outcome of his work through great striving and love.
7. One compelling reason to engage in alchemy is that your internal biological clock is slowing and requires new thought energy to kick it into a higher no-time zone.

8. Look up to see and know the potential you've always had to be a Solar being.

9. The flowering of humanity's divinity is miraculously manifest through alchemy.

10. Bowing to the light within you, we come at sunrise to urge you to try to manifest greater acceptance of your own Solar essence daily.

11. The gracious have what it takes to humble themselves through surrender to joy in becoming fully God-realized alchemists.

12. Solar beingness is all about the blessedness of less and the bliss of what is.

My joy of alchemy is what I have shared and will continue to share with you each day. Every experiment that I have been a party to has been an opportunity to revel in God's beingness and in the sacred processes that manifest themselves through the work that we are about.

I would have you understand joy in the sufficiency of God as beingness in your life by commending you to that Solar essence who you are in reality. Truly, blessed hearts, your divinity is all you have to bank on. If you would precipitate greater abundance, then go to that bank and deposit, by your devotion, the light energies of your spirit. Then, when you require something of that abundance, draw it forth. You see, energy is neither created nor destroyed—it is transformed through your intention. Each and every son and daughter of God receives, upon his or her birth, a divine inheritance of beingness and light. Based on that which you employ of this resource, you can expand that abundance and your personal bank account in heaven from which you may then manifest much greater awareness, presence, and flow.

Therefore, continue in the alchemy of bestowing blessing upon all life. For as you convey light unto one and to many, that blessing accrues to your asset base because the Higher Self of the one blessed receives that offering and returns in kind with divine interest that which you have given and sends it directly to your Solar account. Some of you may be surprised at how much is there. Do not be surprised, for all that you give is multiplied and all that you surrender is received, blessed, and uploaded as a cosmic bestowal to your long-term savings account.

It is a simple equation—the greater the assets and the lesser the liabilities, the more you have available to use. As you use the violet laser-light to diminish and erase those liabilities, your bottom line, your net, will grow. So let us be about our Father's business in increasing our assets and decreasing the liabilities of the old man, the old woman,[104] which will disappear one day when you are subsumed fully into God.

That day is now! I am yours in the Eternal Now,

Saint Germain

32

Daily Drink In the Divine Communion of Solar Beingness from Helios and Vesta

Solar beingness is our goal. I bear a cup of the essence of Helios and Vesta, for my beloved Saint Germain and I have knelt at the altar of the God and Goddess within the sun of this solar system to receive a concentrated essence of their Presence. We extend this elixir of light to your soul to receive of this highest essence of God that can be known within your planetary home.

So, blessed ones, take the chalice that we offer and drink in this golden-pink elixir of cosmic, effervescent light now. You have heard of the love of John the Beloved. Now know the love of Vesta and the wisdom of Helios intertwined within the cosmic frequencies of this celestial liquid. This is the highest communion in which you may share in the new Mass of joy that we, as the hierarchs of the Aquarian Age, bring to the conscious ones upon Earth.

You may call forth again and again, after communing with beloved Helios and Vesta, the reenactment of the partaking of this divine communion, and daily drink in the light of Solar beingness.

O holy ones, know the Lord thy God—the All in all—within, and then you will know the light within all, always.

Portia

33

Attune and Identify
with Your Solar Essence

1. Develop complete fealty to the Sun.
2. Spherical spiritual awareness eventually leads to Solar beingness.
3. Potent possibilities for self-mastery and victory await the just alchemist within the wisdom of the sun's light rays.
4. Divine intervention arises through God's willingness to excite the fires of freedom within his children.
5. God compounds his interest in you daily as you likewise focus your attention on the abundance of his love-wisdom Solar fires.
6. Let your human appetites be tempered by the nourishing rays of the sun.
7. Every moment offers a new spiral of Solar beingness through the alchemy of love.
8. Gently awaken, clothe, and feed all your inner children each morning through compassionate Solar identification.
9. Enjoy the spiritual warmth of your own Sun Source while meditating with Helios and Vesta each day.
10. Your Sun Source offers a constant self-replenishing stream of abundant light for you to accept and radiate to all.
11. I have learned how the alchemy of divine justice always leads to a higher reality.

12. God is beautiful to behold and even more radiant in becoming.

Saint Germain

DCL: The statements that follow illumine each of the above twelve spirals:

1. Your allegiance, or fealty, to the Sun sets the sail for the Lord to trust you to be like himself. Consider evolution and how the divine traits are passed from generation to generation. God trusts the process, and so should you. Let that which you pass along be the highest of Self by merging into the great genealogy of the Divine.

2. As you feel the circumference of your own Solar light around you and you become sensitized to that which God may pour forth as Presence into the chalice of your being, you begin to understand the nature of the sun and the science of emanation. A simple transfer of awareness from the below to the Above may occur within the alchemist whereby, through identification, concentration, and surrender, the very same essence of Solar beingness that resides within the sun of this system may, in an appropriate apportionment, be sustained within your own world by your awareness of Presence. This is how a golden age is born—son by son by son, daughter by daughter by daughter, each a Sun Presence of love-wisdom in the Earth. Yes, the golden-crystal age is up to you to define, and through your own awareness it may be here and now.

3. This spiral, "Potent possibilities for self-mastery and victory await the just alchemist within the wisdom of the sun's light rays," is on lines two, five, eight, and eleven of the cosmic clock. In sequential order, these lines correspond to the God-qualities of self-mastery, wisdom, justice, and victory—the yellow cross. The spiral progresses counterclockwise from the two o'clock line to the five, in order to

unwind the un-wisdom of the lesser self and redefine you in God's image as a Sun.

4. Are you excited today? Allow God to exalt himself within you each moment as the freedom flame manifest within Solar beingness. This is your daily infusion through divine intervention.

5. Is God interested in you? Yes! Allow that interest to compound and grow as you focus on the Source.

6. As you drink in the sun and its nourishment, your human appetites will diminish—gradually, naturally, even as you continue to honor your body's current requirements. Be willing to undergo change in this way despite what the FDA says of the minimum daily requirements to live as a human.

7. The master asks that you meditate as you listen to the song "Alchemy of Love."[105] Listen to it with new ears to hear the inner message behind both the words and the melody, which can sing within you.

8. The inner man of the heart is the voice of conscience, your Higher Self. What of the inner child of your heart? Identify with the Solar essence of the child of God, who you still are even in an adult body. Be reborn childlike and free.

9. If the seed can grow in the earth based on the light and warmth of the sun and sufficient water, how much more can you accelerate and become who you are by attuning to your Sun Source and by worshiping the Mother principle in life?

10. Meditate on your crystal cord daily and that which flows within it to understand how you can sustain youthfulness, beauty, joy, and the eternal complexion of the Divine.

11. Cosmic-clock scientists know that justice is on the eight o'clock line and reality on the nine. Saint Germain said that the alchemy of divine justice always leads to a higher reality. Portia sponsors the eight o'clock line; she supports you at that point of overcoming where you move from the emotional quadrant (lines six, seven, eight) into the physical quadrant (lines nine, ten, eleven).

Getting past the eight o'clock line is a key for many. This is because, in precipitating any alchemy, if you have any anxiety, frustration, sense of injustice, or any blockage on that line, then the spiral of your vision, having descended through the etheric and mental quadrants and progressed into the emotional quadrant, cannot fully take hold in the physical until you resolve and accept the joy of justice within you. Therefore fully accept this joy—the principles of the outpicturing of the Alpha and Omega spirals that flow through the twin flames of justice on the two halves of the scales of justice. When you sustain that balance, God can fully trust that what you then see manifest physically will be endowed with that balance and that joy in your life. To manifest any alchemy, you must have harmony, gratitude, and balance.

12. The responsibility is upon you to be God fully. This is not another's responsibility or something that you can postpone any longer. The time is here; the place is now.

David Christopher Lewis

Benediction

I am your beloved master Saint Germain. I charge forth the light now through your chakras and through your aura for the strengthening of your resolve to accomplish this divine alchemy.

May you win through love, blessed hearts. God bless you.

Saint Germain

Acknowledgments

I am expressing my deep gratitude to the advanced alchemists whose gifts, talents, and love assisted in bringing forth this offering:

Beloved Saint Germain and Portia—Aquarian Alchemists of Joy.

Bob and Verla and Lanello and Ma, for your overshining spiritual guidance during the alchemy of this creative enterprise.

My loving wife and dearest friend, Mona, for your energetic support throughout this endeavor.

My three children, for being the amazing, creative, and giving people who you are. You honor all with your conscious awareness.

Cathleen, for helping codify and organize the words of the master into a whole offering with your keen mind and creative skills.

Our editor, whose experience and attunement kneaded the material into a harmonious whole.

Nancy, Boyd, and Denis, for your conscientious, detailed work and helpful attitudes, especially in the formatting of the book.

Steve and Deborah, for believing in and holding the vision for this project from the beginning, including all your assistance with legal and copyright issues.

Claire, for your friendship, positive spirit, and help overseeing the tens of thousands of details in editing and finalizing the book.

The Creative Arts Team, for your inspired offerings for the book cover and promotional images.

Lenore, Anita, and numerous other unnamed transcribers, whose daily work creates the foundation for our many offerings.

Maria, for all your audio editing of the HeartStreams, which have now became the "Word made flesh" of this holy book.

Patricia, for your gentle spirit and mindful input in presenting our best within all promotional wording and media offerings.

All unnamed heartfriends, whom I see as modern-day alchemists, including our amazing Meru University and Hearts Center board, staff, and volunteers who have been supportive of this tome.

And all divine beings that daily inspire us with your love-wisdom to co-create a beautiful, harmonious, and enlightened cosmos.

Notes

Foreword by David Christopher Lewis

1. Revelation 15:1; 21:9.

2. Meru University offers a wide spectrum of live and on-demand courses offering living teachings directly from the ascended masters. Courses are designed to help you attune to and merge with your own Divine Presence. For more information, go to HeartsCenter.org and select "Meru University" from the menu at the top.

Preface by Saint Germain

3. Psalm 82:6; John 10:34–36.

4. Matthew 22:37–40.

PART ONE: INSTRUCTION IN ADVANCED ALCHEMY

Chapter 1: Establish the Platform for Your Advanced Alchemical Works

5. "The all-chemistry of God" is one of the ways Saint Germain defined alchemy in his first alchemy book. See Mark L. Prophet and Elizabeth Clare Prophet, *Saint Germain On Alchemy: Formulas for Self-Transformation* (Corwin Springs, Mont.: Summit University Press, 1993).

6. The 1894 novel *Brother of the Third Degree,* by Will L. Garver, provides some indication of the testing and initiations that occur under the masters.

7. Matthew 11:12.

8. See glossary entry for *siddhis.*

9. For the full-length version of "Opening Invocation for Prayer Services" (9.007), "Crystal-Diamond Tube of Light" (0.001), and "Solar-Sphere Invocation" (20.022), see *Prayers, Decrees and Mantras,* available through The Hearts Center's online store, item #3200-1-0019. A selection of The Hearts Center's prayers and songs is available individually to listen to and/or download in PDF format at no charge at HeartsCenter.org. From the top menu, select "Broadcast," then "Prayers and Songs." In addition to the text, many prayers and songs are also accessible in audio format.

10. Malcolm Gladwell, *The Tipping Point: How Little Things Can Make a Big Difference* (Boston: Little, Brown and Company, 2000; Back Bay Books, 2002).

11. See glossary entry for *threefold flame.*

12. For more on establishing a flowfield as a magic circle, see Meru University Course #1204, "Self-Transformation through Divine Magic."

Chapter 2: Wield Engrams of Fire and Fohatic Light in Your Creative Process

13. See glossary entry for *Hermes Trismegistus.*

14. See glossary entry for *Omraam Mikhaël Aïvanhov.*

Chapter 3: Activate the *Siddhis* through Resonance

15. 1 John 4:18.

16. The Hindu Trinity of Creator (Brahma), Preserver (Vishnu), and Destroyer (Shiva) parallels the Judeo-Christian Trinity of Father, Son, and Holy Spirit.

17. John 1:14.

18. 1 Thessalonians 5:17.

19. *Kuan Yin's Rosary of Mercy,* 33-minute DVD plus 23-page booklet, item #3200-8-0019; available through The Hearts Center's online bookstore. DVD and booklet are also available separately.

20. See Kuthumi, May 8, 2011, "Accept the Mother Light as a Holy Presence of Love Flowing through You; Allow That Co-Creative Process to Occur Within." Published HeartStreams are available to listen to and/or read, at no cost, at HeartsCenter.org. From the top menu, select "Teachings and Blogs," then "HeartStreams and Discourses," then "HeartStreams Database."

Chapter 4: The Science of Acceptance

21. Luke 15:11–32.

22. Romans 8:16, 17.

23. 1 John 3:1–3.

24. Euclid's ten axioms, or postulates, are outlined in his comprehensive and enduring mathematical work, the *Stoicheia,* or *Elements.*

25. Meru University offers classes on music and harmony and the music of the spheres. To learn more about this science, the cosmic law of harmony, and to attend these classes online, see MU #1206, "The Science of Harmony and the Science of Aquarian Music and Song"; and MU #1210, "The Holy Kumaras on Venusian Alchemy, Architecture, Art, and Music."

Chapter 5: Accelerate Your Vision into Full Realization

26. See "'Create!' and the Cloud," in *Saint Germain On Alchemy*, Book 2, Chapter 6.

27. See glossary entry for *Surya Yoga*.

28. See glossary entry for *immaculate concept*.

29. *Sacred Surrender: Ritual of the Divine Interchange.* This prayer and meditation service on Sweet Surrender with El Morya contains key teachings on the law of surrender. 16-page pocket-sized booklet is available through The Hearts Center's online store, item #3200-1-0023.

30. John 14:12.

Chapter 6: Become the Instrument of the Divine Alchemist

31. John 9:4.

32. John 1:14.

Chapter 7: Be Forewarned and Forearmed

33. See Mark L. Prophet, *The Soulless One: Cloning a Counterfeit Creation* (Summit Publications, Inc., 1965, 1981); and Mark L. Prophet and Elizabeth Clare Prophet, *Climb the Highest Mountain: The Path of the Higher Self* (Summit University Press, 1972; 2003).

34. See glossary entry for *akasha (akashic records)*.

35. See "Release of the Fire Breath of God through the Seven Rainbow Rays," 9.018 in *Prayers, Mantras and Decrees*.

36. See Bruce H. Lipton and Steve Bhaerman, *Spontaneous Evolution: Our Positive Future and How to Get There from Here* (Hay House, 2010).

37. Exodus 3:14, 15.

Chapter 8: Accelerate into Cosmic Consciousness with the Crystal Rays

38. See Henry Wadsworth Longfellow, "A Psalm of Life."

39. See glossary entry for *Mighty Cosmos*.

40. Matthew 12:37.

Chapter 9: Call Forth Energies of Cosmic Light Substance into Your World

41. Matthew 24:22; Mark 13:20.

42. Omraam Mikhaël Aïvanhov, *Life and Work in an Initiatic School: Training for the Divine* (Prosveta Publishing House: 2007), p. 206; available through The Hearts Center's online store, item # 3200-2-0038.

Chapter 10: On Purity of Heart and the Inner Sciences
  43. Matthew 8:23–27; Mark 4:36–41; Luke 8:22–25.
  44. John 2:1–11.
  45. Matthew 14:22–33; Mark 6:45–51; John 6:16–21.

Chapter 12: The Sacred Exchange of Energies between the Heaven
          World and the World of Matter
  46. The name Saint Germain comes from the Latin *Sanctus Germanus,*
  which means Holy Brother. By the law of congruence (see chapter 4),
  when all our chakras resonate with Saint Germain's, then we are coequal
  with him and we too can be called Holy Brother or Holy Sister.

Chapter 13: The Purpose of Divine Ritual
  47. John 16:23, 24.

Chapter 14: A New Matrix for Quicker Precipitation
  48. John 10:10.
  49. Hebrews 11:1.

PART TWO: ANSWERS TO 33 QUESTIONS FROM DISCIPLES

  50. John 5:19, 30; 8:28.
  51. "Divine Director, Lead the Way!" 10.008 in *Prayers, Decrees and
  Mantras.*
  52. 1 Kings 19:12.
  53. Luke 17:21.
  54. See glossary entry for *chohan.*
  55. For more on the practice of Ho'oponopono, see Joe Vitale and
  Ihaleakala Hew Len, Ph.D., *Zero Limits: The Secret Hawaiian System for
  Wealth, Health, Peace, and More* (Hoboken, New Jersey: John Wiley and
  Sons, 2007). Available through The Hearts Center's online store, item
  #3200-2-0076.
  56. John 8:32.
  57. Percival was the spotless, guileless Arthurian knight who quested for
  the Holy Grail.
  58. See glossary entry for *animal magnetism.*
  59. 1 John 4:18.
  60. Genesis 1:29.

61. Matthew 15:11, 17–20; Mark 7:15.

62. Matthew 18:3; Mark 10:15; Luke 18:17.

63. See glossary entry for *seven rays.*

64. Among the ancient stories of the manifestations of the Godhead are the epic tales in the Ramayana.

65. See Shakespeare, *Hamlet, Prince of Denmark,* Act 3, scene 1, line 56.

66. See Daniel 5.

67. For information on pilgrimages, prayer circles, and other activities, go to HeartsCenter.org and select "Events" from the menu at the top.

68. "I AM My Victorious Abundance Here and Now," 20.026 in *Prayers, Decrees and Mantras.*

69. "Maitreya's Loving-Kindness," 20.010 in *Prayers, Decrees and Mantras.*

70. Proverbs 29:18.

71. 1 Peter 3:4.

72. The four cosmic forces have been identified variously as the hierarchs of the elements and as the living creatures mentioned by Ezekiel and the four beasts spoken of in the Revelation.

73. Matthew 18:19, 20.

74. Matthew 3:1–3, 11.

75. John 15:13.

76. 1 Corinthians 12:4–11.

77. See Vladimir Megré, *Anastasia* (Kahului, Hawaii: Ringing Cedars Press, 2d ed., 2008). Available through The Hearts Center's online store, item #3200-2-0042.

78. Genesis 1:3.

79. See glossary entry for *cosmic being.*

80. 1 Corinthians 15:51–53.

81. See Gardenia, May 15, 2011, "It Is Your Purpose to Bless Life through Your Presence: The Floral Light Waves and Aromas of the Spirit May Be Yours to Bless Every Creature, Every Blade of Grass."

PART THREE: ALCHEMICAL ELIXIRS: 33 SPIRALS OF DIVINE ALCHEMY FOR SOLAR BEINGNESS

Spiral 2: Fulfill Your Assignments and Prepare for All That Is Coming

82. John 9:4.

Spiral 3: Let Solar Beingness Flow through You
   83. Matthew 6:9–13; Luke 11:2–4.

Spiral 4: Understand the Presence of God-Love Within
   84. Psalm 46:10.
   85. Luke 2:14.

Spiral 9: Make Your Magic Presence Real Today
   86. The lady members of the Karmic Board are the Goddess of Liberty, Nada, Pallas Athena, Portia, and Kuan Yin. See the glossary entry for *Lords of Karma.*

Spiral 11: Being in God Here and Now
   87. James 1:17.

Spiral 12: Embrace Your Real Self Ever More
   88. 2 Peter 1:10.

Spiral 13: Grasp the Import of Your Personal Ascent
   89. Saint Germain has taught that in the word *try* is a sacred alchemical formula: "Theos (God) rules you."

Spiral 14: The Ancient Dream of God: Heaven upon Earth
   90. The Hearts Center holds a conference at summer solstice each year, often in Livingston, Montana. Information about conferences and other events is available at HeartsCenter.org.

Spiral 15: All Are Tested in the Alchemical Fires of Ruby Love
   91. Malachi 3:2.
   92. Psalm 46:10.

Spiral 16: I Bring a New Spiral of Divine Justice
   93. Matthew 13:24–30.
   94. Revelation 12.
   95. Revelation 7:4; 14:1, 3.

Spiral 17: Be About the Father-Mother God's Business Now
   96. Luke 2:49.

Spiral 19: The Alchemy of Picture-Perfect Presence
   97. John 14:2.

Spiral 20: Each New Day Is an Opportunity to Be God in Manifestation
98. Genesis 3:21.

Spiral 22: Defend the Light! Secure the Bastions of Freedom
99. See Matthew 25:29; Mark 4:25; Luke 8:18; 19:26.
100. John 14:6.

Spiral 26: The Bonding of Our Hearts in the Sacred Alchemy of
Community
101. See glossary entry for *Knights and Ladies of the Flame.*

Spiral 27: You Are God's Great Alchemical Experiment
102. The mystery schools teach that Jesus Christ held the key to the incarnation of God for the Age of Pisces. During the Age of Aquarius, Saint Germain holds that key.

Spiral 30: Merge into the Cosmic Stream of God's Solar Beingness
103. In William Shakespeare's *The Merchant of Venice,* Portia saves Antonio from losing a pound of flesh to the vengeful Shylock.

Spiral 31: Your Divinity Is All You Have to Bank On
104. Ephesians 4:22, 23; Colossians 3:8–10.

Spiral 33: Attune and Identify with Your Solar Essence
105. "Alchemy of Love," by David Christopher Lewis, song 57 in *HeartSongs,* available through The Hearts Center's online store, item #3200-1-0021.

Glossary

Akasha: A Sanskrit term for a dimension of energetic vibration capable of absorbing and archiving every activity—thought, word, action, feeling—of every sentient being from the beginning of time. Related term: *akashic records.*

Alpha and Omega: Our Father-Mother God residing in the Great Central Sun in the center of the known physical creation, or cosmos. As a uniplurality of being, they outpicture the perfect balance of the masculine and feminine polarities within the Godhead.

Animal magnetism: Gravitation into a lower level of awareness than that divinely ordained for the sons and daughters of God, who are destined to be co-creators. A state in which one vibrates in consonance with a herd mentality within a group-soul consciousness, such as is commonly found in many animal species. That which pulls or draws the consciousness of mankind down in a devolutionary spiral of darkness through a lack of Christic awareness.

Ascended masters: The saints, teachers, and sages of all religions, cultures, and ages whose mastery over the world in which we live has allowed them to return to the heart of God through the sacred ritual of the ascension. In the heaven world, these ascended masters work together with the angels and cosmic beings to assist mankind in attaining that selfsame mastery. See also *saints robed in white* and *Great White Brotherhood.*

Astral plane: A more subtle world or vibratory field of awareness between the physical and mental planes of being within which desires, feelings, and emotions are accentuated. The physical plane relates to earth, the astral plane relates to water, the mental plane to air, and the etheric plane to fire. During sleep or heightened meditation, the soul may leave its "seat," its local attachment to the body temple, to travel or project its awareness to, through, and beyond the astral plane to reach the more subtle etheric world, where the universities of the spirit exist within the retreats of the ascended masters around the world.

Builders of Form. See *Elohim.*

Causal body: Our causal body is composed of seven spheres-within-spheres of light surrounding our Solar Presence. In the Buddha Nature Chart depiction (see our website, HeartsCenter.org), the spheres are seen in cross-section, appearing as rings. These color spheres are the accumulation of every compassionate act that we have ever performed throughout our incarnations. Every person's causal body, then, is unique in appearance with some spheres of larger size than others. We receive our energy, strength, and inspiration from the light of our causal body through invocation and intention.

Chakra: A Sanskrit term meaning "wheel" or "discus." Chakras are spinning centers of energy that receive and emanate the flow of God's light; they can also be seen as generating stations, or power stations, of light. There are seven main chakras aligned along the spinal column and head. The crown chakra is located at the top of the head, the third-eye chakra between and a bit above the physical eyes, the throat chakra at the Adam's apple, the heart chakra in the middle of the chest, the solar plexus chakra in the diaphragm area, the seat-of-the-soul chakra below the navel, and the base chakra at the tip of the spine. Five lesser-known chakras, called the secret-ray chakras, are located in the thymus area, hands, and feet.

Chohan: From the Sanskrit, meaning "chief" or "lord." A chohan is a spiritual leader of great attainment who works with mankind from the ascended state. The seven chohans for the Earth each serve on one of the seven rays. They currently are El Morya (blue ray), Lanto (yellow ray), Paul the Venetian (pink ray), Serapis Bey (white ray), Hilarion (green ray), Nada (purple and gold ray), and Saint Germain (violet ray). The Maha Chohan, the "Great Lord" who is the representative of the Holy Spirit, appoints and oversees the work of the chohans. See also *seven rays.*

Cosmic beings: Individual identities that have attained cosmic consciousness. Their auric emanations have expanded to embrace not just one planet but often entire solar systems and galaxies. Some cosmic beings are given the title of "God" or "Goddess" to denote an attainment of celestial awareness while focusing for vast evolutions one particular God-quality.

Crystal-diamond tube of light: A cylinder of divine light that encompasses, protects, and seals us in an energy field of inviolate perfection (illustrated in the Buddha Nature Chart on our website). This tube of shimmering radiance descends from our Solar Presence at our call. See prayers 0.001 and 0.005 in The Hearts Center's *Prayers, Decrees and Mantras* book; available in our online store; also downloadable as separate prayers at HeartsCenter.org.

Crystal rays: Spiritual frequencies beyond the seven rainbow rays in vibration that proceed from out of the white-fire core of being of the Great Causal Body of the Godhead in the Great Central Sun. Also known as the *secret rays,* these five light-energies are focalized in Man within the sacred chakras in the palms, feet, and in the secret chamber of the heart, corresponding to the stigmata, the marks of Christ where Jesus was pierced during his crucifixion. The crystal rays are streams of light through which the higher *siddhis,* Buddhic virtues, and divine quintessences are utilized in higher mindfulness through meditation and heart-centered, conscious living.

Decrees: *Power prayers;* spoken, poetic, rhythmic, and often rhyming prayers or mantras that invoke the light of God to radiate forth in, to, and throughout our beings and around the Earth. When repeated with loving devotion and focus, spiritual light intensifies within the chakras and aura of the decreer, producing positive change and planetary transformation. For a free sampling of decrees, prayers, and mantras, visit HeartsCenter.org.

Devas: Nature spirit beings or archetypal elemental forces within nature that each have a unique natal intelligence which guides the development of the nearly limitless species of life evolving on Earth. Devas oversee the outpicturing of life forms in various domains according to the Creator's original blueprint or seed ideation of those beings. Devas are often seen by those with inner vision as colorful, angel-like beings whose expansive awareness may embrace large valleys, mountain ranges, rivers, seas, and oceans. The more evolved *solar devas* live in the sun and support the evolution of life throughout the solar system.

Divine Director: The (Great) Divine Director is a cosmic being on the blue ray, or first ray, of power, protection, and the will of God. Known in his role as the Guru of Saint Germain, he is available to each child of God to assist, as his name attests, in guiding us to walk in the highest will of God. He is also the manu (progenitor, lawgiver, and sponsor) of the seventh root race and a member of the Great Karmic Board, which adjudicates divine justice in the affairs of mankind and in the individual lives of the sons and daughters of God.

Divine spark: The eternal fire of the Creator individualized for every son or daughter of God within the secret chamber of the heart. Also called the *spirit-spark* or the *threefold flame,* it is that essence that animates beingness and life itself.

Elementals: See *nature spirits.*

Elohim: The "Lords of Creation" referred to in the Book of Genesis, the "Seven Spirits of God" in the Book of Revelation, and the "Morning Stars" in the Book of Job, the Elohim are beings of immense light and power who ensoul galaxies and universes. They are also known as the "Builders of Form," because it is they who created the physical universe in which we live. Serving under the Elohim are the four hierarchs of the elements and the elemental kingdom of gnomes, sylphs, salamanders, and undines.

Emerald Tablet: See *Hermes Trismegistus.*

Etheric plane: The etheric plane is divided into two portions. The lower etheric overlaps denser planes called the mental, the astral, and the physical. In the higher etheric, souls who have balanced a certain percentage of karma by devotion to God, consistent prayer lives, and service to others reside between embodiments or in preparation for their ascension. In comparison to the physical plane, the etheric is so accelerated that it cannot be seen with the human eye. In this higher etheric plane, the records of mankind's entire evolution can be accessed. These records are referred to as *akasha* or the *akashic records*. Levels of the higher etheric plane are where the ascended masters dwell, where their magnificent retreats and cities of light are located.

Five Dhyani Buddhas: Celestial Buddhas that can be visualized in meditation. The Five Dhyani Buddhas are Vairochana, Akshobhya, Ratnasambhava, Amitabha, and Amoghasiddhi, and each represents different aspects of the enlightened consciousness. All are potent healers whose assistance and powers can be invoked to facilitate inner transformation.

Flowfield: A stream of spiritual light through which a continuous flow of divine radiance may be sustained. A flowfield typically results from the constant prayers, meditations, and spiritual services offered by one or more devotees. It may become an ever-expanding reservoir of divine energy that can protect and bless our auras, both individually and collectively. Our auras may become a dynamic flowfield when we are in alignment with God's will, wisdom, and love.

Four and Twenty Elders: Highly evolved spiritual beings, enlightened counselors who sit in judgment on their own thrones before the Great Throne (Three-in-One) of Almighty God. Mentioned in the Book of Revelation, the Four and Twenty Elders adjudicate the destiny of the sons and daughters of God based on their love and applied faith or life works. Within our galaxy, the Elders rule at the Court of the Sacred Fire on the God Star Sirius.

Gnosis: Direct knowledge through personal experience. True, enlightened wisdom through intimate communion with God rather than by a vicarious experience through an intermediary.

Great Central Sun: The Source; the Center; the Great Hub; the Cosmic Sun behind the Sun. A massive energy vortex in the heart center of the cosmos and the nucleus from which all life originated. Sirius is the focus of the Great Central Sun in our section of our galaxy.

Great White Brotherhood: Also referred to as the Universal White Brotherhood and the Universal Great White Brotherhood. An association of saints and sages from all paths and religions that also includes angels and cosmic beings. "It is the authority and governing body that represents the Godhead in this system of worlds."* Many members of the Great White Brotherhood walked the path of mastery on Earth or other planets in our system; others never descended into physical form. "White" does not refer to race; it signifies each one's purity of consciousness. The purpose of the Great White Brotherhood is the upliftment of mankind so that each individual may attain that selfsame mastery and the ultimate joy of divine reunion through the ascension.

*Excerpted from a darshan with the Maha Chohan, June 1, 2008.

Heartfriends: Individuals who have been drawn to the universal message of The Hearts Center Community and the radiance of the ascended masters through our *HeartStreams* and are kindred spirits of divine love. *Heartfriends* are also any and all who are heart-centered and serve God's purposes on Earth, whether they are associated with our movement or not.

HeartStreams: Up-to-the-minute messages and teachings from the ascended masters through their anointed messenger(s) in The Hearts Center movement. Delivered in the form of dictations, discourses, or darshans, these messages vibrate with the masters' love and wisdom, and they anchor light in the Earth as they are being released and also when they are replayed in video or audio format. They teach, exhort, bless, uplift, and direct us in specific actions which, when fulfilled, may yield great blessings for ourselves and our planet.

Hermes Trismegistus: Also known as the God Mercury, Hermes Trismegistus was a great philosopher, priest, and king in antiquity. He also wrote alchemical and astrological works as well as other sacred texts. Trismegistus means "thrice greatest." In his *History of Chemistry,* James Campbell Brown writes, "A series of early Egyptian books is attributed to Hermes Trismegistus, who may have been a real savant, or may be a personification of a long succession of writers. . . . He is identified by some with the Greek god Hermes [equated with the Roman god Mercury] and the Egyptian Thoth. . . . The Egyptians regarded him as the god of wisdom, letters, and the recording of time."

The **Emerald Tablet** became known to European alchemists when it was translated from Arabic into Latin during the twelfth century. The work is attributed in the text to Hermes Trismegistus; however, its origin remains unknown. Within it is the axiom "That which is above is from that which is below, and that which is below is from that which is above, working the miracles of one" (http://www.sacred-texts.com/alc/emerald.htm; accessed 11/30/2014). *The Kybalion: A Study of the Hermetic Philosophy of Ancient Egypt and Greece,* by Three Initiates (Chicago: Yogi Publication Society, 1908, 1940), a source of Hermetic principles and teaching, is at http://www.kybalion.org/kybalion.php (accessed 11/30/2014).

Immaculate concept: A consciousness that sees and believes only perfection of a person or situation. It is a consciousness that refuses to denigrate or gossip, to criticize or judge, to blame or shame. In the Buddhist tradition, this concept is called *absolute bodhichitta. Picture-perfect presence,* a term shared by the ascended masters through The Hearts Center, is another way of expressing it. God holds an immaculate concept of each individual. The term *immaculate concept* and the teaching explaining it were given by Mother Mary to her devotees in the 1990s through the messenger Elizabeth Clare Prophet.

Holy Christ/Buddha Self: See *Solar Presence.*

Karmic Board: See *Lords of Karma.*

Knights and Ladies of the Flame: Initiates who lovingly serve at a spiritual Round Table within a Holy Order that is part of the greater Hearts Center Community worldwide. Through daily prayers and invocations, they are the primary spiritual support of the messenger or spiritual director, of other knights and ladies, and of lightbearers worldwide. Each one serves on a line of the cosmic clock based on his or her astrological birth sign. As spiritual co-equals, knights and ladies uphold the motto All for One and One for All.

Kundalini: Also called the *sacred fire,* kundalini power is an aspect of the indwelling Holy Spirit of God. The kundalini rests in coils of dynamic potential in the base-of-the-spine chakra. The practice of yoga and the offering of prayers and devotion to the Divine Feminine gently raise this energy up the spinal altar, accelerating each of the seven chakras as it travels to the crown. The raising of the kundalini allows the soul access to the *siddhis,* or gifts of the Holy Spirit, and also brings a greater degree of integration and mastery to the soul.

Logos: The Word, or Universal Christ Consciousness. According to Greek philosophy, *Logos* is the guiding principle of the universe. In Hindu teachings, *Shakti,* a synonym for Logos, means "original knowledge or divine reason." The Logos is the creative and dynamic intelligence that permeates and helps to sustain the universe.

Lord of the World: The chief executive officer or divine governor who holds the highest spiritual office for planet Earth. This seat of authority is currently held by Gautama Buddha and was previously held by Sanat Kumara (now the Regent Lord of the World), who came with 144,000 advanced souls to save our Earth many tens of thousands of years ago during our planet's darkest night.

Lords of Karma (or Karmic Board): A heavenly council that deliberates upon ways and means to best assist the citizens of Earth in terms of dealing with the weight of karmic burden imposed upon this planet by its inhabitants. The members of the Karmic Board are the Divine Director, the Goddess of Liberty, Nada, Cyclopea, Pallas Athena, Portia, Kuan Yin, Vairochana, and Gautama Buddha.

Mighty Cosmos: A being whose God consciousness is so vast that it encompasses the entire cosmos. Mighty Cosmos assists us in the use and mastery of the crystal rays, which he ensouls.

Nature spirits (or elementals): Beings of earth (gnomes), water (undines), air (sylphs), and fire (salamanders) that lovingly provide the platform for the evolution of life in the natural world upon Earth. Though most of mankind do not see elementals (young children often do), these gentle beings respond to our loving appreciation for their sacred work in outpicturing the beauty of the flora and fauna all around us. Walt Disney brought to television and movies a colorful representation of some of the workings of the nature spirits, especially in the epic film *Fantasia*.

Omraam Mikhaël Aïvanhov: A Bulgarian master and spiritual teacher who lived between 1900 and 1986. His oral teachings on many spiritual topics, ranging from the importance of meditating upon the sun to commentary on the Book of Revelation, have been transcribed into publications by his students, published by Prosveta Publishing House, and are now in print in English. Available through The Heart Center's online bookstore.

Portia: Twin flame of Saint Germain and hierarch of the Aquarian Age. She serves on the Great Karmic Board as the Goddess of Justice and is also known as the Goddess of Opportunity. She remained in the octaves of light during Saint Germain's embodiments upon Earth to hold a spiritual focus for him to support his work on behalf of mankind.

Saints robed in white: Masterful souls East and West who have reunited with the Divine Light in the ascension through obedience to the Law of Love, and who now wear garments of white light, symbolic of their humility, purity, and attainment. These are free from the rounds of rebirth and have their names written in the Book of Life (Daniel 12:1; Revelation 20:12). See also *ascended masters* and *Great White Brotherhood.*

Sanat Kumara: The *Ancient of Days* (Daniel 7:9, 13, 22), the original Keeper of the Flame, and the spiritual ruler of the planet Venus, whose evolutions exist in an etheric plane beyond our mortal vision. Many eons ago, he offered his assistance to a doomed Earth, karmically scheduled for destruction. Its evolutions no longer acknowledged or were connected to their Source, having extinguished the divine spark within their hearts. Sanat Kumara was granted permission from a cosmic council to come to Earth with 144,000 lightbearers to help Earth's citizens awaken to their true divinity and regain their soul freedom. He is also known as *Dipamkara* in Buddhism, *Kartikeya* (second son of Shiva and Parvati) in Hinduism, and *Ahura Mazda* in Zoroastrianism.

Secret chamber of the heart: A sacred place within the heart chakra, a holy altar in the center of our being where we may go in meditation to meet with God as our own Holy Christ/Buddha Self. It is in the secret chamber that we commune with the Divine and receive the testings that strengthen us to more perfectly embody the qualities of God here on Earth. The *threefold flame* resides in the secret chamber of the heart.

Seven rays: The seven rays emanate from the *Great Central Sun* as well as from our individual *Solar Presence,* through which the Great Central Sun focuses its light. These rays compose the color spheres that surround the Solar Presence. (See the Buddha Nature Chart on our website, HeartsCenter.org.) As concentric spheres of the *causal body,* the seven rays bless the Earth with the vibrations of their qualities, helping mankind to progress in the mastery of each ray. See also *chohan.*

The ray, its color, God-qualities, and the day of the week on which it is most easily attuned to, are as follows:

- Blue—the first ray: will, faith, protection, and power; Tuesday
- Yellow—the second ray: wisdom, illumination, understanding, Sunday
- Pink—the third ray: divine love, compassion, creativity; Monday
- White—the fourth ray: purity, holiness, the light of the ascension; Friday
- Green—the fifth ray: wholeness, healing, abundance, science, music; Wednesday
- Purple and gold—the sixth ray: service and ministration to life; Thursday
- Violet—the seventh ray: forgiveness, mercy, soul-freedom; Saturday

Siddhis: The Sanskrit word *siddhi* is derived from Siddhartha, the given name of the great Buddha Gautama, enlightened teacher of the Middle Way and the Four Noble Truths. According to Eastern spirituality, *siddhis* are spiritual powers that can arise naturally as the mind empties, opens, and becomes clearer. Some of the *siddhis* are clairvoyance, clairaudience, telepathy, psychometry, levitation, premonition, healing, discernment, and bilocation. In the Christian tradition, these higher senses are referred to as the gifts of the Holy Spirit (see 1 Corinthians 12). These gifts may be requested by devotees who in humility desire to minister to life more effectively and powerfully.

Solar Presence (or Higher Self, Holy Christ/Buddha Self): A term introduced by the ascended masters through The Hearts Center in 2005, it describes that portion of our being that is God. It is depicted as the upper figure in the Buddha Nature Chart on our website. Also called the *I AM Presence*, the *Divine Presence*, and the *God Presence*, it is the individualization of the One, our true divine identity. The words *Solar*

Presence provide us with the image of our total being as a radiating sun center that continually emanates divine love and every virtue to all life.

Surya Yoga (sun yoga): Omraam Mikhaël Aïvanhov taught: "Each of the other types of yoga helps to develop one particular aspect of oneself, whereas Surya-yoga activates all our psychic centres. When we unite ourselves with the sun we are bound to get results, for we are uniting with the central power that governs and animates all the planets of our universe. This is why I say that all the other kinds of yoga, which were once considered so wonderful—and which are, indeed, still wonderful—will one day be replaced by Surya-yoga which surpasses them all, for when you work with the sun you are working with God Himself" (*The Splendour of Tiphareth: The Yoga of the Sun [Prosveta Publishing House, 2009],* p. 19).

Threefold flame: The threefold flame is nothing less than God, blazing within our physical form, individualized in each person. This flame is placed in the secret chamber of the heart at birth and is withdrawn at the time of transition. Three identifiable plumes, vibrating as blue, yellow, and pink, compose the threefold flame. These plumes rise from the same source, a tiny sphere of white Mother Light energy. The blue plume blazes as the will of God, the faith of God, and the power of God; it is also the flame of protection. The yellow plume represents the right use of knowledge—a wisdom and discrimination based on the standards and principles of truth. The pink plume represents love—adoration, devotion, compassion—the very nature of God. When the three plumes are in perfect balance through a virtuous life, Christ consciousness is attained.

Twelve archangels and archeiai: An *archangel* is the highest-ranking position in the order of angels. An *archeia* is a feminine archangel. Seven archangels and archeiai each represent one of the seven rays, or the seven major aspects of God's consciousness that are depicted in the causal body rings surrounding our Solar Presence. There are also five crystal-ray archangels and archeiai, recently revealed through the dispensation of The Hearts Center. Just as every soul has a twin flame, every archangel has an archeia. As an example, Mother Mary is an archeia on the ray of healing, the green ray. Her twin flame, also on the green ray, is Archangel Raphael.

Twin Flames: Each soul, as well as each heavenly being and every planet and star, was created by God in the beginning with a sacred complement or counterpart—a loving companion, opposite in polarity. When solar twins, twin rays, or twin flames of incarnated beings are able to work together to fulfill their combined divine mission, whether they are both embodied, or one is embodied and the other has ascended, the positive results for Earth are immense. Most embodied souls have been separated from their solar twins by karma. One day, a glorious reunion will occur—a reuniting in heaven that creates an atmosphere of cosmic-love oneness that initiates the explosive action of concentric waves of light moving ever outward to encompass a universe and more.

Virya: A Sanskrit word meaning "energy, zeal, vigor."

Wonderman of Europe: A title for *Le Comte de Saint Germain*, appropriately given him because of the amazing alchemical feats and spiritual works that he performed throughout the courts of Europe in the eighteenth and nineteenth centuries, such as transmuting the flaws in precious stones, bi-locating, speaking numerous languages fluently, masterfully playing musical instruments, and sharing an intimate knowledge of events around the world.

About the Author

David Christopher Lewis is a spiritual teacher, author, composer, and talk-radio contributor. He is the cofounder of The Hearts Center, a spiritual movement and community dedicated to helping people everywhere realize their highest potential. He conducts seminars worldwide and hosts regular online webinars and live broadcasts on diverse spiritual topics. His published works include *Advanced Studies of the Human Aura: How to Charge Your Energy Field with Light and Spiritual Radiance; Now, Zen and Always: El Morya's Treasury of Spiritual Quips;* and *Mother Mary's Missions: Messages from the Divine Mother.* For more information on his other published works, music CDs, broadcasts, and seminars, visit HeartsCenter.org. David lives with his wife near Livingston, Montana.